THE DRIVING INSTRUCTOR'S HANDBOOK

Twenty-first edition

The Driving Instructor's Handbook

John Miller

First published in Great Britain in 1982 by Kogan Page Limited
Twenty-first edition 2018

2nd Floor, 45 Gee Street
London
EC1V 3RS
United Kingdom

c/o Martin P Hill Consulting
122 W 27th Street
New York, NY 10001
USA

4737/23 Ansari Road
Daryaganj
New Delhi 110002
India

© Autodriva Training Systems 1982, 1983, 1986, 1988
© John Miller and Margaret Stacey 1989, 1991, 1993, 1994, 1996, 1997, 1999, 2002, 2004, 2006, 2007, 2009, 2011, 2013, 2015
© John Miller 2017, 2018

ISBN   978 0 7494 8393 7
E-ISBN   978 0 7494 8394 4

British Library Cataloguing-in-Publication Data

A CIP record for this book is available from the British Library.

Typeset by Integra Software Services, Pondicherry
Print production managed by Jellyfish
Printed and bound in Great Britain by CPI Group (UK) Ltd, Croydon CR0 4YY

CONTENTS

Appendices

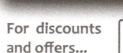

Training to be an ADI?

DeskTop Driving have all the training products to help you pass!

- Training Manuals
- Visual Aids & Cue Cards
- DSA recommended books
- 'Part 3' DVDs
- Lesson Plans & Diagrams
- DSA Question Bank books & DVDs
- Hazard Perception DVDs

Already an ADI?

Join the thousands of ADIs who are earning extra money selling driver trainin products to their pupils!

- Car Theory and Practical Books
- Car Theory and Practical DVDs/CDs
- All DSA Official Publications
- LGV/PCV and Motorcycle Publications
- Hazard Perception DVDs

ABOUT THE AUTHORS

John Miller has been involved in the driver training industry for over 35 years and was an ADI for more than 30 years. For most of that time he ran his own driving school for both car and lorry drivers, as well as an instructor training facility in Chichester. He is now a training consultant to the industry.

As well as *The Driving Instructor's Handbook*, John is also the author *of Practical Teaching Skills for Driving Instructors* (also published by Kogan Page).

Practical Teaching Skills for Driving Instructors is a useful resource book, not only for new instructors who are training for the ADI exams, but also for experienced instructors in their everyday work in driver training at all levels. It is particularly helpful for anyone wanting to improve and extend their teaching and coaching skills and for enhancing their 'continuing professional development'.

Both *The Driving Instructor's Handbook* and *Practical Teaching Skills for Driving Instructors* are listed by the Driver and Vehicle Standards Agency as essential material for the ADI examinations.

John Miller can be contacted at **johnmiller07@btinternet.com**.

For many years, **Margaret Stacey** was co-author with John Miller of both *The Driving Instructor's Handbook* and *Practical Teaching Skills for Driving Instructors*. During that time she devised and produced The Autodriva Home Study Programme, which was used by numerous trainee instructors and training organizations.

Margaret served on several national committees within the industry and was instrumental in setting up the original 'Register of Driving Instructor Trainers' as well as helping to develop the NVQ in driver training.

Since Margaret's death in 2005 both books have been regularly updated by John Miller.

Note: While every effort has been made to ensure that the book is as up to date as possible, continual changes take place in the driver training industry and with legislation. This means that some changes may have occurred since going to print. To keep yourself completely up to date, we recommend that you sign up for regular e-mail updates from the DVSA and refer to the DVSA's website at **www.gov.uk**. You will also benefit from joining one or more of the national associations as well as your local group.

ACKNOWLEDGEMENTS

There are several people to whom I am indebted for help in producing this, the 21th edition of *The Driving Instructor's Handbook*.

Special thanks to:

Susan McCormack of Tri-Coaching Partnership for advice and assistance on all matters relating to coaching and client-centred learning.

Jacqui Turland, Neil Wilson and John Caradine at DVSA for providing the foreword and for advice regarding the ADI exams.

Thanks also to those ADIs and colleagues in the industry who regularly provide comments, feedback and support.

FOREWORD

2017 saw changes to the tests that potential instructors must pass to qualify as an ADI.

The Part 2 test changed to reflect the changes to the category B licence acquisition test.

The Part 3 test moved away from a fault-based assessment, which relied on pre-set tests and role-play exercises, and was both unrealistic and restrictive. Trainee instructors must now provide a 'real' pupil. If the trainee doesn't teach learners, the pupil can be a full licence holder. The lesson needs to reflect the true learning goals and needs of the pupil.

The Driving Instructor's Handbook will help you achieve these new objectives.

Looking forward, we're exploring the use of a log book in which trainee instructors and their trainer can record the subjects covered, the different levels of instruction given and overall progress. This is to ensure that they obtain the required range of skills, knowledge and understanding. Most, if not all, instructor trainers already record progress like this and DVSA is happy for them to continue to use or adapt their existing processes.

We are also working with those on the Official Register of Instructor Trainers to refresh the scheme, which has been largely unchanged for over 15 years. We have revised the terms and conditions, simplified the fee arrangements and will bring the assessments into line with the National Driver and Rider Training standards. The new scheme will be launched in 2018.

The Driving Instructor's Handbook has been regularly updated to ensure that the learning material is current and valid. The DVSA, therefore, continues to list the book as recommended reading for the ADI exams and we welcome this latest edition.

Jacqui Turland
Registrar of Approved Driving Instructors
Driver and Vehicle Standards Agency
Nottingham

Introduction

The Driving Instructor's Handbook was first published in 1982 and since 1989 it has been listed by the Driver and Vehicle Standards Agency (DVSA) as recommended reading for the Approved Driving Instructor (ADI) exams. It contains up-to-date information on all aspects of driver training, ranging from driving licences, driving tests, teaching and coaching skills, to the ADI Register Exams and the ADI Standards Check. The latest edition includes practice questions and a mock test for the ADI Part 1 exam, detailed information on driver training, structuring the lesson, dealing with disabilities and impairments and the National Syllabus for Driving.

Over the years, the *Handbook* has been regularly updated by John Miller and continues to be recommended by the DVSA both for new entrants and for qualified instructors. To quote a previous DVSA ADI Registrar: 'With the many changes taking place over the whole range of activities in the driver training industry, those involved at all levels of training are strongly recommended to use *The Driving Instructor's Handbook* as resource material.'

The driving instructor's role is now much more challenging than when the driving test was first introduced in 1935. Over the last few years, the function of the instructor has changed at an even greater rate than in the past as a result of new practices and methods in the way that new drivers are tested and how they learn.

This edition, the 21st, covers in detail the requirements for the new-style ADI Part 3 test. This part of the qualifying exams is now based on an assessment of the instructor's competences in relation to client-centred learning and how the pupil has benefitted from the instruction given. In this respect it is very similar to the requirements of the existing Standards Check that was introduced in 2014.

The emphasis on client-centred learning and coaching has, of course, made a great improvement in the way instructors teach their pupils and the way in which learners are learning a life skill rather than being taught how to pass a test.

Although most qualified ADIs focus their businesses on teaching new drivers, there are various opportunities to add interest and variety to the job, including:

- pre-driver training;
- teaching people who have disabilities;
- 'Pass Plus' training;
- defensive and advanced driver training;
- company and fleet driver training;
- minibus driver training;
- training in the towing of trailers and caravans;
- corrective driver training for traffic offenders;
- assessments for older drivers;
- driver training schemes run by local authorities and police.

To become an effective driver trainer you need to be much more than a good driver who enjoys motoring. The speed and density of today's traffic, together with increasingly complex driving situations, make the ADI's job an extremely demanding one. The aim of the truly professional instructor should be to improve the standards of new and experienced drivers in order to reduce the numbers of accidents, deaths and casualties suffered on our roads.

You will need to:

- have a thorough understanding of the rules and principles involved in safe driving;
- be able to put these principles into practice by driving thoughtfully and efficiently;
- be able to patiently teach your pupils how to apply those principles, while other drivers around you are trying to get from A to B as quickly as possible;
- instil safe attitudes into clients at all levels of driving.

One of your main aims should be to produce drivers who will help make our roads safer, but at the same time to ensure that they will enjoy their lessons and future motoring.

Practice questions for the Part 1 exam and a mock test are in Chapter 2. These are not the actual exam questions, but they give an indication of how to prepare for the Part 1 theory test. When preparing for this part of the exam don't rely simply on memorizing the answers to several hundred questions – make sure you fully understand the explanations and detail of each topic.

In this edition, Chapter 1 deals with the ADI Register – how to apply to become an instructor and how to prepare for the exams; the format of the exams; various options for training; and the qualities needed to become a successful driver trainer.

All ADIs are required to take the Standards Check at regular intervals. The Check is designed to ensure that the instruction being given is up to the standards set out in the National Standards for qualified instructors and is becoming much more demanding in its assessment of the ADI's skills. Full details of the Standards Check are given in Chapter 6. A number of instructors with years of experience have difficulty retaining their ADI grading, with an increasing percentage now being graded as substandard. ADIs who have not kept themselves up to date with modern teaching and coaching skills should appreciate that new entrants to the Register are much better placed to compete for customers who are nowadays much more discerning in their expectations. Rather than finding themselves in a situation where they are downgraded, they might find it well worth their while to consider taking some form of refresher training prior to their Standards Check. Coaching and teaching skills are dealt with in Chapter 7, with more detail in *Practical Teaching Skills for Driving Instructors* (new edition published by Kogan Page in 2017).

Teaching people to change attitudes and to fully understand the requirements for driving a car in today's road and traffic conditions is far more complex than simply teaching practical vehicle control skills. This is why there is now a move to encourage instructors to use more up-to-date methods of coaching and client-centred learning, rather than just 'instructing'.

Training to become a driving instructor is neither cheap nor easy; in fact, it can be relatively costly and certainly time-consuming. However, the time, effort and expense involved in preparing for all three parts of the ADI exam should be considered as an investment in your future. Latest figures show that 9,000 people start the application process each year, but only about 3,000 candidates actually complete the programme and qualify as ADIs.

A wide variety of training courses are available to the prospective instructor. Before you make your choice or pay out any large sums of money in advance, consider all the implications carefully. Chapter 1 explains the structure of the examination and how long it may take you to qualify. Chapters 2, 3 and 5 go on to explain, in more detail, the training you will require and the different types of course available.

Chapter 12 includes details of how to help pupils with disabilities and other impairments. Methods of teaching, instructor qualifications and courses available are all covered in this chapter.

The driving test is dealt with in Chapter 9. Details of the theory test, including the hazard perception test are explained and the revised practical test are covered in detail. The changes to the test that were introduced by the DVSA in December 2017 include a revision to the vehicle safety questions, driving while using a sat nav and the introduction of several new manoeuvres, including the 'pull up on right' exercise.

To qualify as an ADI you need to pass all three parts of the exam, but an alternative option is to take out a 'trainee licence' after passing the first two parts of the ADI exam. The licence requirements, regulations and responsibilities are dealt with in Chapter 4. The chapter includes how to apply for a licence, qualification, training and supervision.

It's important that you select a tutor who is completely up to date with the examination syllabus and who is a qualified and experienced trainer of ADIs. The Official Register of Driving Instructor Trainers (ORDIT) is a useful guide to available trainers in your area. However, the fact that a trainer is not on the ORDIT register is not necessarily an indication of the quality of the training. Many trainers – for various reasons – do not register. For details of ORDIT, visit **www.gov.uk**. Bear in mind that, although a local driving instructor may be extremely good at teaching new drivers, there is a vast difference between 'teaching to drive' and 'teaching to teach'.

As there is a limit of three attempts on the Part 2 Test of Driving Ability and the Part 3 Test of Ability to Instruct, you should make sure you are well prepared before you attempt these elements of the examination. The pass rate for the Part 3 exam is now running at less than 30 per cent, so it pays to make sure that you receive a realistic amount of good quality practical training from a qualified and experienced ADI tutor. Listen carefully to the advice given by your tutor. There are no short cuts! Remember, if you fail, there will be more pressure on you at the next attempt.

Details of the revised Part 2 and Part 3 tests are covered in chapter 3 and 5. The new-style Part 3 test, which was introduced in 2017, is an assessment of your ability to teach new drivers in a client-centred way, using the National Standard for Driver and Rider Training. The Standard is included in Practical Teaching Skills for Driving Instructors and should be used as a reference in both the ADI Part 3 test and the Standards Check. The complete version can be downloaded from **www.gov.uk/national-standard-for-driver-and-rider-training**.

The Car and Light Van Driving Syllabus is based on the National Driving Standard and provides a structured approach to acquiring the skills, knowledge and understanding to be a safe and responsible road user. The Syllabus is included in full in Chapter 11.

All driver and instructor training and testing (including the ADI Standards Check) is based on these National Standards and the Syllabus, so it is important that you are familiar with the requirements in preparation for the exams and for your work as a professional driver trainer.

Rules and regulations for the driver are in Chapter 10, with sections covering the main points of traffic law, driving licences, offences and penalty points. Vehicle regulations and documents are included in these sections.

The number of qualified instructors has increased over the past few years, with about 40,000 currently on the ADI Register. This figure has been increasing steadily each year although there are now some indications that it may be dropping slightly. Therefore, with a changing market and the sustained level of competition in the industry, you cannot afford to sit back and wait for the telephone to ring. You must be proactive and prepared to seek out new markets and prospective customers for yourself.

As a practising ADI, are you happy with the grading you achieved in your last test? Even though you may have a reasonable pass rate, your teaching style may be a little out of date – especially if you qualified some years ago. Although the Standards Check is covered in Chapter 6, you will find it helpful to update your knowledge and teaching style so that your methods are comparable to those of your newly qualified competitors, who may well have had more rigorous and thorough training. In this respect, listen to any advice given to you by the DVSA Examiner at the time of your regular Standards Check. Make sure that you are completely up to date with modern driving and teaching techniques and that you are working with the latest editions of *The Highway Code*, *The Official DVSA Guide to Driving – The essential skills* and *The Official DVSA Guide to Learning to Drive*. These publications should also form the basis of preparing your pupils for the theory test.

Qualifying as an Approved Driving Instructor 01

This chapter includes information on the 'Approved Driving Instructor' regulations, how to apply for the exams and an overview of the processes involved. Also covered are some suggestions about the qualities needed to become an effective driver trainer and training for the exams.

The ADI qualification

To comply with the requirements of the Road Traffic Act, anyone giving driving instruction for money or money's worth must either be registered with the Driver and Vehicle Standards Agency (DVSA) as an Approved Driving Instructor (ADI) or hold a current 'licence to give instruction' issued by the DVSA.

The Register of ADIs, which is operated in England, Scotland and Wales by the DVSA, has now been in existence for more than 40 years and in that time there have been considerable changes to the structure of the exams and the standards required for entry to the Register. This means that candidates now have to demonstrate a much higher standard of knowledge, driving and instructional skills in order to qualify for and remain on the Register.

If you wish to teach driving for reward, to either complete beginners or experienced drivers, the only official qualification is that of Driver and Vehicle Standards Agency (DVSA) Approved Driving Instructor (ADI) (Car). You must have had a minimum of four years' experience as a driver and meet all of the other requirements laid down in the Road Traffic Act.

To qualify as an ADI, you have to pass an examination that is conducted in three separate tests:

Part 1: Theory and Hazard Perception Test;
Part 2: Eyesight and Driving Ability Test;
Part 3: Test of Ability to Instruct.

You must take and pass all three tests within a two-year period.

Pre-entry qualifications

To become an ADI you must:

- hold a full UK or European Union (EU)/European Economic Area (EAA) unrestricted car driving licence; any EU/EAA licence must be exchanged for either a GB licence or a Community Licence.

- have held the licence for a total of at least four out of the six years prior to entering the Register after qualifying. A foreign driving licence, an automatic car driving licence or a provisional licence held after passing the driving test all count towards the four years.

- not have been disqualified from driving at any time in the four years prior to being entered in the Register.

- be a 'fit and proper' person to have your name entered on the Register. All spent and unspent convictions, both motoring and non-motoring, are taken into account when your application is assessed by the DVSA. This includes fixed penalty offences such as speeding. The decision in this respect rests with the Registrar, who will take into account any motoring convictions acquired in the last six years as well as your criminal record, if any. Any motoring offences that result in current endorsements totalling five penalty points or more will be looked at closely and could result in the application being refused.

- pass the two qualifying practical exams within two years of passing the theory and hazard perception tests.

- apply for registration within 12 months of passing the final part of the exam.

Full details about the qualifying process, pre-entry qualifications and registration can be downloaded from **www.gov.uk/guide-to-the-approved-driving-instructor-register**.

In Northern Ireland, the Register is administered by the Driver and Vehicle Agency. Application forms and the Guide to Becoming an Approved Driving Instructor are available to download from **www.nidirect.gov.uk** or from Business Support Unit, Driver & Vehicle Agency, Balmoral Road, Malone Lower, Belfast BT12 6QL (tel: 0289054 7933).

Application for registration

The initial application to have your name entered into the ADI Register is made at the same time as applying for the Part 1 Theory and Hazard

Perception Test. Application forms are available online or by phoning the DVSA on 0300 200 1122. You can apply online at **www.gov.uk** or by downloading the application form and applying by post. Your name will only be entered into the Register when you have passed the final part of the exam and have sent off your pass certificate with the registration fee, which is currently £300 (at February 2018). Examination and registration fees are reviewed from time to time. For details of the current fees you should ask your tutor, enquire by phone with the DVSA or check the website.

To provide driving tuition for money or the equivalent, you must:

- have passed all three parts of the qualifying examination and be a DVSA ADI (Car);

- have paid the current registration fee;

- agree to take a test of 'continued ability and fitness to give instruction' (Standards Check) when required to do so by the Registrar.

Alternatively, you must have passed Parts 1 and 2 and hold a Trainee Licence. This allows you to gain experience before taking the Part 3 instructional ability test.

For details of the three parts of the exam, see Chapters 2, 3 and 5. Full details of the requirements for a trainee licence are in Chapter 4.

Criminal history checks

Having a criminal record does not necessarily mean that you would be barred from becoming an ADI or that an existing ADI would be removed from the Register. In general terms, the DVSA would look at various factors when assessing the suitability of an applicant.

These factors include:

- the seriousness of the offence and its relevance to the safety of customers;

- the length of time since the offence;

- whether the offence was part of a history of offending, or just a one-off;

- whether the applicant's circumstances have changed since the offence was committed, making re-offending less likely;

- the degree of remorse, or otherwise, expressed by the applicant.

Full details about the suitability of ex-offenders are available from the DVSA and through its website. If you are in doubt, or have any queries about criminal record disclosure, you can contact the DVSA or its contractor at **www. onlinedisclosures.co.uk** or telephone 0845 51 5000.

Trainee licence

With a trainee licence you are allowed to work for payment for a driving school or an ADI while preparing for the instructional test. Under the provisions of the Road Traffic Act, a six-month licence to give instruction can be issued to suitable applicants (the fee at February 2018 is £140).

If you wish to take up this option, you can apply for a licence after you have passed Part 2 of the ADI exam, have completed the required amount of specified training and you have a sponsoring ADI. Only one licence will normally be granted and a second licence may only be issued in exceptional circumstances.

To qualify for a licence to instruct you must:

- have passed Parts 1 and 2 of the qualifying examination;
- have undergone 40 hours of training with a qualified ADI;
- be sponsored by an ADI.

Trainee licences are granted under the following conditions:

- The trainee instructor is only authorized to give instruction from the address on the licence.
- The trainee must receive 40 hours' practical training from an ADI. This period of training must start no earlier than six months before, and be completed by, the date of issue of the licence.
- You must not advertise yourself as a fully qualified instructor.
- You must receive a further period of 20 hours' training or be supervised on 20 per cent of your lessons. In Northern Ireland there is no requirement for specified training, but the 20 per cent supervision still applies.
- Whenever a trainee is giving driving lessons under this scheme, the licence must be displayed in the left-hand side of the car's windscreen.
- If requested by a police officer or anyone authorized by the Secretary of State, the licence must be produced.

For more detail about the training and supervision requirements for the trainee licence, see Chapter 4.

The rules for a trainee licence in Northern Ireland are slightly different: two licences, each of six months, are allowed, but the application for the second licence must be made before the expiry of the first one.

Examination structure

You must take and pass all three parts of the examination in the following sequence:

Part 1: theory and hazard perception test.
Part 2: eyesight test and a practical test of your driving.
Part 3: a test of your ability to give driving instruction.

From the date of passing the theory and hazard perception test, you have two years in which to pass the two practical tests. You may take the theory and hazard perception tests as many times as it takes you to pass both on the same occasion. However, there is a limit of three attempts on the driving and instructional tests.

(Note that in Northern Ireland you are limited to a maximum of three attempts at each part of the exam in a two-year period.)

Part 1: theory and hazard perception

The test covers a wide range of subject knowledge, including:

- the rules and regulations for driving on our roads;
- mechanical principles;
- teaching techniques;
- dealing with disabilities.

Tests are conducted, in English and Welsh, at 'L' test theory centres through-out the UK. If you are dyslexic it may be possible for special arrangements to be made. However, you must state this condition on your application form and you will need to supply some proof of it. Applications can be made online, by phone or by post.

The test uses a touch screen, but don't worry if you are not familiar with interactive computer programs. You will be allowed to work through a practice session before starting. There will also be staff on hand to help if you experience any difficulty.

You have to answer 100 multiple-choice questions by selecting one answer from a choice of four and you have 1hr 45mins to complete the test. The screens are easy to read, with only one question at a time being shown. The program allows you to move backwards and forwards through the questions to check on any you may not be sure about, or to change an answer should you wish to. The system will also alert you if there are questions you have not answered.

The banding system

The questions are banded into four subject groups:

- road procedure;
- traffic signs and signals; car control; pedestrians; mechanical knowledge;
- driving test; disabilities; law;
- publications; instructional techniques.

There are 12 different set tests, and the questions are set randomly for each candidate. This allows for an equal degree of difficulty for all candidates. For details of the subjects in each band, see Chapter 2.

The pass mark

To pass you need to score an overall mark of 85 per cent. However, in order to ensure that you have an adequate knowledge in all of the subject areas, you must score a mark of 80 per cent in each of the four bands. So, for example, if you get a maximum score of 100 per cent in three of the bands but only 76 per cent in the fourth, you will fail.

Following completion of the theory test, you will be given a short break before taking the hazard perception test.

The hazard perception test

This test consists of watching 14 video clips, each lasting about one minute. As with the multiple-choice element of the exam, you are allowed a short practice session before starting the test. Each hazard is allotted a maximum score of five points, and the earlier you spot it the more points you will achieve. However, you have to be careful not to click too many times as this will result in a negative score.

To pass the hazard perception part of the test you must score 57 out of a possible 75 marks. If you fail this part of the test you will have to take both parts again.

Results

You will receive the results for both parts within a few minutes of completing the hazard perception test. If you pass, you will be given information about applying for the Part 2, Eyesight and Driving Ability Test.

If you fail, you may apply for a re-test as soon as you wish. You are allowed to take this test as many times as it takes to pass both elements within the same session. (For more information on the syllabus, sample theory questions and how best to prepare for these two tests, see Chapter 2).

Part 2: driving ability

You may apply as soon as you have passed the theory and hazard perception tests. You will be given a list of test centres when you apply.

Send your application with the current fee (£111 at January 2018) to the DVSA in Nottingham. You will be sent a letter confirming your appointment. When you attend the test, take this and your driving licence and, if necessary, some photographic identification (such as your passport) with you.

The format of the test

The test lasts for about an hour and, if you wish, your trainer may accompany you. Sometimes a senior member of DVSA staff may accompany an examiner on test. This is to ensure uniformity so don't worry – they're not there to test you.

Eyesight

You will first of all be asked to read a number plate from a distance of 27.5 metres, with glasses or contact lenses if you normally wear them. If you cannot read the plate the rest of the test will not be conducted.

Vehicle safety questions

At the start of the test the examiner will ask several questions about vehicle safety. As with the 'L' test, these questions are on a 'show me'/'tell me' basis. Three of the questions ('tell me') will be asked at the start of the test and before moving off. The other two questions ('show me') will be asked while you are driving.

The syllabus for this part of the test includes:

- tyres and brakes;
- steering;
- lights and reflectors;
- direction indicators;

- audible warning devices;
- fluids used in the engine, braking or steering system;
- coolants and lubrication;
- wipers, demisters, brake lights, fog lights, head restraints, ABS warning lights, correct operation of all relevant controls and switches.

Sample questions

'Show me where you would check the engine oil level and tell me how you would check that the engine has sufficient oil.'

'Tell me how you would check that the brakes are working before starting a journey.'

'Show me how you would check that the power-assisted steering is working before starting a journey.'

'Show me how you would check that the headlights and tail lights are working.'

For more detail on the type of question see Chapter 9.

Each incorrect answer is recorded as a driving fault up to a maximum of four faults. If all five questions are answered incorrectly a serious fault is recorded, meaning that you would fail.

Driving technique

The test is of an advanced nature and a very high standard of competence is expected. You must drive in a brisk and 'business-like' manner, demonstrating that you have a thorough knowledge of the principles of good driving and road safety, and that you put them into practice at all times. Routes used include:

- heavy and fast-moving traffic, for example motorways and dual carriageways;
- rural sections;
- urban areas.

You must satisfy the examiner on your:

- expert handling of the controls;
- application of correct road procedure;
- anticipation of the actions of other road users and taking the appropriate action;

- sound judgement of speed, distance and timing;
- consideration for the convenience and safety of other road users.

The result

During the test the examiner will be making an assessment of your personal driving skills and will mark any relevant faults. You will be given the result as soon as the test is completed.

When you pass

To achieve a pass you need to score six or fewer driving faults. Your examiner will give you an oral debrief and explain any driver faults that have been recorded. You will also be given an application form for the Part 3 instructional test.

If you fail

All faults are recorded throughout the test and driving faults (those of a minor nature) will accumulate. You will fail if you commit more than six of these faults, or one serious or dangerous fault. Your examiner will give you a brief explanation of the faults recorded. You will also be given an application form for a further test. If you fail this test three times, you will not be allowed to apply for Part 3.

If you want to continue the process of qualifying after failing a third attempt, you would have to wait until a two-year period has expired from the date you passed the theory test. You will then have to start the whole process again, by taking the theory and hazard perception tests. It therefore makes sense to have sufficient good-quality training to ensure that your personal driving skills are up to the standard required.

For more information on preparing for the ADI Part 2 driving test, see Chapter 3.

Part 3: instructional ability

You can apply for this part of the exam as soon as you have passed the Part 2 driving test. The test is conducted at the centres listed on the application form and, as with the driving test, you can take it at the one of your choice. Send your application to the DVSA with the current fee (£111 at January 2018). The appointment will be confirmed by letter and, when you attend for the test, take this with you along with your driving licence.

The Part 3 test lasts for about an hour and is conducted by a specially qualified DVSA examiner. The test is an assessment of your ability to pass knowledge and skills on to a pupil using a client-centred approach. During the test you are assessed on three main areas of competence:

- lesson planning;
- risk management;
- teaching and learning strategies.

These three main areas of competence are broken down into 17 'lower level' competencies, which are marked individually. Details of the individual competences and how to apply them are in Chapter 5.

For this part of the ADI exam you must provide a suitable car and a pupil. The pupil may be a learner driver or a full licence holder, but they must not be an ADI or someone who has passed the first two parts of the ADI exam.

For full details of the Part 3 test see Chapter 5.

At the end of the test

So that your examiner can make a fair assessment of your overall performance, you will be asked to wait for a few minutes while all elements of your performance are considered. You will then be given an oral debriefing together with the relevant form. If you do not wish to wait, the form will be posted to you.

In Northern Ireland, the procedure is slightly different in that the result is posted on to the candidate within a few days of the exam. The instructor can then arrange a debriefing with the senior examiner by contacting the DVA and making an appointment.

When you pass

You will be given a letter confirming the result and you may apply for entry onto the Register of Approved Driving Instructors (Car) as soon as you wish. Complete the application form on the reverse of the letter and send it with the current fee to the DVSA in Nottingham. This must be done within 12 months of the date you pass.

Registration declaration

When you apply for registration, you must sign a declaration to the effect that you will:

- notify the Registrar of any change of name, address or place of employment;

- notify the Registrar if convicted of any offence;
- return the certificate if your registration lapses or is revoked;
- agree to undergo, when requested by the Registrar, a Standards Check conducted by DVSA staff.

The ADI certificate

You should receive your official green ADI Certificate of Registration within a week. This will remain valid for four years. You will then have to renew your registration. The certificate incorporates:

- your name;
- your photograph;
- your ADI number;
- the date of issue;
- the date of expiry of the certificate.

Displaying your ADI certificate

As a qualified instructor, whenever you are giving tuition for money or the equivalent, you must display the official green certificate on the left-hand side of the car's windscreen, and produce your certificate if requested by a police officer or any person authorized by the Secretary of State. Failure to do so constitutes an offence. If you can satisfy the Registrar that your certificate has been lost, damaged or destroyed, a duplicate can be issued on payment of the current fee.

If you fail

Using the application form on the reverse of the letter, you may apply for a further test if you are still within the two-year qualifying period and the failed test was your first or second attempt. Otherwise, if you wish to continue, you will have to wait until a two-year period from passing the theory test has elapsed before you can apply for Part 1 again. It therefore makes sense to have sufficient good-quality training to ensure that your instructional skills are up to the standard required to become an effective driving instructor!

Northern Ireland – a summary

ADI certificates and licences are issued by the Driver Vehicle Agency (DVA), Balmoral Road, Malone Lower, Belfast BT12 6QL (tel: 02890 547 933).

For detailed information, you should make sure you have an up-to-date copy of the ADI 1 *Your Guide to Becoming an Approved Driving Instructor*, which is available from the DVA (tel: 02890 547 933; website: **www.nidirect.gov.uk/motoring**).

As indicated previously in the chapter, the processes and procedures for ADI registration in Northern Ireland are very similar to those in the rest of the UK, but with a few significant differences, including:

Part 1 exam

You are allowed a maximum of three attempts.

Trainee licence

Two licences can normally be issued, but an application for the second licence must be made before the expiry of the first one. A third licence would only be granted in 'very exceptional circumstances'.

Supervision

A trainee instructor must be under 'direct personal supervision' for 20 per cent of all instruction time during the period of the licence. There is no requirement for specific training.

Part 3 exam (Instructional Ability)

Part 3 tests are conducted in Belfast and Londonderry.

ADI certificate

An ADI certificate issued in England, Scotland or Wales can be exchanged for a Northern Ireland certificate, but a registration fee is payable.

Fees (at January 2018):

ADI Part 1 (theory): £64
ADI Part 2 (driving): £130
ADI Part 3 (instruction): £138
Registration/renewal: £240
Trainee licence: £120.

Training to become an ADI

Selecting a course

One of the most important decisions to be made is on the method of training that can best be fitted in around your other commitments, particularly if you are currently in full-time employment. You also need to bear in mind that, although appointments for theory and hazard perception tests are usually available fairly quickly, the waiting time for practical test appointments is sometimes as long as three months.

Learning to become a driving instructor needs a significant commitment in terms of the time needed to:

- study the recommended books and other materials. Not only do you need to prepare yourself for the theory and hazard perception tests, but if you are to become an effective instructor you will need a thorough understanding of all the principles covered in the full syllabus. This means that learning the questions and answers by rote will not be sufficient!

- enhance your personal driving skills. This is not only so that you are properly prepared for the ADI Part 2 exam, but also so that your own driving will be to a consistently high standard.

- invest in sufficient good-quality training. This is necessary so that you are prepared for the instructional test, and also so that your teaching techniques will assist you in the future to produce better drivers to share the roads with us.

Statistics from the DVSA indicate that only about one-third of those beginning the process of training will eventually qualify as ADIs. Before you commit yourself to paying out large sums of money on training, it is sensible to arrange for an assessment with an experienced tutor. Obtaining an honest opinion of your potential can avoid unnecessary expense and wasted time in not eventually qualifying.

Teaching someone to teach driving is totally different from teaching someone to drive. It doesn't follow that good drivers will always make good instructors. Similarly, it is also very true that not all ADIs, though very good at teaching people to drive, will have the complex skills required to train new instructors. A local ADI may have an extremely good reputation for getting learners through the 'L' test, but because of the higher level of skills and knowledge involved, you may have to look further afield for a qualified and experienced tutor who is fully up to date with the requirements of the exams, trains instructors on a regular basis and is listed in the Official Register for Driving Instructor Training (ORDIT).

With the current pass rate for the instructional test running at about 30 per cent, most failures occur at this stage. It's vital, therefore, that your training is effective and is conducted by someone experienced in the coaching of new instructors.

Types of course available

The structure of the examination means that you will have to apply for, and pass, each test in sequence and there is often a long waiting list for the practical tests – sometimes as long as three months. You should also bear in mind that, should you fail Part 2 three times, you will not be eligible to take the third part of the exam. Make sure that you will not be paying for what you can't have.

Courses vary a great deal in content, duration and cost. Before deciding on the type of course that most suits your needs, you should make every effort to find out what you will be getting for your money. Ask for a full description of the syllabus and the format of the training in relation to each element of the exam.

Remember, everyone has a different rate of learning. The training you receive to develop your driving and teaching skills should, therefore, be adapted to suit your particular needs. Some examples of the types of training available are:

- distance learning programmes for studying at home for the theory test, with practical training for the driving and instructional tests;

- intensive courses to prepare candidates for all three tests;

- courses preparing candidates for obtaining a trainee licence and working for a driving school while preparing for the instructional test.

Before committing yourself, you should ask for information on the following points:

What proportion of the training for the practical elements will be conducted in the car?

How much individual training will I be getting and how much will be on a shared basis?

If the practical training is shared, how many trainees will be in the car at the same time?

Does the course allow for training to be structured to suit my particular learning abilities?

What are the tutor's special qualifications and experience?

And, if you opt for working under the Trainee Licence Scheme:

Will I be receiving proper training and support – particularly prior to being sent out with learners?

Course syllabus

As well as considering these points, you should compare the syllabus of the courses on offer with that of the examination. A good training establishment should prepare you properly for each of the three tests. The course should include:

- up-to-date books and materials with questions and answers for the theory test;
- computer-based practice at the hazard perception element;
- sufficient training for Part 2, Eyesight and Driving Ability Test;
- plenty of training, preferably on an individual basis (certainly no more than a ratio of two trainees to one tutor) for the instructional ability test.

(If you opt to take up a trainee licence, certain criteria must be met. For example, you must be prepared to have additional training and/or be properly supervised during the licence period. The trainee licence scheme is dealt with in more detail in Chapter 4.)

Course material

To prepare yourself properly for the examination, you will need the following materials, all of which are recommended by the DVSA:

The Official DVSA Guide to Driving – The essential skills.

The Highway Code.

The Official DVSA Guide to Learning to Drive.

Practical Teaching Skills for Driving Instructors by John Miller (10th edition, published by Kogan Page in 2017).

How long it will take to qualify

To be realistic, the qualifying procedure is likely to take around 8 to 10 months – that is, if you pass each element at the first attempt and there is no waiting for test appointments. It can take considerably longer than this if:

- there is a long waiting time for appointments;
- tests are postponed;
- you fail any of the tests.

This exam structure and time span should be taken into consideration if you are thinking of taking an intensive course. It is highly likely that you will have to return for 'top-up' training nearer the date of your Part 3 test appointment – and this will probably involve additional fees.

Making the decision

Make sure that you are fully aware of the degree of difficulty of the ADI exams.

Out of 9,000 candidates applying for a theory test in any one year, only about one-third actually qualify as an ADI.

Part 3 has the lowest pass rate at below 30 per cent, so for this test you will need plenty of expert training and preparation.

This change of career will involve a great deal of input in terms of time, commitment and cost. Before committing yourself and enrolling on a course, you should seriously consider the following aspects:

Do I have the potential to become an effective ADI?

Can I really afford the expense, given that there are no guarantees of qualifying?

Does the course allow for training to be tailored to the structure of the exam?

Will I be getting sufficient individual training in preparation for Parts 2 and 3?

Will the course be structured to suit my own needs?

Does my tutor have plenty of experience in the training of new instructors?

Practising before your test

To supplement your training, you may wish to practise without giving up your current job to work for a driving school. It is permissible to teach friends or relatives during your period of training, as long as you do not make any charge or receive payment of any kind, for example in petrol or goods. Alternatively, you may opt to work for another instructor under the Trainee Licence Scheme.

ORDIT – the Official Register of Driving Instructor Training

ORDIT is a voluntary registration scheme administered by the DVSA, using criteria that were set originally by representatives of the driver training industry. The Register consists of a list of training establishments that, following inspection by the DVSA, have satisfied the criteria of minimum standards.

Members of ORDIT offer professional training to a minimum and consistent standard. They are subject to regular inspections to ensure minimum standards are maintained. ORDIT members offer professional facilities and training courses that are designed to develop the skills of those wishing to become driving instructors and further develop the skills of existing driving instructors.

All training courses are structured to ensure clients are fully prepared to teach driving as a life skill.

Qualities of the driver and instructor

To be able to enhance your personal driving skills and ensure that you are driving in line with modern techniques, you need to be aware of the qualities required by the good driver as described by the DVSA in its book, *The Official DVSA Guide to Driving – The essential skills*. Additionally, you will need similar attributes to become an effective instructor.

Responsibility

As a driver: you should always show proper concern for the safety of yourself, your passengers and all other road users. You should also be aware of the need to drive economically and in an environmentally friendly manner.

As an instructor: always have the safety and well-being of your pupils at heart, particularly those in the early stages of their driving careers. Avoid taking them into situations they are unable to cope with. Remember: you are responsible for their safety.

Concentration

As a driver: you must concentrate at all times. Just a moment's distraction from the driving task can have disastrous effects in today's heavily congested and fast-moving traffic.

As an instructor: sitting next to inexperienced drivers, your concentration is even more vital. You have to read the road much further ahead than they will, taking into account any developing situations so that you can keep your pupils safe, relaxed and eager to learn.

Anticipation

As a driver: the ability to predict what might happen is an important part of the skills needed to avoid danger. You need to be aware of any possible hazards in time to safely deal with them.

As an instructor: anticipation is even more important. You will be sitting in the passenger seat beside someone much less able at the controls of your car. You will have to learn to recognize the needs of each individual and anticipate how different pupils may or may not respond to changing situations.

You have to plan as far ahead as possible and anticipate any potential hazards. This will allow time for you to give either positive instructions or prompts, so that your pupil will be able to take any action necessary to avoid problems.

Patience

As a driver: always show patience and restraint with other drivers when they make mistakes. Not everyone is as thoughtful as you!

As an instructor: displaying a positive attitude to your pupils will not only set a good example to them but, if you have your name on your car, it will also be good advertising.

Remember, we all had to learn to drive, and some find it more difficult than others! If you lose patience with a pupil it will only make matters worse. Most people are aware when they have made a mistake anyway, so be patient and always willing to give more help – even when you have explained things several times before.

Demonstrating tolerance will also go a long way in building up your pupils' confidence and also their belief in you.

Confidence

As a driver: the conscientious and efficient driver displays confidence at all times. This confidence results from being totally 'at one' with the vehicle. You should always be travelling at a speed to suit the road, weather and traffic conditions, with an appropriate gear engaged and in the correct position on the road. Planning well ahead and anticipating hazards, the confident driver can avoid the need to make any last-minute, rushed, and usually unsafe, decisions.

As an instructor: not only do you need to be confident yourself, but you will also need the skills required to help develop your pupils' confidence. To do this, you will need to ensure that the routes you select for teaching each aspect of the syllabus are matched to each individual's ability. Avoiding situations where a pupil is not ready will help build up their skills and confidence.

Knowledge

As a driver: not only do you need a sound knowledge of the rules and regulations contained in *The Highway Code* and *The Official DVSA Guide to Driving – The essential skills*, but you also need to be able to apply them in all situations.

As an instructor: you will need to pass on this knowledge so that the drivers you teach will also be able to apply the same principles for driving safely. Remember – they will eventually be sharing the roads with us!

Be prepared to make the effort to keep yourself up to date with the changes taking place so that you are able to:

- handle your vehicle sympathetically and economically;
- apply modern teaching techniques;
- maintain a safe teaching environment;
- recognize the need for keeping your vehicle roadworthy;
- offer advice to pupils on driver licensing requirements, basic mechanical principles, and the rules and regulations for safe driving on all types of road;
- answer pupils' queries confidently.

As well as enhancing your driving skills, having a sound knowledge and understanding will help in your preparations to become an effective instructor.

Remember:

- your knowledge will be tested in the theory element of the ADI examination;
- how you apply this knowledge will be assessed in the driving ability test;
- how you pass the information on to pupils will be assessed in the instructional ability test.

Communication

As a driver: you have to continually communicate your intentions to other road users. Methods of signalling these intentions include:

- using the indicators and arm signals;
- brake lights;
- early positioning on the road;
- reversing lights;
- horn and flashing headlights;
- hazard warning flashers;
- eye contact.

As an instructor: you will need to develop ways of communicating effectively with the wide variety of pupils you will be dealing with. You may sometimes have to adapt the terminology you use so that all your pupils understand exactly what you mean. Not only will you need to be able to teach your pupils how to apply the relevant procedures and driving techniques, you also need to be able to explain why these procedures need to be followed. This 'why' reasoning should lead to a better understanding that will result in safer drivers sharing the road with us.

There are various ways in which you can communicate with your pupils, including:

- establishing the level of understanding of the individual pupil;
- finding the most appropriate method and style of communication;
- explaining new principles in a clear and straightforward way;
- using visual aids so that the pupil can 'see' what you mean;
- giving practical demonstrations of any complicated procedures;
- developing confidence and success by talking the pupil through any new procedures;
- giving your directional instructions clearly and in good time so that the pupil has time to respond safely;
- giving encouragement through positive feedback and praise where deserved;
- finding out whether the pupil has fully understood your instructions by asking appropriate questions;
- encouraging the pupil to ask questions if you feel that he or she does not understand.

Awareness

Modern driving techniques are becoming relatively easier through advances in technology and design, making cars much more efficient and safe. However, road and traffic conditions are becoming more and more complex and congested, and in order to keep your clients safe, you need to be aware of the major causes of road accidents. These include:

- other drivers' ignorance of, or total disregard for, the rules of the road;
- lack of concentration and response to developing situations;
- carelessness;
- driving while under the influence of drink or drugs;
- driving when feeling unwell;
- driving with deficient eyesight;
- some drivers' willingness to take risks;
- using vehicles that are not roadworthy;
- driving while under the stress of modern needs to rush everywhere;
- using mobile phones or other in-car equipment.

All these elements mean that new drivers have to be taught to a far higher standard than ever, with hazard awareness playing a major role in their development. It will be up to you to ensure that you teach drivers at all levels to:

- handle their vehicle sympathetically and economically;
- drive with courtesy and consideration;
- look and plan well ahead, anticipating what may happen;
- take early action to avoid problems;
- compensate for the mistakes of others;
- understand what they are doing and why they are doing it.

To be able to do all these things, you should be prepared to keep yourself up to date with the changes taking place relevant to driving and the teaching of it. We all need to update and adapt our driving procedures and habits from time to time and adjust them to meet current rules and regulations, as well as to deal with ever-changing road and traffic conditions.

ADI Part 1:   02
Theory test and
hazard perception

This is the first of three parts of the ADI exams. The test takes about 1 hr 45 mins in total and is in two sections:

- a multiple-choice question paper of 100 questions; and
- a hazard perception test using video clips

You must take and pass both sections on the same occasion at the same time.

There is no limit to the number of times you can take the test.

See **www.gov.uk/adi-part-1-test** for more information.

Note: In Northern Ireland you are allowed only three attempts.

Booking the ADI theory test

You can book the theory test if your application to start the qualifying process has been accepted by the DVSA. At that stage, you will be given details of the booking arrangements.

The most convenient way to book is online at **www.gov.uk/book-your-instructor-theory-test**. To do this you will need:

- a valid UK or EU driving licence;
- your personal reference number from the DVSA;
- debit or credit card details.

Alternatively you can book by phone on 0300 200 1122.

The cost of the ADI theory test at February 2018 is £81 (£64 in Northern Ireland), but up-to-date fees are shown at **www.gov.uk/approved-driving-instructor-adi-fees**. To cancel or postpone the test you need to give at least three clear days' notice otherwise you are likely to lose the fee.

Special needs

Facilities are available for candidates who have special needs.

If you have reading difficulties, including dyslexia, you can request a voice-over in English. You may also be allowed extra time to complete the multiple-choice part of the exam. To use these facilities you must send evidence of your particular reading difficulty to the DVSA at the time of your application.

The postal address for enquiries about the theory test is:

DVSA, PO Box 1286, Warrington, WA1 9GN.

If you have another type of special need you can contact customer services at the DVSA to discuss your particular requirement and the facilities that might be available.

Multiple-choice questions

This part of the test consists of 100 questions, with four alternative answers, one of which is correct.

The questions are banded into four subject groups:

- road procedure;
- traffic signs and signals; car control; pedestrians; mechanical knowledge;
- driving test; disabilities; law;
- publications; instructional techniques.

You are allowed 90 minutes to complete this part of the test.

Example questions

Band 1 – Road procedure

Q You should not attempt to overtake a cyclist:

    a on a dual carriageway;

    b on a left-hand bend;

    c just before turning left;

    d on a one-way street.

Q You are moving off from behind a parked car. You should:

    a look round as you move off;

    b always give a signal;

c look round before starting to move;

d use all three mirrors as you pull out.

Q You are driving at night and are dazzled by the headlights of an oncoming vehicle. You should:

a use full beam headlights;

b switch on your front fog lights;

c slow down and stop if necessary;

d flash your headlights to warn the other driver.

Q You are about to turn left into a side road where pedestrians are crossing. You should:

a wait for them to cross;

b move out round them;

c sound the horn to warn the pedestrians;

d flash your headlights.

Q If traffic is moving slowly in lanes:

a you should change lanes as much as possible to make progress;

b you must not overtake on the left;

c you should keep to the right-hand lane where possible;

d you are allowed to overtake on the left when traffic in the right-hand lane is moving more slowly.

Q Approaching a right-hand bend your position should be:

a well to the left;

b middle of the lane;

c either left or centre, depending on the type of bend;

d more to the right.

Q A large vehicle in front of you is signalling left but moving out to the right. You should:

a overtake on the left;

b overtake on the right;

c flash your headlights to warn the driver;

d stay back until the vehicle has completed the turn.

Q When reversing you should:

   a be ready to give way to other traffic;

   b complete the manoeuvre as quickly as possible;

   c assume that other traffic will give way;

   d give a signal to warn other road users.

Q When following a large vehicle, you should not be too close because:

   a the driver may not be able to see you in their mirrors;

   b the vehicle may stop suddenly;

   c it would be more difficult to overtake on the left;

   d you might not see road signs.

Q You are waiting to emerge from a side road. A vehicle on the main road is signalling to turn left into your road. You should:

   a move as soon as possible to keep the traffic flowing;

   b wait until you can see that the other vehicle is actually turning;

   c stop until the other vehicle has gone;

   d move out carefully.

Band 2 – Traffic signs and signals; car control; pedestrians; mechanical knowledge

Q If you can see regular street lighting, but no speed limit signs, the limit is usually:

   a 20 mph;

   b 30 mph;

   c 40 mph;

   d 50 mph.

Q Flashing amber lights at a pelican crossing mean that you should:

   a give way to pedestrians who are waiting;

   b proceed, but carefully;

   c give way to any pedestrians who are on the crossing;

   d stop.

Q A bus lane showing no indication of times of operation means:

   a there is no restriction on entering it;

   b it operates 24 hours a day;

  c it only operates during peak hours;

  d you can enter it if there are no buses.

Q On a wet road, the back of your car is sliding to the right. You should:

  a steer to the left;

  b steer to the right;

  c brake firmly in a straight line;

  d accelerate gently.

Q To supervise a learner driver you must:

  a be an ADI or hold a trainee licence;

  b hold a full licence;

  c be over 25;

  d be at least 21 and have held a full licence for at least three years.

Q A prohibitory sign tells the driver:

  a about a hazard;

  b what they must do;

  c what they must not do;

  d to slow down.

Q A single broken white line along the centre of the road with long markings and short gaps means that it is a:

  a centre line;

  b warning line;

  c hazard warning;

  d no overtaking line.

Q A straight pelican crossing with a central refuge is:

  a treated as one continuous crossing;

  b treated as two separate crossings;

  c up to the pedestrian how to deal with it;

  d governed by the lights on each side.

Q A 'Toucan' crossing is for:

  a pedestrians and cyclists;

  b cyclists only;

c pedestrians only;

d horse riders.

Q A green traffic light means that you can:

a go, but only if it is safe to do so;

b go promptly;

c go if the green filter light is on;

d only go if you are turning left or going straight on.

Band 3 – The driving test; disabilities; the law

Q A person who is profoundly deaf would be allowed to drive:

a any category B motor vehicle;

b specified vehicles only;

c with a special note on the licence;

d no motor vehicles.

Q After passing the driving test, you develop a health problem that could affect your driving. You need to:

a inform the police;

b not do anything;

c inform DVLA;

d notify DVSA.

Q During a lesson, your pupil is involved in an accident where no one is injured, but there is damage to someone else's property. The property owner is not about. You are required to:

a report the accident to your insurance company;

b report the accident to the police as soon as possible;

c try to contact the property owner;

d tell someone who lives nearby.

Q A driving test pass certificate is valid for:

a one year;

b two years;

c three years;

d an unlimited amount of time.

Q To avoid losing the fee if cancelling or postponing, a driving test candidate must give:

   a three working days' notice;

   b seven days' notice;

   c 24 hours' notice;

   d as much notice as possible.

Q A driving test examiner will:

   a give advice if the learner asks;

   b help if appropriate;

   c only give help and take action in an emergency;

   d give help to the learner in the first few minutes of the test.

Q Out of 50 questions in the theory test for learners, the pass mark is:

   a 39;

   b 41;

   c 43;

   d 45.

Q A driving test pass certificate is valid for:

   a two weeks;

   b until the licence expires;

   c two months;

   d two years.

Q A driver who has a hearing loss will:

   a be issued with a restricted licence;

   b need to take a special test;

   c not be allowed to drive;

   d have no restriction on their licence.

Q When applying for a driving test a person with a disability will need to:

   a complete a separate form;

   b pay an additional fee;

   c contact the driving test centre;

   d give information about the disability when applying.

Band 4 – Publications; instructional techniques

Q When teaching a pupil to stop they should be taught:

a to select a lower gear;

b to change down through the gears;

c that a gear change is not always necessary;

d to use first gear.

Q You are approaching a set of traffic lights that are out of action. You should teach the pupil to:

a stop and look each way;

b be prepared to stop for traffic from any direction;

c stop, unless someone is close behind you;

d only stop if there are any large vehicles about.

Q In order to start learning effectively, the pupil should:

a want to learn;

b understand some basic car mechanics;

c have good hand/eye coordination;

d be technically minded.

Q If a pupil gives only a part answer to a question you should:

a give praise, but ask a supplementary question;

b offer a full explanation;

c tell the pupil to study the subject in more detail;

d repeat the question.

Q Giving feedback means that you should:

a comment on all errors;

b provide information about the pupil's performance;

c always praise the pupil;

d instruct at all times.

Q A course of lessons should be structured by moving from:

a complex to simple;

b known to unknown;

c unknown to known;

d one part of the syllabus to another in a strict timetable.

Q Studying *The Highway Code* will increase the pupil's:

   a knowledge;

   b skill;

   c awareness;

   d attitude.

Q The usual way to give directional instructions is:

   a direct, identify, alert;

   b alert, direct, identify;

   c identify, direct, instruct;

   d identify, instruct, alert.

Q There are three recognized types of route for learners:

   a town, country, test route;

   b primary, secondary, dual carriageway;

   c nursery, intermediate, advanced;

   d rural, residential, town.

Q You should only use the word 'stop':

   a when there is approaching traffic;

   b when approaching a traffic light on amber;

   c in an emergency;

   d at a junction.

You are allowed 90 minutes to complete the questions. During the test you do not necessarily have to answer the questions in order – you can move between questions and 'flag' any that you may want to come back to later.

One hundred questions are set randomly in 12 different papers to allow an equal degree of difficulty for all candidates, and the questions will not appear in 'banded' order.

The question bank is not published, but official revision questions covering the same topics and subject areas are available from the DVSA.

You must take your driving licence with you. If you have an old-style paper licence you must also produce a valid passport as visual identity. Make sure you arrive in good time. If you are late or you do not have the correct documents, you may not be allowed to take the test and you will lose the fee.

You are allowed plenty of time for this test – don't rush. As you can see, the questions are very wide-ranging and some will need careful consideration. Don't worry if you see people leaving after only half an hour. Learner drivers use the same centres and their test only takes about 35 minutes compared with the 90 minutes allowed for the ADI exam. If you have been thorough with your studies, you should have no problems, but make sure you:

- take your time;
- read each question carefully and at least twice;
- carefully consider the choice of answers;
- eliminate the obviously wrong answers quite quickly, where possible, but take time to consider the options when faced with negatively worded questions;
- leave questions you're not sure about and go back to them when you've answered those you find easier;
- check that you've answered all the questions.

The overall pass mark is 85 per cent. However, to show that you have an adequate knowledge in all the subject areas, you need a score of at least 80 per cent in each band to pass. This means that, even if you score 100 per cent in three of the bands and 76 per cent in the fourth, you will fail. This emphasizes the need for a thorough understanding of the principles covered in all the recommended materials.

After you have completed the theory test you will be given a short break before taking the hazard perception test.

Hazard perception test

Before starting this part of the test, as with the theory element, you will be allowed a short practice session.

The test consists of 14 computer-generated imagery clips showing various developing hazards. A 'developing hazard' is one that may cause you to take some action, such as changing speed or direction.

One of the clips has two potential hazards, the others all have just one. You must watch carefully and respond to the hazards by clicking on the mouse. As each hazard develops, you need to keep registering a response to the changing situation – just as you would be assessing and reassessing developing situations when driving.

Each hazard is allotted a maximum score of five points, and the earlier you spot the hazard, the more points you will achieve. Provided your responses are made to correspond with the potential hazards or changing situations, you should be able to achieve a maximum score.

Be careful not to click too early, or at random, as this will result in a negative score.

To pass you must score 57 out of a possible 75 marks. If you fail this part of the test you will have to take both parts again.

Resource materials

To ensure that you cover all the elements included in this syllabus, the DVSA recommends that you study the following materials:

- *Driving – The essential skills.*
- *The Highway Code.*
- *The Official DVSA Theory Test for Approved Driving Instructors Pack.*
- *Know Your Traffic Signs.*
- *Practical Teaching Skills for Driving Instructors.*

The multiple-choice theory test questions are based on information in these books. Make sure that you have the latest editions of these publications.

For details of all books and resource materials, see Appendix III.

It's sensible to practise your skills at responding to 'on-screen' hazards. Your trainer should be able to supply you with one or more of the wide variety of CD-ROMs and DVDs that are now available.

The DVSA produces a very effective interactive DVD on hazard perception. As well as preparing you for the ADI theory exam, it is useful material for your pupils. For more information, see **www.tsoshop.co.uk/bookstore.asp**.

After the test

When you pass you will receive a pass certificate letter showing the marks for each part of the test.

This certificate is needed when you apply for and take the ADI Part 2.

You have two years from the date of passing the Part 1 to complete all three parts of the exam and qualify as an ADI.

If you fail, you can apply again straight away. There is no limit to the number of theory tests you can take.

Note that in Northern Ireland you are allowed only three attempts at the Part 1 test within the two-year period.

Preparing for the Part 1

To be a safe driver and an effective instructor, you need a thorough understanding of the principles, rules and regulations included in all the reading materials recommended by the Driver and Vehicle Standards Agency (DVSA).

As a professional driver trainer, you should be able to:

- apply these principles, rules and regulations whenever you are driving;

- pass on all this information to your pupils to help them acquire the skills needed to put them into practice effectively;

- give accurate answers to any questions your pupils may ask.

To be able to carry out your work as a responsible ADI, you need a wide range of subject knowledge and skills. For this reason, the theory test syllabus includes:

- The principles of road safety in general and their application in specified circumstances.

- Correct and courteous driving techniques:
  - car control;
  - road procedure;
  - hazard recognition and proper response;
  - dealing safely with other road users and pedestrians;
  - the use of safety equipment.

- The theory and practice of learning, teaching and assessment.

- The tuition required to instruct a pupil in driving a car, and:
  - the identification, analysis and correction of errors;
  - your manner and the relationship between instructor and pupil;
  - simple vehicle adaptations for drivers with disabilities;
  - a knowledge of *The Highway Code*;
  - a knowledge of *The Official DVSA Guide to Learning to Drive*.

- A knowledge of basic mechanics and the design of cars adequate for the needs of driving instruction.

Studying the syllabus

Don't be misled into thinking that it will be enough to just learn a set of questions and answers by rote! Learning something 'by rote' means memorizing through repetition. This way of learning, although useful for remembering such things as multiplication tables and other basic facts, will not give you the understanding you need to be properly prepared to:

- be able to discriminate between the correct and incorrect answers given in the theory test;
- gain the maximum benefit from your practical training;
- pass the practical tests within the limited number of attempts allowed;
- effectively carry out your role as an ADI.

You should also consider that, if you are not properly prepared, there is the additional expense of failing two or three tests.

You need to prepare yourself properly for the exam for all the reasons indicated above, especially as it is highly unlikely that you will be able to memorize the answers to specific questions. This is particularly relevant when you consider that the questions are not presented in 'banded' order.

Even if you enrol on an intensive course, you will still have a lot of studying to do in your own time. There are no shortcuts to gaining all this knowledge and understanding. Be prepared to exercise a good deal of self-discipline and set enough time aside for your studies.

Simply using the practice questions or reading a book will not necessarily benefit you – even if you have a photographic memory!

You need to really know and understand all the topics and subject areas thoroughly.

Develop your study skills by:

- making time available;
- finding the best place to carry out your studies;
- formulating a study plan.

Make the best use of your time by:

- organizing study periods to fit in with your existing commitments;
- setting yourself achievable objectives;
- not overloading yourself by trying to learn too much at once;

- following a properly structured study programme;
- dividing the materials into related topics;
- monitoring your progress throughout your course;
- seeking the advice of your tutor if there are any points you don't understand.

You will find more information on how to develop your study skills in *Practical Teaching Skills for Driving Instructors*.

Theory mock test

These questions are designed to test your knowledge of the syllabus for the ADI Part 1 exam.

They are not actual DVSA official practice questions, but they are very similar in content and are taken from all parts of the syllabus.

Although the questions are not in any particular order, they cover the complete syllabus, with a balance of questions in each.

Band 1:

Road procedure – 25 questions.

Band 2:

Traffic signs and signals – 5 questions.

Car control – 10 questions.

Pedestrians – 5 questions.

Mechanical knowledge – 5 questions.

Band 3:

Driving tests – 10 questions.

Disabilities – 5 questions.

Law – 10 questions.

Band 4:

Publications – 10 questions.

Instructional techniques – 15 questions.

Remember that you need to achieve at least 80 per cent in each band as well as the overall pass mark of 85 per cent.

This means that you need to have 85 correct answers, with at least 20 correct in each band.

You should be able to complete the test in about 90 minutes. Mark one answer unless otherwise indicated.

1 At traffic lights, amber means:

   a) Keep going if it's safe to do so.

   b) Stop under any circumstances.

   c) Stop, unless it would be unsafe to do so.

   d) All other lights will be showing red.

2 A theory test pass certificate is valid for:

   a) 6 months.

   b) 12 months.

   c) 18 months.

   d) 24 months.

3 Signs giving directions are usually:

   a) Rectangular.

   b) Triangular.

   c) Circular.

   d) Hexagonal.

4 A long white line with short gaps down the centre of the road is an indication of:

   a) A deviation.

   b) An entrance to property.

   c) A hazard.

   d) An urban clearway.

5 *The Highway Code* says that you should never reverse:

   a) From a major road into a minor road.

   b) On one-way streets.

   c) From a minor road onto a major road.

   d) Into narrow driveways.

6 Reflective studs along the left edge of the road are:

a) Blue.

b) White.

c) Amber.

d) Red.

7 Pupils should apply for the theory test:

a) Within three months of receiving their provisional licence.

b) When they have studied and the ADI advises them to do so.

c) Only after they have had some practical lessons.

d) Only after passing the hazard perception test.

8 Unless exempt, passengers travelling in cars must wear seat belts in:

a) The front seats only.

b) Any seat of the car.

c) The rear seats only.

d) Towns and on motorways only.

9 You must report to the licensing authority any medical condition that:

a) Warrants a visit to the doctor.

b) Is likely to last more than one month.

c) Is likely to last more than three months.

d) Requires you to take medication.

10 Car passengers under three years of age are the responsibility of:

a) Their parents.

b) The adult sitting next to them.

c) No one in particular.

d) The driver.

11 The speed limits for learner drivers are:

a) The same as for full licence holders.

b) 10 mph less than for full licence holders.

c) 10 per cent less than for full licence holders.

d) Maximum 50 mph.

12 You should control the speed of your car when driving downhill by:

a) Using the highest gear possible.

b) Slowing down and then changing to a lower gear.

c) Coasting while using the footbrake.

d) Braking firmly all the way down the hill.

13 What is 'client-centred learning' about?

a) Always doing what the pupil wants to do in the lesson.

b) Constantly asking the pupil questions.

c) An ongoing conversation with the pupil to ensure that you understand their learning needs.

d) Always looking the pupil in the eye when you give them feedback.

14 To ensure uniformity of tests, examiners are:

a) Allowed to apply their own standards to individual tests.

b) Never transferred from one test centre to another.

c) Closely supervised by a senior examiner.

d) Influenced by each ADI's standards.

15 A full driving licence is valid until the driver's:

a) 60th birthday.

b) 65th birthday.

c) 70th birthday.

d) 75th birthday.

16 If you are involved in an accident and do not have your insurance certificate with you, it must be produced at a police station within:

a) 24 hours.

b) 48 hours.

c) Five days.

d) Seven days.

17 Children under 14 should wear seat belts:

a) If travelling in the front or rear of the car.

b) When they are the only passenger in the car.

c) If they decide for themselves to do so.

d) Only if there is no child harness available.

18 In built-up areas, a 30-mph speed limit applies unless there are:

   a) Signs indicating otherwise.

   b) Houses on one side of the road.

   c) Signs stating 'urban clearway'.

   d) No pavements.

19 A provisional licence holder is allowed to drive a vehicle of up to:

   a) 1.5 tonnes.

   b) 3.5 tonnes.

   c) 7.5 tonnes.

   d) 2.0 tonnes.

20 Using the gears to slow down should:

   a) Result in better fuel economy.

   b) Be normal practice for learners.

   c) Not be normal practice.

   d) Save wear and tear on the gearbox.

21 Groups of people marching on the road should:

   a) Keep to the right.

   b) Keep to the left.

   c) Have a red flag showing at the back of the group.

   d) Have a white flag showing at the front of the group.

22 Approaching a green traffic light, you should:

   a) Speed up in case the light changes.

   b) Give an arm signal for slowing down.

   c) Expect traffic in other directions to stop.

   d) Be ready to stop if the lights change.

23 When walking with children, you should:

   a) Cross the road only at pedestrian crossings.

   b) Walk between the child and the road.

   c) Make sure the child is wearing reflective clothing.

   d) Cross the road with the child in front.

24 Unless you are receiving higher-rate Disability Living Allowance, the minimum legal age for driving a car is:

a) 17.

b) 16.

c) 18.

d) 21.

25 As a general rule, driving test routes are designed to incorporate:

a) A wide variety of road and traffic situations.

b) Level crossings or motorways.

c) Very steep gradients.

d) As many non-standard situations as possible.

26 The ADI Regulations are part of:

a) The Road Traffic Act.

b) *The Guide to Becoming an Approved Driving Instructor.*

c) *The Official DVSA Guide to Learning to Drive.*

d) *The Driving Instructor's Handbook.*

27 When turning right at a junction where an oncoming vehicle is also turning right, the DVSA book, *Driving – The essential skills*, advises:

a) Turning nearside to nearside.

b) Turning offside to offside where possible.

c) Holding back until the road is clear.

d) Waiting behind the give-way line.

28 According to *The Highway Code*, you should not park on:

a) The right-hand side of the road.

b) Any broken yellow line at night.

c) Any road where there are no street lights.

d) A road marked with double white lines.

29 *The Highway Code* says that, at night, you should use:

a) Sidelights in built-up areas.

b) Dipped headlights in built-up areas.

c) Sidelights on all roads.

d) Sidelights and fog lights.

30 Serious faults committed by the pupil in the first few minutes of a driving test:

a) Will be ignored by the examiner.

b) Never result in failure.

c) Will not be recorded.

d) May result in failure.

31 One of the basic teaching principles is:

a) Demonstration–practice–explanation.

b) Practice–explanation–demonstration.

c) Explanation–demonstration–practice.

d) Explanation–practice–demonstration.

32 When attending for a theory test, candidates must produce:

a) A current valid provisional driving licence.

b) A copy of *The Official DVSA Guide to Learning to Drive*.

c) Acknowledgement of their application.

d) Their instructor's ADI certificate.

33 The instruction for turning left should be:

a) Turn next left, please.

b) Next left turn, please.

c) Take the next opening on the left, please.

d) Take the next road on the left, please.

34 For an instructor to accompany a pupil on test, the:

a) Candidate must ask the examiner.

b) Instructor must ask the examiner.

c) Request must be made on the original application.

d) Instructor must sign not to take part.

35 *The Highway Code* says that the minimum tread on tyres should be:

a) 1.0 mm.

b) 1.6 mm.

c) 2.0 mm.

d) 2.6 mm.

36 A white stick with a red band is used by someone who is:

   a) Blind and mute.

   b) Partially sighted.

   c) Deaf and blind.

   d) Registered as blind.

37 A pupil on test who commits only one serious fault will:

   a) Pass the test.

   b) Fail the test.

   c) Be judged at the examiner's discretion.

   d) Be taken back to the test centre.

38 To cancel a driving test without losing the fee requires:

   a) Three complete working days' notice.

   b) Three days' notice including weekend days.

   c) Three days' notice including Bank Holidays.

   d) Three days' notice including the day of the test.

39 When first introducing a novice to the use of mirrors, emphasis should be placed on:

   a) Correct adjustment.

   b) Effective use of all mirrors.

   c) Full, all-round observations.

   d) Checking the nearside blind areas.

40 For a first attempt at reversing, most emphasis should be on:

   a) Taking effective observations.

   b) Maintaining control of the car.

   c) Finishing in a perfect position.

   d) Using the handbrake at each pause.

41 According to the DVSA book, *Driving – The essential skills*, it is:

   a) Essential that an ADI is a 'perfect driver'.

   b) Doubtful that the 'perfect driver' exists.

   c) Quite common to achieve driving perfection.

   d) Not worth aiming for perfection in your driving.

42 Anyone supervising a learner driver must:

   a) Be at least 25 and have held a full driving licence for at least three years.

   b) Have passed an advanced driving test.

   c) Have their name on the ADI register or hold a trainee licence.

   d) Be at least 21 and have held a full driving licence for that type of vehicle for at least three years.

43 If an examiner has to take action, this will be recorded on the driving test report as a:

   a) Possible failure.

   b) Driving fault.

   c) Serious fault.

   d) Dangerous fault.

44 Who, of the following, may accompany a learner on a driving test:

   a) Anyone the candidate wishes.

   b) Only an ADI.

   c) Only a parent or guardian.

   d) No one other than DVSA personnel.

45 The purpose of the examiner's driving report, which is given to all successful test candidates, is to:

   a) Help overcome any minor weaknesses in the candidate's driving.

   b) Show how close to perfect the candidate was.

   c) Make sure the successful candidate does not become over-confident.

   d) Highlight the errors in the ADI's teaching.

46 So that learners get the most benefit from each lesson, instructors should organize their teaching plan:

   a) At the beginning of each session.

   b) In short, attainable stages.

   c) In large stages, so that fewer lessons will be needed.

   d) Extensively to cover all aspects.

47 Setting very difficult objectives for a learner driver may:

   a) Help pupils learn more quickly.

   b) Slow down the pupil's learning.

    c) Cause pupils to lose concentration.

    d) Result in more being remembered.

48 At the end of each lesson the instructor should:

    a) Point out all the faults committed during the lesson.

    b) Emphasize each individual fault.

    c) Take the payment for the next lesson.

    d) Recap on what has been learnt.

49 When passing stationary buses you should:

    a) Drive past quickly to minimize the danger.

    b) Pass slowly, looking for people getting off.

    c) Flash your headlights to warn the driver.

    d) Sound the horn to warn any pedestrians.

50 When students reach a 'plateau' in their learning you should:

    a) Go on to a new topic.

    b) Carry on with the lesson you had planned.

    c) Return to a previous topic for reinforcement purposes.

    d) Introduce a more difficult topic.

51 Extreme emotions such as fear or anger:

    a) Can be relieved by going for a drive.

    b) Can enhance concentration when driving.

    c) Should help you to pay attention to hazards.

    d) Can reduce your concentration levels.

52 The exhaust system:

    a) Gets rid of burnt gases.

    b) Only works when the engine is hot.

    c) Takes hot air from the carburettor.

    d) Helps to slow the car.

53 If your car breaks down on a level crossing and the bells start ringing, you should firstly:

    a) Push the vehicle over the crossing.

    b) Try to find out the cause of the problem.

c) Stand well clear.

d) Wave a warning signal.

54 An ADI who is disqualified from driving for 12 months would be barred from giving driving instruction for a total of:

a) One year.

b) Two years.

c) Five years.

d) Six years.

55 You can only be issued with a trainee licence if you:

a) Are preparing for the ADI exams.

b) Have passed Parts 1 and 2 and are sponsored by an ADI.

c) Have passed Part 1 of the ADI exam.

d) Are taking training with an authorized training organization.

56 If you are first to arrive at the scene of an accident and a casualty stops breathing, you should:

a) Tilt their head forward.

b) First check that their airway is clear.

c) Not move their head.

d) Put a pillow under their head.

57 If you are involved in an accident which involves someone else, you should first of all:

a) Drive to the nearest police station.

b) Check your car for damage before driving on.

c) Phone home to let someone know.

d) Stop immediately and exchange details.

58 If a police officer asks you to produce your documents, they must be taken to:

a) A police station nominated by the officer.

b) A police station of your choice.

c) Police headquarters.

d) The nearest police station.

59 The three main factors involved in a skid are:

    a) Driver, vehicle, weather.

    b) Vehicle, road, weather.

    c) Driver, number of passengers, road.

    d) Driver, vehicle, road.

60 You should 'make progress' by:

    a) Always driving up to the speed limit.

    b) Changing up to the highest gear as soon as possible.

    c) Always keeping up with other drivers.

    d) Driving at speeds to suit the conditions.

61 In fog, when waiting to turn right into a side road, you should:

    a) Keep your right foot on the brake pedal.

    b) Use the hazard warning flashers.

    c) Keep well over to the left side of the road.

    d) Give an arm signal as an extra warning.

62 Approaching a junction in an unfamiliar area, you should:

    a) Select the centre lane.

    b) Be guided by the signs and road markings.

    c) Always position well to the left to be on the safe side.

    d) Always stop and ask the way.

63 When driving downhill, gravity makes:

    a) The brakes more effective.

    b) No difference to the braking.

    c) The brakes less effective.

    d) It necessary to use the ABS.

64 Parking at the kerb on the left facing uphill, you should:

    a) Put a brick behind each wheel.

    b) Keep the wheels straight.

    c) Turn the steering wheel to the left.

    d) Turn the steering wheel to the right.

65 When driving on multi-lane roads you should keep:

    a) Close to the lane marking on your left.

    b) Close to the lane marking on your right.

    c) In the centre of your lane.

    d) As far to the left as you can.

66 Before crossing a one-way street, pedestrians should look:

    a) To the left.

    b) To the right.

    c) Both ways.

    d) All around.

67 The PSL routine is used:

    a) Instead of the MSM routine.

    b) As part of the MSM routine.

    c) Before the MSM routine.

    d) Only as part of an overtaking manoeuvre.

68 You may wait in a box junction when:

    a) The exit is clear and you intend to turn right.

    b) You are following the road ahead.

    c) You are turning left, but your exit is blocked.

    d) Your filter light is showing green.

69 *The Highway Code* states that you must not reverse for more than:

    a) The distance you can see to be clear.

    b) 10 metres.

    c) 14 metres.

    d) The distance that is necessary.

70 At zebra crossings, you must not pass:

    a) The moving vehicle nearest the crossing.

    b) Any moving vehicle within the zigzags.

    c) Any vehicle when you are approaching the crossing.

    d) Any cyclist.

71 Anti-lock braking systems:

   a) Are only built into cars with automatic transmission.

   b) Prevent the car from skidding.

   c) Only work when braking gently.

   d) Are designed to prevent the wheels locking during heavy braking.

72 People with disabilities are:

   a) Permitted to drive adapted cars only.

   b) Restricted to driving cars with automatic transmission.

   c) Not allowed to drive on motorways.

   d) Permitted to drive any type of car, depending on their disability.

73 Flashing headlights should be used:

   a) As a warning of your presence.

   b) When giving way to other drivers.

   c) When you are dazzled by oncoming headlights.

   d) When you are greeting another driver.

74 When turning from a main road into a side road, give way to:

   a) All pedestrians who are waiting.

   b) Traffic coming from your left.

   c) All the traffic in the road you are turning into.

   d) Pedestrians who are crossing the road.

75 Approaching a roundabout, you should:

   a) Stop at the give-way line.

   b) Keep moving if the way is clear.

   c) Give way to all traffic.

   d) Always change down to second gear.

76 For pedestrians, the flashing green man at pelican crossings means:

   a) Cross the road with care.

   b) Do not start to cross.

   c) Cross the road quickly.

   d) Drivers have priority over pedestrians.

77 When crossing a dual carriageway you should:

    a) Wait in the side road until you can cross both carriageways.

    b) Cross one half, then wait in the central reservation until the second half is clear.

    c) Take into account the width of the central reservation before deciding on how to cross.

    d) Turn left onto the dual carriageway, then turn round.

78 The main reason for a skid to occur is the:

    a) Condition of the car.

    b) Condition of the road surface.

    c) Driver not responding to the conditions.

    d) Lack of grit or sand on the road.

79 When reversing in a van, it is usually better to:

    a) Reverse into an opening on the right.

    b) Reverse into an opening on the left.

    c) Use the interior mirrors to get a better view.

    d) Get your passenger to guide you.

80 When waiting to turn right at a box junction where there is oncoming traffic you should wait:

    a) In the yellow box.

    b) At the stop line.

    c) In the box only if your exit is blocked.

    d) Until the light has changed to red.

81 A green filter arrow means:

    a) Only proceed when the main green light is showing.

    b) Proceed if it's safe to do so, regardless of the other light.

    c) All the other lights will be showing red.

    d) It is now safe for you to proceed.

82 Learner drivers should use mirrors to:

    a) Decide if their actions will be safe.

    b) Show examiners that they are using them.

c) Check if the mirrors are adjusted correctly.

d) Check all the blind areas around the car.

83 High-intensity rear fog lights should be used:

a) If visibility falls below 100 metres.

b) Whenever it is misty or raining.

c) When driving on unlit roads.

d) When a following driver is too close.

84 If a candidate attends for the practical test in a car that appears to be un-roadworthy:

a) Another appointment will be given at no extra cost.

b) The candidate will be advised to have the car checked over after the test.

c) The facts will be reported to DVLA.

d) The test may be cancelled, with no refund.

85 When following other traffic on a dry road, you should leave a time gap of at least:

a) Five seconds.

b) Four seconds.

c) Three seconds.

d) Two seconds.

86 Driving test candidates who make a lot of driving faults, but which are not considered serious or dangerous:

a) May fail the test.

b) Are not likely to fail unless a serious or dangerous fault is made.

c) Are likely to make the examiner nervous.

d) Will be obliged to take a further theory test.

87 *The Highway Code* recommends the use of an arm signal when:

a) Turning right or left into a driveway.

b) Stopping at a pedestrian crossing.

c) Stopping on the right-hand side of the road.

d) When taking your driving test.

88 Your following distance on wet roads should be:

   a) Doubled.

   b) Trebled.

   c) Quadrupled.

   d) Twice your distance.

89 According to the DVSA book, *Driving – The essential skills*, the only safe separation distance is:

   a) Your thinking distance.

   b) Your overall stopping distance.

   c) Your normal following distance.

   d) At least two cars' lengths behind others.

90 Pedestrians should show their intention to cross at a zebra crossing by:

   a) Waiting by the beacon.

   b) Raising a hand to approaching drivers.

   c) Stepping onto the give-way line.

   d) Putting one foot on the crossing.

91 At 70 mph the braking distance is:

   a) 21m (70ft).

   b) 38m (125ft).

   c) 75m (245ft).

   d) 96m (315ft).

92 Fuel economy can be maximized by:

   a) Using all the gears progressively when slowing down.

   b) Using engine braking as much as possible.

   c) Using the lowest gears possible.

   d) Using the highest gear possible.

93 When applying for a test for a pupil who has a slight disability, you should:

   a) Not mention it on the application form.

   b) Give as much information as possible.

   c) Inform the DVSA at Nottingham.

   d) Tell the examiner on the day of the test.

94 When dealing with bends, the speed of the car should be lowest when you are:

a) Entering the bend.

b) Halfway round the bend.

c) Leaving the bend.

d) Approaching the bend.

95 Flashing headlights mean:

a) The same as sounding the horn.

b) The oncoming driver is giving way.

c) The oncoming driver is proceeding.

d) The road is clear for oncoming vehicles.

96 If you break down on a level crossing you must first of all:

a) Push the vehicle clear of the crossing.

b) Stand well clear.

c) Get your passengers out.

d) Use your mobile phone to get help.

97 Before emerging at a junction, your pupil should:

a) Keep looking to the right for traffic.

b) Look right, left, then right again.

c) Look left–right, left–right.

d) Look effectively in all directions.

98 The clutch separates the:

a) Fuel and air mixture.

b) Footbrake and handbrake.

c) Drive between engine and wheels.

d) Transmission from the steering.

99 *The Highway Code* advises signalling:

a) As often as possible.

b) To warn or inform others.

c) For moving off and stopping.

d) Only when you can't see into a side road.

100 If the road ahead is flooded, you should:

   a) Stop and check the depth of the water.

   b) Drive through as quickly as possible.

   c) Drive over the verge to avoid the deeper water.

   d) Check the brakes before driving through.

Answers in Appendix IV.

ADI Part 2: Driving ability 03

This is the second of the three qualifying tests and is a check on your own driving ability.

The test lasts about an hour and consists of five elements:

- an eyesight check;
- vehicle safety questions ('show me, tell me');
- general driving ability;
- manoeuvres;
- independent driving.

To pass, you must be able to drive safely in different road and traffic conditions and show, by the way you drive, that you know The Highway Code. The National Standard for Driving Cars tells you what you need to do.

The test is not simply a longer version of the 'L' test – it is a very demanding advanced driving test, with a pass rate currently running at less than 50 per cent. To quote the DVSA:

This test is far more difficult than the learner test. It is of an advanced nature: a very high standard of competence is required. You must show that you have a thorough knowledge of the principles of good driving and road safety and that you can apply them in practice.

Application

When you passed the theory and hazard perception test you will have been given an application form for this part of the exam. You may then apply as soon as you wish and can take the test at any centre of your choice, although if you offer an alternative centre you may find that you can get an appointment at an earlier date.

You can book your test online at **www.gov.uk/book-driving-test** or by phoning the DVSA on 0300 200 1122. The current fee (at January 2018) is £111.

Information on how to book your Part 2 test in Northern Ireland is available at **www.nidirect.gov.uk/motoring** or by phoning 028 9054 7933 for an application form. The fee in Northern Ireland is currently £130.

On the day of the test you must take with you:

- your UK photo-card driving licence;
- your ADI Part 1 pass certificate;
- a suitable car.

If you don't have a photo-card licence you should take your passport (or some other form of visual identity) with you as photographic proof of your identity. The test will not be conducted if you do not produce the correct documentation.

The car

You must provide a suitable vehicle that:

- is properly taxed and is insured for a driving test;
- is roadworthy and has a valid MOT certificate (if it needs one);
- is a saloon, hatchback or estate car (not a convertible) in proper working condition with front and rear seatbelts in working order;
- has no warning lights showing (for example, airbag warning light);
- has the legal tread depth on all tyres and has no tyre damage. (a space saver tyre must not be fitted);
- is smoke-free. You must not smoke in the car just before or during the test.
- is capable of reaching at least 62 mph and have an mph speedometer;
- has 4 wheels and a maximum authorised mass of no more than 3,500kg;
- has an extra interior rear-view mirror for the examiner;
- has a passenger seatbelt for the examiner and a proper passenger head restraint (not a slip on type).

Your car must meet all these requirements otherwise it will not be possible for the test to be conducted and you will lose the fee.

If you use a dash camera, it must:

- face outside the car and not film the inside;
- not record audio from inside the car.

You can hire a car for the test, but make sure that it conforms to all the rules and is fitted with dual controls.

If you have a licence for driving manual cars you can take the test in either a manual or automatic car. You will then be able to train pupils in both types of car when you have qualified.

If your licence covers you for automatics only you must take the test in an automatic car. In this case you will only be able to teach in an automatic car after you qualify.

There are some cars that cannot use be used on test because they do not give the examiner all-round vision. These include:

- BMW Mini convertible;
- Ford KA convertible;
- Toyota iQ;
- VW Beetle convertible.

From time to time a member of the DVSA staff may accompany your examiner to ensure the uniformity of the tests. All seatbelts front and rear must therefore be in working order, otherwise the test might be cancelled. Anyone who accompanies you on the test would also be expected to wear a seatbelt.

Eyesight

You will be asked to read a vehicle number plate from a distance of 26.5 metres for new-style registration plates, or 27.5 metres if it is an old-style number plate with the larger digits. If you need to wear spectacles or contact lenses to do this, you must wear them for the driving part of the test.

If you are unable to complete the eyesight test satisfactorily, you will not be allowed to continue with the driving test and it will be counted as a failure.

Vehicle safety questions

You will be asked five vehicle safety questions.

The examiner will ask three 'tell me' questions at the start of the test, before you start driving and two 'show me' questions while you're driving.

Incorrect answers are marked as 'driving faults', but if all five questions are answered incorrectly this will be marked as a 'serious fault'.

Sample questions:

> 'Tell me how you would check that the brakes are working before starting a journey.'

> 'Tell me how you would check that the headlights and tail lights are working.'

> 'Tell me how you would switch on the rear fog light(s) and explain when you would use them.'

> 'When it's safe to do so, can you show me how you wash and clean the rear windscreen?'

> 'When it's safe to do so, can you show me how you would open and close the side window?'

Note: For full details of the 'show me, tell me' questions, see Chapter 9.

The driving test

During the test you will be assessed on your driving in a variety of situations, including:

- urban areas;
- rural roads;
- motorway or dual carriageways, where possible;
- roads that carry heavy and/or fast-moving traffic.

The assessment is based on your:

- expert handling of the controls;
- use of correct road procedure;
- anticipation of the actions of other road users and then taking appropriate action;
- sound judgement of distance, speed and timing;
- consideration for the convenience and safety of other road users;
- driving in an environmentally friendly manner.

Manoeuvres

You will be asked to do two manoeuvring exercises. The examiner will choose from:

- parallel park at the side of the road;
- reverse into a parking bay and drive out;
- drive into a parking bay and reverse out;
- pull up on the right-hand side of the road, reverse for about two car lengths and then re-join the traffic.

Independent driving

Normally during the test you will be following the specific direction instructions of the examiner, but for a period of about 20 minutes you will be asked to drive 'independently'. You will be asked to follow directions from a sat nav or by following traffic signs to a particular location. The examiner will provide the sat nav equipment and set up a route to be followed.

The result

To pass the test, you must show a high standard of competence, demonstrating the principles of eco-friendly driving. Your driving should be well-planned, positive and progressive, keeping to speed limits but attaining national speed limits when it is safe to do so. If you make a mistake, it probably will not affect the result unless it's a serious error. The examiner will only stop the test if they think that your driving could be a danger to other road users.

Resource material

To be able to drive skilfully and safely, you need a thorough understanding and working knowledge of the rules and regulations. You should have done most of your studying when preparing for the theory test; now you must demonstrate that you can apply the rules sensibly and correctly. To help with your application of the correct routines and procedures you should continually refer to *The Official DVSA Guide to Driving – The essential skills*, *The Highway Code* and *Know Your Traffic Signs*.

For details of reference books and resource materials, see Appendix III.

Preparation

Even if you have already passed an advanced driving test, the syllabus and style of driving of the other motoring organizations may differ from those of the DVSA. You are expected to drive as an experienced motorist and not just as a good learner. It is therefore advisable to have an assessment with an experienced ADI tutor. Although instructors at a local driving school may be extremely good at preparing candidates for the 'L' test, they may not be fully conversant with the higher level of assessment required for this test.

Tutors registered under the ORDIT scheme know what the DVSA's requirements are and are skilled at assessments at this level. They will be able to advise you on any adjustments needed to enhance your driving style and efficiency.

Even if you have been driving for many years, you may need to modify some aspects of your driving to streamline your performance in line with modern driving techniques. It is often said that 'unlearning' something you've been doing for years is far more difficult than learning something from scratch, so be aware that some experienced drivers find it difficult to adapt to a new style of driving.

Effective training

Training with a qualified, experienced tutor is essential for several reasons:

- If you are still driving in the style you have been using for many years, you may be applying inefficient or outdated methods.
- Although you will have passed the theory test at this stage, there may still be some deficiencies in areas of your knowledge that could result in failure. A trained tutor will be able to identify these and teach you how to apply the rules and procedures correctly.
- The standard of driving required by the DVSA is higher than that of some other advanced driving organizations.
- You may have some false assumptions about the test and its content – a good tutor will be able to advise you correctly.
- An assessment given under test conditions will be invaluable experience.

- The training you receive from your tutor will provide you with a demonstration of the teaching techniques you will need to acquire to become an effective instructor.

Failure is expensive, and it increases the pressure when attending for retests. In addition, if you do not take training with a specialist, you may well be at a disadvantage when it comes to taking your instructional ability test, as you will not have seen demonstrated the teaching skills you need to acquire. A good tutor will make an objective assessment of the current level of your personal driving skills and be able to guide you along the route to improvement and explain why you might need to make changes to your style or methods.

You are allowed a maximum of three attempts at this test so be prepared to invest in sufficient training.

It is sensible to have a couple of 'mock test' sessions with your tutor prior to taking the test just in case you have any last-minute doubts or queries, and need any advice or reassurance.

Remember – your examiner will be expecting to see you drive with skill and confidence. You are an experienced driver – it will therefore be obvious to the examiner's trained eye if you are trying to put on a show of being 'extra careful'. If you do this, there is the likelihood that it will cause you to make incorrect decisions and to fail to make proper progress.

To prepare for the test, you should:

- take advice from your tutor on the aspects of your driving that need improvement;
- continue to refer to the recommended books;
- get as much practice as possible on different types of road and in differing conditions;
- apply the correct procedures whenever you are driving so that they become natural;
- try to maintain progress in relation to the conditions, the law and your car;
- practise giving yourself commentaries as you are driving along.

As well as making progress, you should also take into consideration vehicle sympathy, economy and the comfort of your passengers. To maximize progress, you should:

- make sure you can reach all of the controls properly;
- use the controls smoothly and progressively;

- hold, turn and straighten the steering wheel properly;
- demonstrate vehicle sympathy by selecting gears at the correct time and in accordance with speed and power requirements;
- plan well ahead so that you can use 'accelerator sense' to avoid unnecessary stops, excessive use of the brakes and engine braking;
- maximize fuel economy by keeping the engine revs at an appropriate level.

To maintain progress and demonstrate your personal driving skills, you should:

- look and plan well ahead, anticipating and preparing for hazards before you reach them;
- adjust your speed to avoid any unnecessary stops;
- start looking early at junctions so that you can take opportunities to proceed as soon as you are sure it's safe;
- always be aware of the speed limit and make progress by driving up to it in relation to the road, weather and traffic conditions.

To protect yourself, your passengers and road users all around, you should:

- be aware of what is happening all around your car at all times by using all the mirrors on a regular basis;
- respond properly to what you see in the mirrors;
- anticipate and make allowances for the mistakes of other road users;
- exercise self-discipline and restraint and avoid confrontation;
- show courtesy and consideration to anyone else using the road;
- always be prepared to give way, even if you have priority.

Show that you can handle your car efficiently in all the manoeuvre exercises by:

- maintaining absolute control on all gradients, using the handbrake when necessary;
- making effective observations throughout, and responding correctly to the presence of any other road users – which means giving them priority when appropriate;
- demonstrating accurate steering skills to complete each exercise effectively;
- stopping the car in a controlled manner, avoiding skidding; but if you do skid, you must demonstrate that you can correct it properly.

Eco-safe driving

You are expected to be an experienced driver and will need to show that you are aware of the need for fuel efficiency and an environmentally friendly approach in all aspects of your driving. As an ADI you will need to be able to encourage your new drivers in the use of all these various techniques. Fuel-efficient driving is now part of the ADI Part 2 exam as well as the 'L' driver test.

Eco-friendly driving can have a significant impact on the global use of conventional fuels and make a positive contribution to the reduction of carbon emissions. This process starts with an awareness of the availability of vehicles with alternative fuels such as electric and 'dual fuel' power.

To make an improvement in fuel efficiency, you can consider several areas of your own style of driving, including:

Acceleration. Your use of acceleration should be steady, smooth and progressive whenever possible, avoiding unnecessary speed peaks. A smooth driving style can save up to 10 per cent of fuel used. Where appropriate, use the cruise control, as this can be more efficient on fuel usage.

Braking. Any use of the footbrake should be smooth and positive, with a certain amount of tapering on and off. Avoid any harsh use of the brakes by easing off the accelerator earlier where possible.

Gear changes. Make gear changes effectively, with block changes up and down where appropriate. Move into the higher gears reasonably quickly. Cars with manual gear change are more fuel efficient than automatics.

Hazard awareness. and forward-planning techniques should be used effectively to minimize any unnecessary or harsh changes of speed or direction.

Vehicle sympathy. Keep engine speeds relatively low whenever possible. Generally, keeping the engine speed to about 3,000 rpm can save a considerable amount of fuel. Use all vehicle controls smoothly to avoid any unnecessary sharp fluctuations in speed.

Manoeuvring. Reversing into a parking space and then driving out forwards is generally regarded as more fuel efficient than reversing out when the engine is cold.

Speed. Keep to all legal speed limits and plan well ahead for any changes. Some experts reckon that reducing your top speed by 10 mph can save a considerable amount of fuel.

Air conditioning. Avoid using air con or climate control unless it is necessary, as this can be detrimental to fuel consumption. Avoid driving with the car windows or sunroof open, as this can create 'drag' and an increase in fuel consumed.

Individually, these savings may not seem much, but collectively they can make substantial reductions, not only on your own costs but also on the global use of carbon fuels.

The main areas that the examiner will be looking for include:

Hazard awareness and planning: hazards are identified at an early stage, giving adequate time to respond and to decelerate as appropriate.

Speed limits: complied with all legal speed limits. Speed is appropriate to all road, traffic and weather conditions.

Starting up and moving off: avoids excessive use of the accelerator. Moves off promptly and smoothly.

Accelerator: used smoothly. Accelerator is properly coordinated with the other controls.

Gears: used efficiently and effectively, with the appropriate gear engaged at all times.

Engine braking: used effectively to take advantage of engine braking power where appropriate.

Engine power and torque: utilized higher gears at lower engine speed where appropriate without causing the engine to labour.

Cruise control: used in appropriate situations, but without compromising road safety.

Remember – this is not just about saving fuel in your vehicle; it is also to do with releasing fewer polluting chemicals into the atmosphere and conserving fuels globally.

Marking system

This test demands a high level of driving skill and, as a result, the marking system is more critical than on other tests. Faults are assessed under three categories:

1 *Dangerous faults* – faults that cause actual danger to you, the examiner, the public or property.

2 *Serious or potentially dangerous faults* – faults that cause potential danger or damage and which, in different circumstances, could have led to a serious situation developing.

3 *Driving faults* – errors that detract from the 'perfect drive'. Individually, these faults may not be dangerous or serious, but if you make the same fault on several occasions it could become a 'serious' fault.

To pass this part of the exam you must have no serious or dangerous faults and a maximum of six driving faults. Examples of different types of fault:

Dangerous faults:

- turning right across the path of an oncoming vehicle;
- emerging from a junction and slowing down another driver;
- driving too slowly for the conditions and missing opportunities to proceed in busy situations.

Serious or potentially dangerous faults:

- failure to respond to the presence of other road users during a manoeuvre exercise;
- cutting a right corner with no other road user present.

Driving faults:

- ineffective use of the mirrors and lack of response;
- making too many unnecessary gear changes;
- signalling incorrectly; lack of observations during manoeuvre exercises.

The examiner will offer a debrief on any of your driving faults and you will be given a copy of the marking sheet. At this stage your trainer may be present, but will not be allowed to take part in the discussion.

When you pass, you can book your Part 3 test or apply for a trainee licence. The trainee licence can help you prepare for the Part 3 test, but it is not compulsory or essential. For details, see Chapter 4. If you fail, you will be given an application form for a further attempt at the driving test.

Remember, you are allowed only three attempts at this test. If you fail on the third, and still wish to continue with the qualifying process, you will have to wait until the two-year period elapses from first passing the Part 1 test. You would then have to start the whole process again by retaking Part 1.

Your driving skills

In preparation for your ADI driving test and for a future of effective, economical and safe driving, you need to know something about the theory behind good driving principles. As driving is mainly a practical skill it can be developed only through effective practice and experience. It involves a complex mixture that combines:

- knowledge;
- understanding;
- awareness; and
- attitude.

In order to practise 'safe driving for life' in your own driving you need to identify all these elements. To become an effective trainer of new drivers there are other aspects of driver behaviour that you need to understand.

It is extremely unlikely that 'the perfect driver' exists. However, perfection is something that we should all try to achieve. As instructors, we should take a pride in our driving and be able not only to analyse and improve our own performance, but also to offer constructive criticism to our pupils. In striving for perfection, we need to recognize some of the main ingredients and characteristics of 'the perfect driver', which include skill, knowledge and attitude elements.

Profile of 'the perfect driver'

Skill

To the perfect driver, 'vehicle sympathy' means being 'at one' with, and in total control of, the car at all times. All actions should be smooth, positive and precise. The vehicle should:

- be in the correct position on the road;
- be travelling at a safe speed for the road and traffic conditions;
- have an appropriate gear engaged to suit the speed and power requirements.

Observation, anticipation and forward planning – all of which require total concentration – are essential at all times. Too often, a driver's ability is judged only on manipulative and control skills. Perfection in these practical skills alone, however, will not compensate for a lack of knowledge or a defective attitude. Optimum performance requires not only the ability to think for oneself, but also the skill to read the road and traffic conditions effectively and to take account of what other road users may do.

Knowledge

The good driver will know and understand the laws, rules and regulations relating to road procedure. Without this knowledge, even the most skilfully adept person cannot become a complete driver. It is generally accepted that knowledge generates positive attitudes. In driving instruction, as in general education, the more the knowledge and understanding are developed, the better and safer the outcomes will be.

Attitude

Knowledge of the subject and skill in handling the car are not sufficient qualities in themselves. They need to be applied in a safe, sensible manner. This means taking into account mistakes other drivers make and being prepared to make allowances for them.

Attitudes have a profound effect on the quality of driving, and although relatively easy to define in general terms, they are more difficult to assess in the individual driver. The perfect driver never drives in a spirit of competition or takes revenge on another road user and is always considerate, courteous and tolerant.

For the instructor, these qualities are even more important. The attitude you display during lessons or on a demonstration drive will be transmitted to your pupils.

Attitude affects the behaviour of drivers, with reckless or unsafe actions being attributed to a negative one. Opinions are not always objective when judgements are made about a traffic situation or another driver. Judgement in any situation may be influenced by attitudes assumed previously in a similar event. An incorrect attitude can sometimes make drivers see things not as they actually are, but as they imagine them to be. One of your most important jobs as an instructor will be to develop favourable attitudes in your pupils and change any negative ones they may have.

Motivation describes the personal needs and drives of the individual. It ranges from the need to survive to a feeling of well-being and achievement of desires. Motivation can be used in a positive way to improve driver behaviour. However, it may sometimes cause illogical and potentially unsafe driving. For example, drivers may take uncharacteristic risks if they:

- are late for work or an important appointment;
- want to get the better of another driver;
- wish to demonstrate a superiority of skill;
- are trying to gain the admiration of friends.

Emotion is the general term used to describe feelings such as love, hate or fear. Intense emotions such as anger, frustration and grief tend to turn the focus of the mind in on itself. This in turn lowers the attention being paid to the driving task and limits perceptive abilities.

Anger may result from an argument. Frustration may result from being held up behind a slow-moving vehicle. Anxiety may be the result of worries about work or other personal problems.

Inexperienced drivers who lack self-confidence may suffer from ill-founded fears that they cannot cope. Driving is in itself a stressful activity, and deficient knowledge or skill can result in frustration and may generate destructive emotions.

Personality is described as 'distinctive personal qualities'. However, what we may think of ourselves may be completely different from the way in which others see us. Personality tends to be inconsistent and, faced with varying circumstances, drivers may display different sides of their personality.

There is some evidence to suggest that extrovert drivers are more likely to be involved in accidents than someone who is more introverted. This may be partly explained by the extrovert driver's inability to concentrate on the driving task for longer periods.

Perception is the brain's interpretation of information it receives from the eyes, ears and other senses. The perception of a particular traffic hazard is carried out by the primary information-processing functions of the brain. This involves a need to compare the current situation with existing knowledge and previous experience.

Hazard recognition requires an active and rapid assessment of the potential risks involved in a particular situation, and the driver must anticipate events before they occur. This anticipation relies heavily on stored memories of similar experiences.

Perception is the driver's visual and mental awareness, and it provides information on:

- speed;
- position;
- timing.

Drivers may have limited perceptual capacity and are often faced with an overload of information from the environment. In order to maintain safety when this happens, it becomes necessary to prioritize. This means that the important pieces of information will need to be attended to while other aspects will have to be ignored.

Road sense

Driving is a continuous process of observing, responding and attending to constantly changing needs involving the vehicle, the road layout and traffic conditions. You need to continually recognize, assess and reassess hazards and respond correctly in good time. These responses involve the M–S–M (mirror–signal–manouevre) and P–S–L (position–speed–look) routines.

Within the individual elements of these routines, you should:

- look, assess and decide what action can safely be taken in relation to the information received from the all-round situation;
- look, assess and decide whether a signal is required;
- assess whether the signal is having the required effect on others;
- look, assess and decide what effect any changes in position and speed are likely to have on others;
- decide what further looks may be required.

To be a good driver you need to assess the part you are taking in the changing road and traffic environment. For example, you should not only respond to developing situations, but you should also see yourself as an active part of those situations – often contributing to them. Assessing risks, and deciding on the appropriate response to a hazard, involves a continuous process of assessing and reassessing the constantly changing traffic situation. This means:

- assessing the degree of risk;
- deciding on the priorities;
- focusing attention on the most important aspect;
- deciding on a specific course of action;
- responding in good time;
- reassessing.

Anticipation is having the ability to predict the actions of other road users and is part of the visual search skills. As a good driver, you need to know:

- why, where and when you must look;
- the kind of things to look for;
- what to expect;
- how to see effectively as opposed to just 'looking'.

Risk assessment is influenced by knowledge and previous experience. It can be learnt on a trial-and-error basis or through controlled exercises. Most drivers will recognize that there is a bend in the road; however, they might not all think of the possibility of there being an obstruction hidden from view.

Most collision accidents result from deficiencies in a driver's information-processing skills and not from deficient car control. A large proportion of accidents could be avoided if drivers were more aware of the risks involved, knew what to look for and what to expect, and were prepared to drive defensively by taking avoiding action.

Visual awareness

The good driver is constantly gathering information from the all-round traffic scene. An active visual scan not only provides more information at an earlier stage, but also gives more time to respond. The eye movements of experienced drivers need to be very rapid, moving quickly from one point of interest to another, checking and rechecking areas of risk. Drivers should practise an effective visual search system that involves:

- looking well ahead – allowing you to steer a safe and smooth line;
- keeping the eyes moving – to help you build up a more complete picture and improve awareness;
- getting the big picture – looking all around assists with the judgement of speed and position;
- allowing others to see you – positioning your car so that you can see and be seen;
- looking for alternatives – working out an action plan that may be required if events change.

Hazard recognition

The natural inclination of many drivers is to keep going, unless it is obviously unsafe, for example by steering away from a moving hazard rather than slowing down to avoid it. You need to:

- actively search the road ahead;
- assess the safety of proceeding;
- recognize the consequences of your actions.

When reading the road ahead, rather than waiting for something to happen, you need to anticipate it and respond in good time so that you attempt to avoid any potential problems. To do this you need to obtain as much relevant information about the road and traffic situation as you can. For example:

- *To steer accurately and adjust to safe speeds before reaching a hazard,* look well ahead for bends, gradients, road signs, junctions and obstructions such as parked cars, road works and traffic hold-ups.

- *To maintain tyre and road surface adhesion,* drive smoothly and approach hazards at a suitable speed, taking into account weather conditions, road surface and any camber on bends.

- *To anticipate and act on the actions of other road users,* scan the road for anything with a potential for moving into or across your path.

- *To be able to stop well within the distance you can see to be clear,* you need to identify any blind areas and adjust your speed accordingly.

- *To avoid problems with road users to your sides and rear,* make full use of all the mirrors and use your peripheral vision. You also need a good understanding of the principles of communicating with other road users. You also need to exercise good lane discipline.

Making decisions

Some drivers' decisions often polarize between 'stop' and 'go' where neither is necessarily the correct decision. Inadequate information and hurried assessments are often major causes of incorrect decisions. Try to make decisions early enough to create extra time and leave you with alternatives. For example, when you are approaching a parked vehicle where there is a line of slow-moving traffic approaching from the opposite direction, there could be three choices:

1 It is safe to proceed.

2 It is unsafe to go now.

3 We need more information to reassess the situation before a decision can be made.

Any decision – whether it is to proceed, hold back, give way, or stop – must be continually reassessed. Make your assessments in advance and keep all options open. For example, when approaching a green traffic light, you should be anticipating the possibility of it changing and be ready with the decision to stop. At some point on the approach, however, you will be too close to pull up safely, and the only safe decision is to continue. When approaching any traffic lights, no matter what colour is showing, you need to continually reassess what to do if they change.

Response and control skills

Communication

Methods of communication between road users are complex, and involve much more than merely using the commonly recognized means of signalling by using:

- indicators;
- brake lights;
- arm signals;
- horn;
- flashing headlights;
- hazard warning lights.

An effective communication system involves:

- the position of the vehicle on the road;
- the speed of the vehicle;
- implied signals of intent;
- eye contact;
- courtesy signals and acknowledgements.

Signalling by position

In general, the driver who maintains a correct course, speed and position on the road should not need to signal. Although this is not completely valid for all circumstances, there is an element of truth to it, and you can often anticipate an intended act from another vehicle's position.

Taking up the correct position will help to confirm your signals. Where the position does not appear to confirm a signal, other drivers may become confused. For example, a vehicle may be signalling left, but if the car's position is more towards the centre of the road, other drivers may understandably become confused as they are receiving conflicting information.

Signalling by speed

Changes in speed can also be used as an indication of a driver's intended action. For example, in a situation where a vehicle is signalling to turn left, is positioned correctly and is obviously slowing down, there is a combination of evidence to suggest a left turn will be made, and other road users do not have to rely on one single factor.

Other examples of where speed clearly signals another driver's intentions are when a car is approaching a junction far too quickly for it to give way, and when a driver is accelerating rather than slowing down near a zebra crossing. By slowing down well before crossings, you can clearly signal your intentions to the pedestrians waiting to cross as well as letting any other drivers know what you are doing.

Defensive signals

These are the signals you might use to warn other road users of your presence. They include the use of flashing headlights, the horn and hazard warning lights. The use of the horn would normally be considered in relatively slow-moving traffic conditions. Use it when you think another road user might not be aware of your presence, for example when approaching blind summits, sharp bends on narrow roads, or when you see vehicles reversing from driveways. In faster-moving traffic such as on a motorway, flashing headlights would usually be more effective than sounding the horn because the traffic noise will tend to drown other sounds.

Use the hazard warning lights only when stationary or in an emergency, unless you are coming to a stop for a traffic hold-up on a motorway.

Implied signals, eye contact and courtesy

Not only do you need to recognize and interpret the speed and movement of other traffic, but you must also be alert to implied or potential movement, for example the pedestrians standing at the edge of the pavement near a zebra crossing.

A vehicle waiting at a give-way line always has the potential to move into your path. Treat the implications with respect and be ready to slow down.

Eye contact is another valid form of communication. For example, when you are slowing down on the approach, or waiting at a pedestrian crossing, it helps to reassure pedestrians they have been seen; or when you are waiting to pull into a line of slow-moving traffic it may persuade others to hang back and allow you to move out into the traffic stream.

Speed adjustment

The senses used in the judgement of speed are sight, hearing, balance and touch.

The interpretation of speed can be very difficult at times, particularly in a modern car with a sound-insulated interior. In the absence of vibration and noise on a smooth road that has no nearby side features such as buildings, speed can seem deceptively slow.

Speed is usually assessed through a combination of factors that involve an established speed 'norm' learnt from previous experiences. It can be judged from:

- the rate at which visual images disappear to the sides;
- road, wind and engine noise;
- the sense of balance when changing speeds and direction;
- the general 'feel' of the vehicle on the road;
- comparisons with established 'speed norms'.

These speed norms can sometimes be misleading, for example when approaching the intersection at the end of the slip road after leaving a motorway.

Speed adjustments are required to maintain sufficient safety margins so that you can stop well within the distance you can see to be clear and in accordance with the traffic conditions, visibility and regulations. These adjustments must take into account the critical perceptual and attention overload limitations of any driver.

As your speed increases your focus point needs to be farther ahead, with a corresponding reduction in your peripheral vision. Where you need to attend to foreground detail, you must reduce your speed. Peripheral vision will assist in the judgement of your speed and position. If you do not reduce your speed you may well miss important risk factors, and your awareness of lateral position and safety margin will be limited.

To attain maximum awareness you need to apply an active visual scanning process for observing the road and traffic environment in its entirety, including signs, markings and traffic flow. By using this scanning process, and by maintaining proper control of your speed, you should be able to maintain a safe course while at the same time watching for the potential movement of other road users and compensating for them in good time.

You should always be travelling at a speed at which you can stop safely within the distance you can see to be clear. This means also taking into consideration how closely you are being followed. If a driver is far too close for comfort, you will need to take responsibility for his or her safety as well as your own. To do this you should:

- ease off the gas gradually;

- drop back from the vehicle ahead;

- look and plan as far ahead as possible;

- slow down early, braking gently when you see a hazard.

By allowing more space between you and the vehicle ahead, and braking early and gently, you will be creating more time for the following driver to respond.

Position

As well as being in the correct position in relation to the type of road and any change in direction you may be considering, you also need to consider your distance from the vehicle ahead. Positioning properly, safely and with consideration involves:

- your driving position in the road;

- driving in the centre of your lane;

- changing lanes early and gradually;

- allowing sufficient safety cushion between you and the vehicle ahead;

- allowing sufficient safety margins when passing parked vehicles or other obstructions;

- maintaining safety margins that will allow for the unexpected movement of others;

- selecting safe parking positions;

- taking up suitable positions on the approach to junctions so that you can make effective observations;

- positioning correctly when turning so that minimum disruption is caused to the traffic flow.

To position yourself correctly in order to maintain good sightlines and visibility of the road ahead, you need to position out towards the centre of the road when approaching parked vehicles, and be prepared, when giving way to oncoming traffic, to wait well back from the obstruction.

Other considerations when waiting in traffic include not obstructing crossings or access to side roads and entrances, and not stopping so close to the vehicle ahead as to be unable to pull out around it should the need arise.

Gathering information

Failing to take precautionary measures in doubtful situations can often result in the situation becoming critical and making extreme measures necessary. Before making any commitment to act, you need to gather relevant information so that you can deal with any situation safely and effectively.

Driving is not just a series of decisions to stop or go. In many situations you will need to put into effect an information-gathering exercise. For this, you will need to slow down to create time for the situation to develop, and keep your options open before making a definite commitment to keep moving or stop. Take precautionary measures when your vision is restricted or where there may be an unseen hazard, for example over the brow of a hill or around a bend.

Hold-back procedure

There are various ways of holding back from problems, including momentarily easing off the accelerator to maintain a safe gap. Maintaining safety where there are hazards normally means:

- looking and planning well ahead;
- anticipating any changing circumstances and potential hazards;
- maintaining good vehicle control at all times;
- slowing down early enough to hold back from the hazard.

Hold-back procedure involves actively reducing the speed with a view to looking, deciding or waiting, and maintaining safe options in moments of uncertainty to create a safety cushion.

Progress

Whereas the hold-back procedure involves slowing down with a view to looking, waiting and deciding on what action is required, *powered progress* involves proceeding after considering all the available information and deciding it's safe to go. This often includes *creeping and peeping*. Using first-gear clutch control, slowly edge forwards so that you can look round any obstruction, or in all directions at blind junctions, before making any commitment to proceed.

For making powered progress away from hazards, the point at which the decision to go is taken will dictate which gear to select. Remember, *gears are for going – not for slowing!* Select a gear that will be appropriate for the speed and power requirements.

Speed control and steering

The control skills required will depend on the need either to make powered progress or to hold back. Powered progress involves holding the car still or moving off under full control on all gradients, then making efficient progress through the gears, taking into account changing conditions and gradients. Holding back involves slowing down using either deceleration or controlled rates of braking, depending on gradients, and stopping if the need arises and securing the vehicle. Which procedure is necessary depends on the road and traffic environment.

You need to demonstrate that you have a thorough knowledge of all the different skills involved in proper speed control. You also need to demonstrate that you understand about the safe use of speed in relation to the acceleration, braking and cornering limitations of your vehicle, and the qualities of adhesion between the tyres and the road surface. You should be aware of the overall stopping distances in both good and poor driving conditions, and have the ability to apply them.

Pay particular attention to signs and markings so that you are aware of the speed limit for the road you are using. You should be aware of the need to make proper progress according to the road and traffic conditions. Demonstrate that you are a confident driver – if you put on a show of being over-cautious, you may inconvenience other people or put them in danger. Maintain all-round awareness by keeping a check on what is happening all around your vehicle before you make any changes to your speed or direction.

System of car control

An efficient system of car control should take into account the natural and mechanical forces that affect the stability of a vehicle in motion. Your system of driving must take into consideration other road users' actions by having built-in safety margins that should help to compensate for:

- human error;
- deficient skills;
- minor lapses in concentration;
- mistakes by other road users.

Applying an efficient system should ensure that you will always have time to maintain control of your vehicle in a sympathetic manner. Points to remember are:

- The speed of your vehicle should always be such that you can stop in a controlled manner well within the distance you can see to be clear. To do this you need to look for and respond to:
  - obstructions on your intended course;
  - the potential for other road users to move into your intended course from blind areas;
  - restrictions to your sightlines caused by road features such as bends, hill crests or dips in the road;
  - obstructions that may be hidden by restricted sightlines.
- Control and speed should take into account the natural and mechanical forces that affect the stability of vehicles in motion. You should demonstrate an awareness of the:
  - physical road-holding and handling limitations of your car;
  - tyre and road surface adhesion;
  - increased stopping distances in wet and icy conditions;
  - effects of camber and gravity;
  - aerodynamic forces acting on the vehicle.
- To minimize the effects of the forces that affect the stability of vehicles in motion, you should:
  - use the accelerator, brakes and steering smoothly and progressively;
  - avoid excessive acceleration or braking when negotiating bends and corners;
  - avoid changing gear when your hands would be better engaged on the steering wheel, for example when negotiating sharp bends and turns;
  - avoid unnecessary gear changes when selective changing is more appropriate;

- keep both hands on the wheel when braking, accelerating and cornering;
- accelerate progressively when negotiating a curved path.

- If you are sympathetic to the needs of your vehicle, you will improve fuel efficiency and prolong the vehicle's working life. Try to:
  - avoid unnecessary or fidgety movements on the accelerator;
  - use the accelerator and footbrake early and progressively;
  - avoid excessive clutch slip, drag and unnecessary coasting;
  - avoid excessive tyre wear by cornering at lower speeds;
  - avoid using the gears to reduce speed;
  - use cruise control if it's available.

Handbrake

Use the handbrake:

- when the vehicle is stationary on up- and downhill slopes;
- if you're going to be stationary for more than a few seconds, that is, for longer than the time it would take to apply and then release it again; and, of course,
- when parked.

However, if you plan ahead properly and anticipate any changing circumstances, you should be able to minimize the number of times you need to come to a complete stop. By planning and creeping slowly forwards, you are creating time for the hazard to clear, making the stop either unnecessary or minimal. For such short stops the use of the handbrake is obviously unnecessary.

Brakes and gears

When slowing down, keep both hands on the wheel and (unless you are on an uphill gradient) use the footbrake to reduce speed. After slowing down, change to a gear that is appropriate for negotiating the hazard. For example, when approaching a left turn in, say, fourth or fifth gear, brake to reduce the speed sufficiently and then change into the gear required to negotiate this particular corner. When approaching a T-junction where your view of the main road is restricted, brake to slow down until the car has almost stopped, push down the clutch and release the pressure from the brake to allow the vehicle to roll slowly. Just before stopping, change into first gear, ready to go again. As well as being a waste of fuel, changing down to reduce the speed is unsympathetic and causes unnecessary wear and tear on the clutch, gearbox and transmission.

However, it is sometimes useful to use a lower gear on downhill gradients to offset the effects of gravity. In these circumstances, use the brakes initially to bring the speed under control before selecting the appropriate gear. This provides increased engine braking and reduces the risk of brake failure from overheating due to continuous use on long downhill stretches of road.

Factors influencing stopping distances

The overall stopping distance consists of two separate components: the thinking distance and the braking distance. Thinking distances are based on the average person's reaction time of about two-thirds of a second in normal driving conditions. This reaction time is the interval between recognizing an emergency and the act of beginning to apply the footbrake. In an artificial 'emergency stop' situation this reaction time may be reduced – but only slightly.

The conversion of speed from miles per hour to metres per second shows that, at a speed of 60 mph with a reaction time of two-thirds of a second, the 'thinking distance' will be about 18 metres (or 60 feet). This distance is proportional to the speed. The exact distance may vary slightly from one driver to another and from one situation to another, depending on the driver's fitness, health, reactions and state of mind.

A combination of factors can affect the braking distance, including the:

- size and weight of the vehicle;
- effectiveness of the vehicle's braking system;
- type of tyres, their pressure and depth of tread;
- condition of the road surface.

Whereas thinking distances increase proportionally with speed, braking distances increase much more rapidly at higher speeds. For example, if you increase your speed from 20 to 40 mph it is going to take four times the distance to stop (24 metres instead of 6 metres). At 60 mph, the braking distance is nine times the distance covered at 20 mph.

Table 3.1   Stopping distances

Speed			Thinking distance		Braking distance		Overall stopping distance	
Mph	Metres per sec	Feet per sec	Metres	Feet	Metres	Feet	Metres	Feet
20	9	30	6	20	6	20	12	40
30	14	45	9	30	14	45	23	75
40	18	60	12	40	24	80	36	120
50	23	75	15	50	38	125	53	175
60	27	90	18	60	55	180	73	240
70	32	105	21	70	75	245	96	315

With good brakes and tyres on a dry road, the car should normally stop in the distances shown in Table 3.1. On wet or slippery roads, these distances will be much greater, and can be up to 10 times the braking distance in extreme conditions.

The cause and correction of skidding

Although the vehicle and road surface condition may contribute to a skid, the main cause of most skids is without any doubt the driver. There are three different types of skid and these are usually caused by:

- excessive speed for the road conditions and/or traffic situation;
- excessive acceleration, braking and/or cornering forces being applied to the tyres;
- a combination of both.

The rear-wheel skid occurs when the rear wheels lose their grip. It is usually the result of excessive speed and cornering forces. Sometimes it also occurs in combination with harsh acceleration or, more usually, excessive braking. This type of skid is more easily recognized because the rear of the car slides away from the centre of the corner. If uncorrected it could cause the vehicle to turn completely round.

It is essential to eliminate the cause, for example to release the accelerator and/or footbrake and compensate with the steering.

Because, in this type of skid, the driver will see that the vehicle is pointing in the wrong direction, the natural reaction will be to steer back on course.

There is a danger however, particularly with the quick response of radial tyres, for drivers to over-steer, causing the vehicle to spin the other way.

The front-wheel skid occurs when the front wheels lose their grip, leaving the driver with no directional control. It usually occurs because of turning sharply into a corner or bend at excessive speed and/or under hard acceleration or braking. It can be recognized when the vehicle fails to go in the direction in which it is being steered.

To correct the skid, the cause must be eliminated and steering control regained by momentarily straightening the wheels and/or reducing pressure on the accelerator or brake.

The four-wheel skid occurs when all four wheels lose their grip. It is usually caused by excessive speed for the road conditions or traffic situation, resulting in uncontrolled over-braking. On a wet or slippery surface the driver may even feel that the speed is increasing. Steering control is lost and the vehicle may turn broadside. The control can be partially restored by momentarily releasing the brake to allow the wheels to start turning again and then quickly reapplying the brake in a rapid on–off action. Many new cars are fitted with an anti-lock braking system that will work in the same way, allowing the driver to regain control much more easily.

More information on skids is in *The Official DVSA Guide to Driving*. The prevention of skids is better than the cure! It is important to recognize danger signs early and act on them. For example, slowing down early when you see a group of children playing near the road will mean less braking pressure would be needed if one of them dashes out. Concentration, planning and the early anticipation of the possible actions of others is essential.

In snow and ice, slow down early with light braking pressure. Gentle braking is less likely to cause skidding than changing into a lower gear. Use gradual acceleration and keep in the highest gear possible without distressing the engine. When going uphill in snow, try to maintain a steady momentum by staying well back from the vehicle ahead.

Drive at safe speeds for the road surface conditions. Accelerate, brake and corner gently. Drive more slowly on wet, icy and slippery surfaces. Watch out for loose gravel, fallen leaves and damp patches under trees. Make sure your tyres are correctly inflated and that they have a minimum of 2 mm of tread all around. Never mix cross-ply and radial tyres on the same axle. If you must use a mix of tyres, fit the cross-ply to the front and the radials to the rear axle.

Keep off soft verges! Read the surface conditions and slow down well before reaching any bumpy parts and speed humps. Avoid heavy braking on loose gravel and muddy surfaces and when driving through damp patches under trees.

The combination of oil, rubber, dust and water can make the surface very slippery after a light summer shower following a long dry spell. In freezing temperatures, remember that black ice forms on exposed bridges first.

Emergency braking

You need to be realistic about the distance it can take to stop, particularly in wet conditions. When you have to brake quickly:

- pivot promptly from accelerator to brake;
- apply the brake progressively and firmly;
- keep both hands on the wheel to keep the vehicle on a straight course;
- apply maximum braking force just before the wheels lock up.

Avoid braking so hard that the wheels lock up, as this will considerably lengthen the stopping distance.

If the wheels lock up, particularly in wet, slippery conditions, the brake should be released momentarily and then quickly reapplied – this is called cadence braking and it will allow the tyres to regain their grip. This method of rapid on–off braking is how an anti-lock braking system (ABS) works – and should not be used if the car is fitted with ABS, when pressure on the pedal should be maintained. Cadence braking and ABS give the driver greater braking efficiency and increased directional control should the wheels lock.

Whenever you drive, you need to:

- exercise self-discipline;
- concentrate all the time and read the road well ahead;
- drive at speeds at which you can stop safely within the distance you can see is clear;
- anticipate actual and potential hazards;
- be courteous, patient and considerate;
- apply the controls gradually and smoothly;
- drive in a safe, sympathetic, effective and economic manner.

The Cardington Special Test

This high-level driving test is open to all Approved Driving Instructors who want to keep their own driving up to standard as part of their continued professional development. One of the strictest tests available, it is conducted by permanent staff instructors operating out of the DVSA's Training and Development Centre at Cardington near Bedford.

You have to provide your own car for the test. It must have:

- manual transmission;
- an interior instructor mirror;
- integral head restraints for both the driver and the assessor.

The test normally lasts approximately 90 minutes, and covers a variety of road and traffic conditions, including motorways.

You will be assessed on your driving technique, and you are expected to demonstrate a systematic and professional approach to all hazards and to plan expertly for safe progress at all times. In particular, the assessor will be checking your:

- expert handling of the vehicle controls;
- use of correct road procedures;
- anticipation of the actions of other road users and taking the appropriate action;
- sound judgement of distance, speed and timing;

Each individual fault will be fully assessed in the light of the prevailing conditions. The result is normally confirmed by post within 48 hours and, whether you pass or fail, you will receive a report on those faults observed. If you achieve a grade A, you will also receive the Cardington Certificate.

The current fee is £144, but this is continually under review by the DVSA.

To make a booking, download the application form from **www.gov.uk/dvsa-special-tests-for-instructors** or phone the DVSA.

Eco-driving

All advanced driving tests these days – including the ADI Part 2 and the Cardington Special Test – include an element of eco-friendly driving.

Some of the main points that you should bear in mind include:

- Don't leave the car engine to warm up – drive off as soon as practicable after starting the engine.
- Harsh acceleration, sharp braking and generally aggressive driving can all cause an increase in fuel usage.

- Improved engine technology makes it possible to move up through the gears more rapidly – for petrol cars about 2,500 rpm, and for diesel about 2,000 rpm.

- Missing out intermediate gears by 'block changing' up and down through the gears can save fuel.

- Remember that very short journeys of less than two miles produce 60 per cent more pollution than journeys with a warm engine. Catalytic converters can take up to six miles to become really effective.

- Switching off the engine when waiting in queues of traffic uses less energy.

- The optimum speed range for minimum emissions is regarded as being 40–60 mph.

- Make sure that the engine is regularly maintained and properly tuned to keep emissions to a minimum.

- Make sure that tyre pressures are set at the recommended level. If the pressures are low, fuel consumption can be increased by about 2–3 per cent.

- Don't carry unnecessary loads such as roof racks or heavy items in the boot. In these circumstances, fuel consumption can increase by up to 10 per cent. With a heavy trailer – a boat or a caravan, for example – this figure can rise to 30 per cent.

Trainee licence 04

Once you have passed the Part 2 exam you are eligible to apply for a 'Trainee Licence'. It is not necessary to use the trainee licence scheme if you want to go straight on to obtaining full qualification, but it does offer the opportunity to gain valuable work experience with genuine pupils while you are preparing for the Part 3 exam.

A fully qualified instructor has a green-coloured certificate which is displayed in the windscreen of the car during lessons – the trainee instructor's certificate is pink.

As a trainee licence holder you are allowed to charge fees, but only for a limited period and with stringent training and supervision conditions attached.

With good training you should be able to pass the exams and qualify as an ADI more quickly and with less expense without the need to take out a trainee licence. However, some people find that the practical experience gained by working with genuine pupils under a licence does help them prepare for the Part 3 exam.

The trainee licence should be regarded as an extension of your training and not as a job opportunity.

Application

You can apply for a licence online at **www.gov.uk/apply-for-a-trainee-driving-instructor-licence**. Alternatively, send a downloaded copy of the application form (ADI3L), together with a completed ADI21T, to: Approved Driving Instructor Registrar, Driver and Vehicle Standards Agency, The Axis Building, 112 Upper Parliament Street, Nottingham NG1 6LP. The ADI21T form is a declaration that you have taken the required amount of training. Make sure that you put your ADI reference number on the back of the photo. The form will need to be signed by the person who has been responsible for your training and who will be supervising you while you are under licence. The current fee (February 2018) is £140 and in Northern Ireland it is £120.

Qualification

To qualify for a licence you must have taken at least 40 hours of specified training with a qualified ADI, 25 per cent of which must be practical in-car training with a ratio of not more than two trainees to each ADI tutor. All the training must have been received in the six months preceding the application.

When you apply for the trainee licence you have two options:

- you will need to be supervised for 20 per cent of all lessons you give during the period of your licence; or
- you must take an extra 20 hours of training while you have the licence.

You must choose one of these options and you cannot change options at a later stage. Take advice from your trainer or sponsoring ADI about which option would be best for you.

Eligibility

In addition to the training requirement you must be eligible to take the Part 3 test and must not have exceeded the two-year qualifying period. If you are unsuccessful in Part 3 on three attempts the licence would be revoked.

Duration

A trainee licence is valid for six months. A second licence can only be issued under exceptional circumstances.

Your trainee licence shows the name and address of your training organization or sponsoring ADI. You must only work from that address and are not allowed to set up in business on your own account. If you leave the nominated school to join another one you must apply for a new licence.

To continue using the licence, you must:

- be a 'fit and proper person';
- receive the appropriate amount of training;
- make sure that you do not give the impression, either in adverts or elsewhere, that you are fully qualified as an ADI.

Training

Once the licence has been issued there is a requirement for ongoing training or supervision.

You have two options at this stage:

1 Your sponsoring ADI must supervise 20 per cent of all the lessons you give. A record of all lessons given, along with the supervision received, must be kept on form ADI 21S. Both you and your sponsor must sign this form, which must then be returned to the DVSA as soon as the licence expires.

2 Alternatively, a minimum additional 20 hours' training covering all the specified topics must be undertaken. This extra training must take place within the first three months of the issue of the licence or before taking a first attempt at Part 3, whichever is the sooner. (A record of this training must be kept on form ADI 21AT and must be sent to the DVSA before the end of the three-month period, or presented to the examiner who conducts the Part 3 test, whichever is the earlier.)

At least 25 per cent of the period of training has to be practically based and in a car at a maximum instructor-to-trainee ratio of no more than two trainees to one ADI.

If you subsequently fail either your first or second attempt at the Part 3 test, a further five hours of training must be taken before you are allowed to take another test. A declaration signed by you and your sponsor has to be provided to the examiner on the day of the test. Failure to do this will result in the test being cancelled and the licence could be taken away.

Displaying the trainee licence

Whenever you are giving driving lessons under this scheme, the licence must be displayed nearside of the car's windscreen. If requested by a police officer or any person authorized by the Secretary of State, the licence must be produced. Failure to do this is an offence.

If you hold a trainee licence

If you are working under the Trainee Licence Scheme, have signed for the training option, and are attending for your first attempt at the Part 3 exam within the first three months of the licence, you will have to produce your ADI 21T form. Both you and your trainer should sign this form to confirm you have had a minimum of 20 hours' extra training. This is in addition to the 40 hours' training required to obtain the licence.

If you have to take the test for a second or third time, you will need to provide a declaration, signed by you and your trainer, to confirm that a minimum additional five hours' training has been received. If you are not able to produce any of the training declarations your test will be cancelled and you will lose the fee.

Northern Ireland trainee licence

Application forms for the trainee licence are available from: Business Support Unit, DVA, Balmoral Road, Belfast BT12 6QL, tel: 028 9054 7933 or at **www.nidirect.gov.uk/motoring**.

You are allowed a total of two licences, each of six months, irrespective of the number of times you re-enter the qualifying process. The application for the second licence must be made before the expiry of the first one. A third licence would only be issued in exceptional circumstances.

Training is not a statutory requirement for the issue of a trainee licence, but is recommended. DVA suggest that you should make suitable checks regarding the competence of the training organization that you choose and fully understand in advance what to expect from the tuition and the fees paid.

There is currently no requirement to display a trainee licence, but it is a good idea to do so to show your pupils and the enforcement agencies that you are permitted to give professional training.

ADI Part 3: Instructional ability

This is the third and final part of the ADI qualifying exams. It is a test of your instructional ability and is generally regarded as the most difficult of the three tests, with a pass rate of about 30 per cent.

The test takes about one hour and includes an assessment of 17 areas of competence which are marked individually.

During the test, which is conducted by a specially qualified DVSA senior examiner, you will have to demonstrate, through your practical teaching and coaching skills, that you are able to help someone learn in the most effective way. The criteria for doing this are based on the National Standard for Driver and Rider Training.

Application

When you pass the Part 2 Eyesight and Driving Ability Test, you will be given details of how to apply for Part 3. Tests are conducted at various centres and can be taken at whichever one you choose.

The Part 3 Test can be booked online at **www.gov.uk/book-driving-test**. Alternatively, you can book by phoning the DVSA on 0300 200 1122.

Whichever method you choose you will need your driving licence number, the theory test pass certificate and details of your credit or debit card account. If you have lost your original theory pass letter, you can find the number online.

The fee for this part of the exam is currently £111. In Northern Ireland the fee is £138.

Soon after applying you will receive written confirmation of your appointment. Take this confirmation letter with you when you attend for the test, along with your photo-card licence. If you still have the old-style paper licence you will need to take your passport as photographic proof of your identity.

The car

The car you use must be roadworthy, safe and reliable. A soft-top convertible is not acceptable, nor is a car with limited rear seating for the examiner.

'L' plates (or 'D' plates in Wales) must be displayed if the driver is a provisional licence holder. It should go without saying that a clean and tidy car (both inside and outside) will create a professional image. If you normally use the back seat of the car as your 'office' with an accumulation of diaries, reference books, teaching aids and so on, make sure that it is reasonably tidy and that the examiner has sufficient room.

You must make sure that all seatbelts (both front and rear) are in good working order.

Your pupil

If your pupil is a full licence holder rather than a learner, they must not be an ADI or someone who has passed the first two parts of the ADI exams. The most important thing to remember is that the examiner is assessing your ability to teach and not the pupil's ability to drive. You must therefore ensure that your instruction is pitched at the correct level, whatever standard the driver has attained.

Your examiner will ask you for some background information about the pupil, such as how much previous driving they have done and whether they hold a full or provisional licence.

You must demonstrate clearly to the examiner that the needs that you identify have been discussed and agreed with the pupil. You will then be asked to deliver a lesson in exactly the same way as you would normally do.

Assessment

You will be given a grade based on the following marking criteria:

During the assessment, the examiner will want to see whether your instruction helps someone to learn in an effective way. For this reason you will be assessed giving a normal lesson with a real pupil.

The assessment is based on a client-centred approach, with an emphasis on the importance of risk management and involves three areas of competence:

- planning of the lesson;
- risk management; and
- teaching and learning strategies.

Marks are allocated for each of these three competencies:

0 = no evidence of competence;

1 = a few elements of competence demonstrated;

2 = competence demonstrated in most areas;

3 = competence demonstrated in all areas.

The three main areas of competence are broken down into 17 'lower level' competences as shown later in this chapter.

To achieve a pass you must meet three specific criteria:

- score eight or more marks in the risk management section;
- manage critical incidents effectively;
- identify any significant weakness and give correct and sufficient information in order to ensure that safety critical situations do not occur.

Preparation

Your pupil can wait in the car when you arrive at the test centre. When you return to the car, you should introduce the pupil to the examiner.

You should tell the pupil to behave exactly as they would normally. It might help to put the pupil at ease if you explain to them that the examiner is there to check that you are doing your job and to make sure that the quality of instruction they get meets the minimum standards.

You should prepare a normal lesson based on the pupil's learning needs or agreed development strategy.

Before the lesson starts, the examiner will ask you some questions about the pupil, the pupil's strengths and areas for development.

You can show the examiner the pupil's driver's record (if they have one) before the start of the lesson to help explain their current progress in their agreed training programme.

When you arrive at the test centre, the examiner will confirm your identity and complete the necessary paperwork.

You are required to show competence against all the criteria on the assessment form. The examiner will check that you understand, for example by asking:

'Do you have any questions before we start?'

You'll then be asked about the pupil's background and how much experience they've had. For example, the examiner might say:

'Could you tell me how many lessons your pupil has had and what you have been covering recently?'

When the examiner is satisfied that they have the information they need and that you have understood what's going to happen, you will be asked to continue with the lesson, for example by the examiner saying:

'Thank you, carry on with this lesson in your normal way. I won't take any part in the lesson. Would you plan your lesson to be back here in one hour from now.'

Presenting the lesson

The format of the lesson should follow the same pattern as on a normal lesson. After the initial introduction of pupil to examiner and explaining to the pupil the purpose of the test, it is important that you demonstrate that you understand the three broad competences. You need to show that you are competent in lesson planning; that you can manage the risk in order that the goal that has been agreed will be achieved; and that you are able to apply the most effective teaching and learning strategies to achieve the goal.

In the ADI Part 3 test, you will need to adapt your lesson to suit the level and ability of the pupil; and/or the limited amount of time available.

You can do this by:

- using your client-centred learning skills to work to an agreed programme;
- adapting your teaching method to suit progress made during the lesson;
- ensuring some positive learning takes place through practice within the time scale.

During the test you will be assessed on:

Your ability to plan the lesson and be flexible within this plan

If the goal and structure of the lesson have been agreed – along with the most suitable route – and the pupil struggles, are you able to adapt the lesson plan so that the goal will be achieved? For example, if the pupil needs to creep the car forwards to emerge safely at junctions, but keeps stalling because they are not able to hold the clutch around the biting point, take them to a quiet area without junctions and encourage them to just creep along the road using the clutch to control the speed. When you return to the junctions the pupil should now be able to emerge safely, whilst controlling the vehicle with the clutch.

Your ability to manage the risk

Once the car is moving you must ensure that you keep everyone safe, whilst also giving the responsibility for the task to the pupil so that they can focus on achieving the goal. The route you use is important for this because, if it is too challenging, you will end up having to talk your pupil through everything and that won't give them a fair chance to focus on the goal. If you need to step in with a spoken instruction or use the dual controls, you must ensure you give the pupil sufficient feedback so that they understand what the risks might have been if you hadn't intervened.

Your ability to use appropriate teaching and learning strategies

You need to show that you are able to adapt the way you teach to suit the way your pupil learns so that they pupil has the best possible chance of achieving the goal. This includes being non-judgemental and establishing an equal relationship so that learning is most likely to take place.

Once you have finished any reflective discussion with the pupil, you will be told that the test has finished. The examiner will take a few minutes to review the assessment.

The assessment is made against three broad or 'high' areas of competence:

- lesson planning;
- risk management;
- teaching and learning strategies.

The three 'high' areas of competence are broken down further into 17 lower-level competences and a mark is given for each of these.

Assessment structure

Lesson planning

- Did the trainer identify the pupil's learning goals and needs?
- Was the agreed lesson structure appropriate for the pupil's experience and ability?

- Were the practice areas appropriate?
- Was the lesson plan adapted, when appropriate, to help the pupil work towards their learning goals?

Risk management

- Did the trainer ensure that the pupil fully understood how the responsibility for risk would be shared?
- Were the directions and instructions given to the pupil clear and given in good time?
- Was the trainer aware of the surroundings and the pupil's actions?
- Was any verbal or physical intervention by the trainer timely and appropriate?
- Was sufficient feedback given to help the pupil understand any potential safety-critical incidents?

Teaching and learning strategies

- Was the teaching style suited to the pupil's level of ability?
- Was the pupil encouraged to analyse problems and take responsibility for their learning?
- Were opportunities and examples used to clarify learning outcomes?
- Was the technical information given comprehensive, appropriate and accurate?
- Was the pupil given appropriate and timely feedback during the session?
- Were the pupil's queries followed up and answered?
- Did the trainer maintain an appropriate non-discriminatory manner throughout the session?
- At the end of the session – was the pupil encouraged to reflect on their own performance?

For each of these competences a mark is given on a scale of 0–3.

Table 5.1

Score	Criteria
3	Competence demonstrated in all elements
2	Competence demonstrated in most elements
1	Competence demonstrated in a few elements
0	No evidence of competence

These marks are added together to give an overall mark and they will also provide a profile of the areas where you have any strengths and where you might need to do some more development work.

After completing the marking sheet the examiner will then review the training session.

You will fail if:

- You get a score of 7 or less for the 'Risk Management' category.
- The examiner stops the lesson because you have put yourself, the pupil, the examiner or someone else in immediate danger.
- You have a total score of 30 or less (out of a possible 51).

If you get a total score of 43 or more you will be given a Grade A.

With a total score of between 31 and 42 you will be given a Grade B.

Table 5.2

Total score	Grade
0–30	Fail
31–42	Grade B
43–51	Grade A

The key point to understand is that the lower-level competences, on the form, can themselves be broken down into elements. You will have to use a range of skills to ensure each of these elements is in place.

For example, the first lower-level competence, in the lesson planning section, is 'Did the ADI identify the pupil's learning goals and needs?'

To fully satisfy this requirement you must:

- actively recognize the need to understand the pupil's experience and background;

- ask suitable questions;

- encourage the pupil to talk about their goals, concerns, etc and actively listen to what the pupil has to say;

- understand the significance of what the pupil says;

- recognize other indications, eg body language, that the pupil is trying to express something but perhaps cannot find the right words.

Competence standards examples

An instructor who makes no attempt to understand their pupil's needs would be demonstrating no evidence of competence and be marked 0.

An instructor who makes an attempt, asks a few questions, but doesn't really listen and then goes ahead and does what they intended to do regardless, would be demonstrating a few elements of competence and would be marked 1.

This is indicating that your performance is not acceptable and that you may need to do a lot more work, even though you have given evidence of knowing what you are supposed to be doing.

An instructor who grasps the importance of understanding the pupil's needs and makes a real effort to do so, but who finds it difficult to frame suitable questions, would be demonstrating competence in most elements and would be marked 2.

Your performance is regarded as acceptable but there are clear areas where you could improve.

If the examiner gives a score of 3, they are effectively saying that this is an area where you do not need to do any further work, apart from continuously reflecting on your performance.

The examiner's role is to assess your competence to deliver effective driving instruction. The 'National standard for driver training' is expressed in terms of learning outcomes and there may be more than one way for you to achieve those outcomes. Of course if you do, or say, something that is clearly wrong this will be picked up, especially where it could lead to a safety issue. However, the overall approach by the examiner is focused on recognizing achievement and promoting improvement and development, rather than purely identifying faults.

Your task is to provide an effective learning experience for the pupil. An effective learning experience is judged to be one in which the pupil is supported to take as much responsibility as possible for their learning process.

You should, where it is correct and safe to do so, feel free to introduce wider issues from the driving standard into the lesson, such as assessing personal fitness to drive, the use of alcohol or drugs or dealing with aggression. If, for example, a pupil offers an inappropriate comment about the use of alcohol it would be appropriate for you to challenge this.

Similarly, it would be appropriate for you to encourage the pupil to think through what might happen, in particular situations, if the conditions were different. For example, after negotiating a particularly difficult junction it might be helpful to discuss how different it would be at night or in bad weather. The important thing to remember here is that the most effective learning takes place when the pupil finds the answers for themselves.

If opportunities arise for discussion of issues between you and the pupil, while on the move, these can be used, but this needs to be tailored to the pupil's ability and should not create distraction. Too many unnecessary instructions can both demotivate the pupil and create a real hazard.

Typical lessons

Partly trained inexperienced learner

Drivers at this stage of their career are likely to want/need experience of a steadily increasing variety of road and traffic conditions to enable them to develop their basic skills. They may have areas where they are uncomfortable or not yet competent, such as complex junctions or roundabouts, or heavy or fast-moving traffic. They may not have a good understanding of theory, for example, of road signs and markings.

In this context the key objectives of the 'National standard for driver and rider training' include being able to:

- create a climate that promotes learning;

- explain and demonstrate skills and techniques;

- transfer the balance of responsibility for their learning process to the learner as soon as possible.

You should be working to understand where the pupil is having difficulties and how you can help them develop sound basic skills. If you are not making the effort to understand, you are not demonstrating competence. By asking questions or staying silent and listening and watching you are clearly making the effort to understand and demonstrate competence. It doesn't matter if you don't achieve full understanding by the end of the lesson.

In the same way, pupils at this level should not feel they are being patronized or talked down to as this will make them unreceptive. They do not all learn in the same way.

Consequently there is no single, correct way to transfer responsibility to them and, in any case, this is not going to take place instantly. In this context, just as it is unreasonable to expect a pupil to get it right instantly, so it is unreasonable to expect the instructor to transfer responsibility instantly. The key thing that you must demonstrate is that you understand the need to transfer ownership and make the effort to do so.

It is important to understand that, at this level, a pupil will not always 'get it right' as soon as the instructor gives them some direction or coaches them around a problem. You should understand the issue, at least in principle, and what you need to do in theory. You should generally be willing to try to overcome weaknesses, but your efforts may not always be successful. You will not be penalized if you do not immediately 'solve the problem'.

You should use a variety of tools to encourage the pupil to analyse their own performance and to find solutions to problems. You should be supportive and give suitable and technically correct instructions or demonstrations where appropriate. Of course, where a pupil cannot come up with a way forward you should provide suitable input – especially if failure to do so might result in a risk to any party.

Experienced pupil – about ready to take their test

At this stage the key objective of the 'National standard for driver and rider training' is to work with the learner to agree when they are ready to undertake formal assessment of driving competence.

Evidence suggests that, by this stage, some pupils may:

- be technically skilful;
- be able to complete manoeuvres competently;
- have experience of driving on a wide range of roads and in a range of conditions.

They may be confident and feel that they are at the stage of refining their competence around 'what they need to do to pass the test'. On the other hand they may:

- have already developed bad habits, especially if they have been taught by a relative or friend;
- have an inflated opinion of their competence;
- have a poor understanding of risk;
- have not developed the skills of scanning and planning that will help them to cope when they drive independently;
- have not developed the skills of reflection that will help them to be life-long learners.

They may not be used to being challenged to analyse and come up with solutions. They could be impatient and resistant to correction if they do demonstrate 'bad habits'. They may well have forgotten a lot of what they learnt when they did their theory test. Responses at this level could vary from enthusiastic acceptance of the information they need, to real resistance to being told things they do not think are relevant.

You must demonstrate that you understand the key issues that need to be addressed to try to reduce the numbers of newly qualified drivers who crash in the first six months. You should be working to develop a realistic understanding of ability and an enhanced understanding of risk. You should be checking, developing and reinforcing systematic scanning and planning tools. You should be strongly encouraging reflection.

You should be supportive, not over-instruct and give suitable and technically correct instructions or demonstrations where necessary. However, the emphasis is likely to be on the use of tools, such as practical examples, to develop a more joined-up and outward-looking approach.

New full licence holder

This type of pupil will have demonstrated 'competence' against those elements of the national standards for driving that are tested in the theory and practical tests. Remember, however, that these tests are limited in scope. They do not require the pupil to drive on all classes of roads and they do not test understanding of that part of the national standards for driving which calls on learners to reflect on their competence as they go through their driving career.

Your objective at this stage should be to develop the pupil's competence across the full range of driving environments and to support and reinforce their commitment to life-long learning around driving.

Reasons why an individual might come to an ADI at this stage include:

- wanting to refresh their skills if they haven't driven since they took their test;
- moving on to a bigger or technologically different vehicle;
- starting to drive for work;
- starting a family and wanting to improve their skills;
- moving from an urban to a rural environment, or vice versa;
- starting to use motorways;
- a simple desire to become a better-developed driver.

This pupil is likely to be enthusiastic and, in theory at least, open to learning if they have chosen to take training. If, on the other hand, they have been told to take it, perhaps by an employer, they might be resentful and resistant. They may well have already lost the disciplines of the mirror–signal–manoeuvre routine and forward-planning skills. They may not be used to driving in an 'eco-safe' way and may not even understand the term. They may be nervous about increased responsibility and accountability.

Experienced full licence holder

At this stage this type of pupil should be more confident and competent than they were immediately after passing their test. They should have gained experience across all or most of the possible classes of roads, at night and in bad weather. They may already be driving for work and are likely to regard themselves as capable drivers, even though their application of safety routines and forward-planning skills may show they are not quite as competent as they think.

Reasons why an individual might come to an ADI at this stage include:

- being required by employers to undertake additional training to keep insurance costs down;
- wanting to drive more economically to reduce business costs;
- having had an accident or near miss that has shaken their confidence;
- returning to driving after a period of ill-health or loss of licence;
- recognizing that their driving skills are deteriorating through age or ill-health.

The pupil may be an overseas driver who has significant experience but, having been in the UK beyond the statutory period, is now required to take the tests to qualify for a UK licence.

Depending on their reasons for undertaking training these pupils could be enthusiastic or very nervous, willing or very resistant. Older pupils may find it harder to learn new skills or to get out of bad habits. They may have developed unsafe habits such as not leaving large enough separation distances and failing to carry out systematic observation routines.

In assessment, the key thing is that you must demonstrate you can find out exactly what it is the pupil wants from the lesson and put together a plan to deliver that. You must, of course, spot and deal with bad habits that might have been acquired. However, the lesson must take the pupil forward in their learning. If it does not deliver what the pupil is looking for they will not engage with the learning process.

Assessment criteria

Lesson planning

The purpose of all driver training is to assess and develop the learner's skill, knowledge and understanding in relation to the contents of the National Standard for Driver Training. Research indicates that is best achieved by placing the client at the centre of the learning process. In this context, the assessment criteria will be interpreted as follows.

Did the trainer identify the pupil's learning goals and needs?

Usually this process will take place at the beginning of a lesson. If you have not worked with the pupil before, it is perfectly OK for you to ask the pupil to undertake a demonstration/assessment drive. This should give a good idea of the pupil's level of competence and provide a basis for a discussion of the pupil's needs.

As the examiner observes the lesson they will be looking for indications that the elements which go to make up the low-level competence are being demonstrated. In this case the sorts of things that would show an indication of competence include:

- encouraging the pupil to say what they want from the lesson;
- asking questions to ensure understanding;
- checking understanding as the lesson progresses;
- listening to what the pupil is saying;
- taking note of body language.

If you encourage the pupil to say what they want, ask questions to check understanding at the beginning and as the lesson progresses, listen to what they are saying and also pick up on body language you are likely to get a 3. If, on the other hand, you do all the listening bits but fail to spot the learner getting very tense and nervous in a particular situation you would probably get a 2. You would have demonstrated your understanding of the need to listen etc, but have not yet developed the ability to spot non-verbal clues.

Indications of a lack of competence could include:

- making assumptions about understanding or experience;
- failing to note negative or concerned comments or body language that shows discomfort;
- undermining the pupil's confidence by continually asking questions clearly beyond the pupil's knowledge or understanding;
- pushing the pupil to address issues that they are not happy to talk about, unless there is a clear need, such as an identified risk or a safety-critical issue.

Was the agreed lesson structure appropriate for the pupil's experience and ability?

The lesson structure should allow the pupil to progress at a manageable rate; stretching them without overwhelming them. For example, a pupil who is concerned about entering roundabouts should not be asked to tackle a fast-flowing multi-lane, multi-exit junction as their first attempt. Neither should they be restricted to very quiet junctions, unless you identify a potential risk issue that they want to check out first.

Indications that all the elements of competence are in place could include:

- ensuring the pupil understands what they plan to do and agrees with that plan;
- a lesson that reflects the information given by the pupil and the learning goals they want to tackle;
- building in opportunities to check the statements made by the pupil before moving to more challenging situations;
- checking theoretical understanding.

Indications of lack of competence include:

- delivering a pre-planned, standard lesson that doesn't take into account the pupil's expressed needs or concerns;
- failing to build in a suitable balance of practice and theory.

Were the practice areas suitable?

You should use an area or route that allows the pupil to practise safely and helps them to achieve their goals. It should provide some stretch and challenge, but without taking the pupil out of their comfort zone.

Indications that all the elements of competence are in place could include choosing a practice area/route that provides:

- a range of opportunities to address the agreed learning objectives;
- challenges, but is realistic in terms of the pupil's capabilities and confidence.

Indications of lack of competence include taking the pupil into an area that:

- takes the pupil outside of their competence zone – so that they spend all their time 'surviving' and have no space left to look at learning issues;
- exposes the pupil to risks they cannot manage.

Was the lesson plan adapted, when appropriate, to help the pupil work towards their learning goals?

You should be willing and able to adapt if your pupil:

- appears to be uncomfortable or unable to deal with the learning experience that you have set up;
- suggests that it is not providing what they were looking for.

If the pupil's inability is creating a possible risk situation you must adapt quickly. This might require a few extra questions to clarify what is out of line. It may be that the problem is because of the teaching and learning style being used rather than because the overall plan is wrong. Whatever the reason for adapting the plan, you must make sure the pupil understands what they are doing and why.

Indications that all the elements of competence are in place could include:

- comparing the actual performance of the pupil with their claims and clarifying any differences;
- responding to any faults or weaknesses that undermine the original plan for the session;
- responding to any concerns or issues raised by the pupil;
- picking up on non-verbal signs of discomfort or confusion.

Indications of lack of competence include:

- persisting with a plan despite the pupil being clearly out of their depth;
- persisting with a plan despite the pupil demonstrating faults or weaknesses that should lead to a rethink of the plan;
- changing the plan without reason;
- failing to explain to the pupil why the plan has been changed.

Risk management

It is vital that all parties in any on-road training situation understand, and are clear about, where the responsibility lies for the safety of themselves, others in the vehicle and other road users.

There are two aspects to the management of risk in any training situation. At all times you are responsible for your own safety, the safety of the pupil and the safety of other road users. In particular circumstances this can extend to taking physical control of the vehicle to manage a safety-critical incident. From a training point of view, you are also responsible for developing the pupil's awareness of and ability to manage risk (as the driver, the pupil also has responsibilities). This is the objective that is being assessed in this section.

Did the ADI make sure that the pupil fully understood how the responsibility for risk would be shared?

The 'balance of responsibility', between the pupil and the ADI, will inevitably vary in different circumstances. For example, compare the following two scenarios:

A pupil in the very early stages of their training, in a car fitted with dual controls.

In this situation it might be reasonable for you to start a lesson by saying something like:

> At all times I expect you to drive as carefully and responsibly as possible. I will expect you to be aware of other road users and to control the car. However, I do have the ability to take control of the car in an emergency. I will only use these controls when I feel that you are not dealing with the situation yourself. If that happens we will take some time to talk about what happened so that you understand for next time.

A pupil who has passed their driving test but has asked you to give them some additional training in their own car, which is much bigger and more technically advanced than the one they learnt in.

In this situation you might say something like:

> You have passed your test and I will therefore assume that you are taking full responsibility for our safety. I will be talking to you from time to time but I will try to keep that to a minimum so that I don't distract you. If I am quiet don't worry; that just means I am comfortable with what you are doing. I will, of course, let you know if I see any risk that you appear to have missed.

However, such opening statements are not all that is involved in meeting this criterion. You should be managing this process throughout the lesson. So, for example, if the pupil makes some sort of mistake carrying out a manoeuvre you should, ideally, find an opportunity to analyse that mistake with the pupil. Having achieved an understanding of what went wrong you might then ask the pupil to try the manoeuvre again. At that point you should provide the pupil with clear information about what is required of them.

So, for example, you might say: 'Let's try that manoeuvre again. I won't say anything. Just try to remember what we have just been talking about.'

On the other hand you may want to take back a bit of control and might say: 'Let's try that again. I will talk you through it this time. Just follow my instructions.'

You should work with the pupil to decide the best way of tackling the problem and that might mean a temporary change in the 'balance of responsibility'. The important thing is that the pupil knows what is expected of them.

Under test conditions there are no circumstances in which you can assume that the issue of risk management has been dealt with. Even if you and the pupil have had discussions about risk before the observed lesson, you must show that you are actively managing the issue for assessment purposes.

Indications that all the elements of competence are in place could include:

- asking the pupil what is meant by risk;
- asking the pupil what sorts of issues create risk, such as the use of alcohol or drugs;
- explaining clearly what is expected of the pupil and what the pupil can reasonably expect of you;
- checking that the pupil understands what is required of them when there is a change of plan or they are asked to repeat an exercise.

Indications of lack of competence include:

- failing to address the issue of risk management;
- giving incorrect guidance about where responsibility lies for management of risk;

- failing to explain how dual controls will be used;
- undermining the pupil's commitment to being safe and responsible, eg by agreeing with risky attitudes to alcohol use;
- asking the pupil to repeat a manoeuvre or carry out a particular exercise without making sure that they understand what role you are going to play.

Were directions and instructions given to the pupil clear and given in good time?

'Directions' should be taken to mean any instruction, such as 'turn left at the next junction' or 'try changing gear a little later'. Any input from you must be sufficient, timely and appropriate. It is important that you take account of the ability of your pupils when giving directions. Directions given late, or in a confusing or misleading way, do not allow the pupil to respond and can make weaknesses worse.

Too many unnecessary instructions can both demotivate the pupil and create a real hazard. Remember it is an offence to use a mobile phone whilst driving because this is known to create a level of risk equivalent to or, in some cases, greater than driving whilst drunk. It cannot, therefore be good practice to constantly bombard the pupil with unnecessary questions.

Indications that all the elements of competence are in place could include:

- clear, concise directions;
- ensuring the pupil understands what they plan to do and agrees with that plan;
- directions given at a suitable time so that the pupil can respond.

Indications of lack of competence include:

- giving confused directions;
- giving directions too late;
- giving unnecessary directions;
- failing to recognize when your input is causing overload or confusion.

Was the trainer aware of the surroundings and the pupil's actions?

This question lies at the heart of the ADI's professional skill. You should be able to:

- take in the outside world;
- observe the actions of the pupil, including comments and body language;

- judge whether those actions are suitable in any given situation;
- respond accordingly.

Any serious lapses in this area are likely to lead to a 0 marking.

Was any verbal or physical intervention by the trainer timely and appropriate?

The overall approach should be client-centred. Remember that there is a fine balance between giving enough input and giving too much.

When stationary, it would be expected that inputs and interventions would take the form of a dialogue with the pupil. In the moving-car environment, you remaining silent and signalling your confidence in the pupil through your body language is just as much a coaching input as asking a stream of questions. Clearly the most important 'interventions' are those that manage risk in a moving car. You would be expected to point out situations in which a risk or hazard might arise to your pupil. However, direct intervention may be needed to prevent a situation escalating. This criterion is primarily about your response in those situations.

Indications that all the elements of competence are in place could include:

- intervening in a way that actively supports the pupil's learning process and safety during the session;
- allowing the pupil to deal with situations appropriately;
- taking control of a situation where the pupil is clearly out of their depth.

Indications of lack of competence include:

- ignoring a developing situation and leaving the pupil to flounder;
- taking control of a situation the pupil is clearly dealing with appropriately;
- constantly intervening when unnecessary;
- intervening inappropriately and creating distractions;
- undermining the pupil's confidence;
- reinforcing the instructor as the person who is in sole control of the lesson.

Was sufficient feedback given to help the pupil understand any potential safety-critical incidents?

If a safety-critical, or potentially critical incident does occur, it is vital that the pupil fully understands what happened and how they could have avoided or dealt with it better. Ideally the pupil should be supported to analyse the situation for themselves. However, it may be necessary for you to provide feedback if, for example, the pupil simply did not see a problem. That feedback should be given as soon as is practical after the incident.

Indications that all the elements of competence are in place could include:

- finding a safe place to stop and examine the critical incident;
- allowing the pupil time to express any fears or concerns the incident might have caused;
- supporting the pupil to reflect clearly about what happened;
- providing input to clarify aspects of the incident that the pupil does not understand;
- supporting the pupil to identify strategies for future situations;
- providing input where the pupil does not understand what they should do differently;
- checking that the pupil feels able to put the strategy in place;
- agreeing ways of developing that competence if the pupil feels the need.

Indications of lack of competence include:

- failing to examine the incident;
- taking too long to address issues generated by an incident;
- not allowing the pupil to explore their own understanding;
- telling the pupil what the solution is and not checking their understanding;
- failing to check the pupil's ability to put in place the agreed strategy.

Teaching and learning strategies

The important thing to remember when considering teaching and learning strategies is that they are about client-centred learning. The examiner's assessment is about whether you have been able to help the pupil to learn in an active way. Also, remember instruction based around the core competences used currently is pretty good. We must not throw that away. Coaching is a powerful extension of the range of options. It is not an automatic replacement for any of the existing ones.

There will be many times when it is useful to use a coaching technique. The principle that underpins coaching is that an engaged pupil is likely to achieve a higher level of understanding and that self-directed solutions will seem far more relevant. This applies in every situation, including instruction.

Direct instruction is useful in helping a pupil in the early stages cope with new situations or in supporting a pupil who is clearly struggling in a certain situation. Good coaching will use the correct technique at the correct time, matching the pupil's needs. In some cases you may need to give direct instruction through a particularly difficult situation. That instruction forms part of a coaching process if you then encourage the pupil to analyse the problem and take responsibility for learning from it. A good ADI will take every opportunity to reinforce learning.

Was the teaching style suited to the pupil's learning style and current ability?

You should take into account all that you understand about the pupil. You should recognize that different pupils will have different preferred approaches to learning, although these may only emerge fully over a number of lessons. Some pupils may be very willing to learn actively and others may want opportunities to reflect before they make the next step in their learning. You should at least be able to give evidence of their sensitivity to these issues. In a one-off session this will probably be best demonstrated by offering a range of options. You should be able to adjust your approach if evidence emerges of a different preferred style.

It is impossible to force learning on a pupil. Progress is always determined by what the pupil is comfortable with. The skill is in recognizing when the pupil stops learning. The pace of a session should be set by the pupil. On the other hand, a pupil should not be talked out of experimenting, if this is within safe bounds.

When coaching, you should ensure that the tools used are suitable. If a question and answer technique is used, this should match the pupil's level of ability and encourage them to use a higher level of thinking to give a response. Asking closed questions of a pupil who is demonstrating a high level of ability, unless this is to check knowledge, is of little use. Asking open questions of a pupil of limited ability who is finding it difficult to achieve the task they have set for themselves may be very confusing. These are not hard and fast rules. The effectiveness of any question is assessed given the circumstances at the time.

Indications that all the elements of competence are in place could include:

- actively working to understand how you can best support the pupil's learning process (you might not achieve a full understanding in the session – it is the attempt that demonstrates competence);
- modifying your teaching style when or if you realize there is a need to do so;

- providing accurate and technically correct demonstration, instruction or information – giving technically incorrect instruction or information is an automatic fail if that input might lead to a safety-critical situation;
- using practical examples and other similar tools to provide different ways of looking at a particular subject;
- linking learning in theory to learning in practice;
- encouraging and helping the pupil to take ownership of the learning process;
- responding to faults in a timely manner;
- providing enough uninterrupted time to practise new skills;
- providing the pupil with clear guidance about how they might practise outside the session.

Indications of lack of competence include:

- adopting a teaching style clearly at odds with the pupil's learning style;
- failing to check with the pupil whether the approach they are taking is acceptable;
- failing to explore other ways of addressing a particular learning point;
- concentrating on delivering teaching tools rather than looking for learning outcomes;
- ignoring safety issues.

Was the pupil encouraged to analyse problems and take responsibility for their learning?

A key part of the client-centred approach is development of active problem solving in the pupil. This means that you have to provide time for this to happen and you have to stop talking for long enough for the pupil to do the work. The key thing to remember, however, is that different pupils will respond to this invitation in different ways. Some may be able to do it instantly, in a discussion. Others may need to go away and reflect upon a particular problem. They may need to be pointed at readings or other inputs to help them get a handle on the issue. Pushing a pupil to come up with answers on the spot may be unproductive for some.

Indications that all the elements of competence are in place could include:

- providing time, in a suitable location, to explore any problems or issues that arose during the lesson or that were raised by the pupil;

- providing timely opportunities for analysis, promptly in the case of risk-critical incidents;
- taking time and using suitable techniques to understand any problems the pupil had with understanding an issue;
- suggesting suitable strategies to help the pupil develop their understanding, such as using practical examples or pointing them at further reading;
- giving clear and accurate information to fill gaps in the pupil's knowledge or understanding;
- leaving the pupil feeling that they had responsibility for their learning in the situation.

Indications of lack of competence include:

- leaving the pupil feeling that you were in control of the teaching process;
- failing to explore alternative ways of addressing a problem – in response to evidence of different learning preferences;
- providing unsuitable or incorrect inputs.

Were opportunities and examples used to clarify learning outcomes?

While training in technique is core to the learning process it is important to reinforce this input and to link it with theory. The best way to do this is to use real-world situations during the lesson. The use of practical examples and scenarios gives the pupil a better understanding of when, how and why to use a particular technique.

This can be done, for example, by asking the pupil to think about why mirrors are important when changing direction.

Indications that all the elements of competence are in place could include:

- using examples identified in a lesson in a suitable way and at a suitable time to confirm or reinforce understanding;
- exploring different ways to use examples to respond to differences in preferred learning style;
- using examples that are within the pupil's range of experience and ability to understand;
- recognizing that some pupils will be able to respond instantly while others will want to think about the issue.

Indications of lack of competence include:

- using examples the pupil cannot really understand through lack of experience;
- using complex examples that the pupil doesn't have the ability to respond to;
- failing to give the pupil time to think through the issues and come to their own conclusion;
- imposing an interpretation.

Was the technical information given comprehensive, appropriate and accurate?

As noted above, giving incorrect or insufficient information, with the result that a safety-critical situation might occur, will result in an automatic fail.

Remember that good information is accurate, relevant and timely. Failure to meet any one of these criteria makes the others redundant.

Most sessions will require some technical input from you to help the pupil solve problems or to fill a gap in their knowledge. This input must be accurate and appropriate.

Information given must be comprehensive when associated with a recurring weakness in the pupil's driving. Simply telling the pupil that they have done something wrong is unlikely to help them overcome the problem.

Any practical demonstration of technique must be clear and suitable. The pupil should be engaged and given the opportunity to explore their understanding of what they are being shown.

Information given unnecessarily may not be helpful; for example, continually telling the pupil what to do and not allowing them an opportunity to take responsibility.

Unclear or misleading advice should also be avoided. Comments such as 'you're a bit close to these parked cars' could be used to introduce coaching on a weakness but are of little use on their own as they are unclear. How close is 'a bit' and is it significant?

Indications that all the elements of competence are in place could include:

- giving clear, timely and technically accurate demonstrations or explanations;
- checking understanding and, if necessary, repeating the demonstration or explanation;
- finding a different way to demonstrate or explain if the pupil still does not understand.

Indications of lack of competence include:

- providing inaccurate or unclear information, too late or too early in the learning process;

- failing to check understanding;

- failing to explore alternative ways of presenting information where the pupil does not understand the first offering.

Was the pupil given appropriate and timely feedback during the session?

Feedback is an essential part of learning but the process must be balanced. A pupil needs to have a clear picture of how they are doing against their learning objectives throughout the lesson. They should be encouraged when performing well and coached when a problem or learning opportunity occurs. However, a constant stream of words, however technically accurate, given at an unsuitable time, may be demotivating or actually dangerous. Sitting quietly and saying nothing can also be a very powerful form of feedback in some situations.

All feedback should be relevant, positive and honest. It is not helpful if the pupil is given unrealistic feedback which creates a false sense of their own ability. Where possible, feedback should not be negative. Rather than saying somebody has a weakness, consider expressing it as a learning opportunity. However, if they need to be told something is wrong or dangerous there is no point in waffling. The pupil should have a realistic sense of their own performance.

Feedback is a two-way street. It should, ideally, be prompted by the pupil with you responding to the pupil's questions or comments. The pupil's feedback should never be overlooked or disregarded.

Indications that all the elements of competence are in place could include:

- providing feedback in response to questions from the pupil;

- seeking appropriate opportunities to provide feedback that reinforces understanding or confirms achievement of learning objectives;

- providing feedback about failure to achieve learning objectives that helps the pupil achieve an understanding of what they need to do to improve;

- providing feedback that the pupil can understand;

- providing consistent feedback that is reinforced by body language.

Indications of lack of competence include:

- providing feedback a long time after an incident so that the pupil cannot link the feedback to what happened;

- providing feedback that overlooks a safety-critical incident;
- continuously providing feedback when this may be distracting the pupil;
- failing to check the pupil's understanding of feedback;
- providing feedback that is irrelevant to the pupil's learning objectives, for example commenting on their personal appearance;
- refusing to hear reasonable feedback about your own performance.

Were the pupil's queries followed up and answered?

Direct questions or queries from the pupil should be dealt with as soon as possible. The response may involve providing information or directing the pupil to a suitable source.

Remember that, wherever possible, the pupil should be encouraged to discover answers themselves. However, if you do need to provide information you must ensure that the pupil completely understands the information given.

Pupils may not always have the confidence to ask direct questions. You should be able to pick up comments or body language that indicates uncertainty or confusion and use suitable techniques to explore possible issues.

Indications that all the elements of competence are in place could include:

- responding openly and readily to queries;
- providing helpful answers or directing the pupil to suitable sources of information;
- actively checking with pupils if their comments or body language suggest they may have a question;
- encouraging the pupil to explore possible solutions for themselves.

Indications of lack of competence include:

- refusing to respond to queries;
- providing inaccurate information in response to queries;
- avoiding the question or denying responsibility for answering it.

Did the trainer maintain an appropriate, non-discriminatory manner throughout the session?

You should maintain an atmosphere in which the pupil feels comfortable to express their opinions. You should create an open, friendly environment for learning, regardless of the pupil's age, gender, sexual orientation, ethnic background, religion, physical abilities or any other irrelevant factor.

This implies active respect for the pupil, their values and what constitutes appropriate behaviour in their culture.

You must not display inappropriate attitudes or behaviours towards other road users and should challenge your pupil if they display these behaviours.

Indications that all the elements of competence are in place could include:

- keeping a respectful distance and not invading the pupil's personal space;

- asking the pupil how they wish to be addressed;

- asking a disabled driver to explain what you need to know about their condition;

- adopting an appropriate position in the car;

- using language about other road users that is not derogatory and that does not invite the pupil to collude with any discriminatory attitude.

Indications of lack of competence include:

- invading somebody's physical space;
- touching the pupil, including trying to shake hands, unless it is necessary for safety reasons;
- using somebody's first name unless they have said that this is acceptable;
- commenting on the pupil's appearance or any other personal attribute unless it has a direct impact on their ability to drive safely, such as wearing shoes that make it difficult for them to operate the vehicle's pedals.

End of the session – was the pupil encouraged to reflect on their own performance?

At the end of the session the pupil should be encouraged to reflect on their performance and discuss their feelings. You should encourage honest self-appraisal and use client-centred techniques to highlight areas that need development if the pupil has not recognized them. Once development areas have been identified the pupil should be encouraged to make them part of future development.

Review

In most situations you will maintain your awareness of what is going on around you, give reasonably clear and timely direction and intervene in an appropriate and timely way to ensure that no safety-critical incidents occur.

However, from time to time, situations will arise in which your actions or instruction are of such poor quality that the examiner may decide that they are putting themselves, the learner or any third party in immediate danger.

Example: the learner is approaching a closed junction. They ask the instructor whether they should stop at the give-way line. The instructor is completely unable to see down the joining roads but tells the learner to 'go, go, go'.

In these circumstances the examiner would be entitled to stop the lesson and mark it as an immediate fail.

When you pass

You can apply for entry onto the Register of Approved Driving Instructors (Car). The application can be made at **www.gov.uk/apply-first-approved-driving-instructor-adi-badge**. You must do this within 12 months of the date you pass. Registration then becomes renewable every four years.

With your application for registration you will need to enclose the appropriate payment and a recent passport-style photo.

Registration declaration

When you apply for registration, you must sign a declaration to the effect that you will:

- notify the Registrar of any change of name, address or place of employment;
- notify the Registrar if convicted of any offence;
- return the certificate if your registration lapses or is revoked;
- agree to undergo, when requested by the Registrar, a Standards Check.

If you fail

You may apply for a further test if you are still within the two-year qualifying period, and if the test was your first or second attempt. Otherwise, if you wish to continue, you will have to wait until the two-year period has elapsed before you can apply for Part 1 again. It is therefore sensible to be prepared to invest in sufficient training with an experienced tutor before taking your Part 3.

The ADI certificate

After passing the Part 3 test and making your application, you should receive your official green ADI Certificate of Registration within a week. It shows details of your name, photograph, ADI number, the date of issue and the date of expiry of the certificate, which will be four years from the date of its issue. As a qualified instructor, whenever you are giving tuition, you must display the official green certificate on the left-hand side of the car's windscreen, and produce your certificate if requested to by a police officer or any person authorized by the Secretary of State. If you can satisfy the Registrar that your certificate has been lost, damaged or destroyed, the DVSA will issue a duplicate on payment of the current fee.

ADI Standards Check

When you have completed all three parts of the exam and qualified as an ADI, you are obliged to undertake a 'Standards Check' at regular intervals to retain your qualification.

The format and criteria for the Part 3 exam are virtually the same as for the existing Standards Check. For this reason, Chapter 6 gives an overview of the Standards Check, with the criteria as in this chapter on the ADI Part 3.

The ADI Standards Check 06

The ADI Standards Check is a legal requirement for all ADIs. You must take at least one Standards Check in each four-year period of registration as an ADI.

You will be assessed on your delivery of instruction to the pupil based on the criteria set out in the *Standards Check form SC1* and the National Standard for Driver Training.

The national standard sets out the skills, knowledge and understanding you need to be an effective driver trainer. The standards check assesses how well you meet the standard. The aim of the Standards Check is to allow the DVSA to assess an ADI's ability to instruct and to assess whether their instruction helps a person to learn in an effective way. The Standards Check is conducted with a DVSA examiner observing the ADI delivering a normal one-hour lesson.

The Standards Check looks at whether your instruction helps the pupil to learn effectively. It is designed to help ADIs to understand, demonstrate and develop the competencies in the national standards and allows you to demonstrate to the examiner what you do in your normal daily work.

You should familiarize yourself with the assessment check form (page 127) and areas being assessed and consider whether the instructional techniques you use will allow you to meet and demonstrate the competences.

Individual ADIs are responsible for their own Standards Check lessons. The DVSA suggests that you should make sure you have a sound knowledge of the area around your chosen driving test centre so that you can plan your lesson and will be able to give appropriate directions to the pupil during the Standards Check. You must take the Standards Check even if you do not have your own instruction car or you are not actively working as an ADI. The Registrar can consider taking someone off the register if they repeatedly don't attend for a Standards Check.

You will normally be invited for a Standards Check at your local driving test centre. You will get a letter confirming the time and place of the

Standards Check and which explains the procedure. A sample letter can be downloaded from **www.gov.uk/adi-standards-check**. You must respond by phone or to the e-mail address on the letter within 10 days, indicating whether you will be able to attend.

The appointment

Checks are conducted during the examiner's normal working hours and the invitation to attend will specify the date, time and place – normally local to the area you work in, and often the local driving test centre. You must acknowledge receipt of the invitation.

You do not necessarily need to accept the date given in the invitation letter. It is quite acceptable to change the date if it is inconvenient – for example, a pre-arranged holiday or other important commitments. However, you must contact the DVSA promptly, and they will require evidence such as a driving test application number or holiday booking confirmation.

If you do not attend at the agreed time, you will be asked to attend at a time and place nominated by the DVSA. It is important that you attend – not having a pupil, not having a car or not working as an ADI are not regarded as acceptable reasons for non-attendance.

Classroom-based and 'off-road' lessons are not allowed for the Standards Check.

In Northern Ireland, the procedures are slightly different. For details see the ADI 1 *Your Guide to Becoming an Approved Driving Instructor*. This document is available from the Driver and Vehicle Agency (DVA), County Hall, Castlerock Road, Waterside, Coleraine BT51 3HS. Telephone: 0845 601 4094. E-mail **dva@doeni.gov.uk**. Website: **www.nidirect.gov.uk**.

The car

The car you use for the Standards Check must be roadworthy, safe and reliable. A soft-top convertible is not acceptable, nor is a car with limited rear seating for the examiner. 'L' plates must be displayed if the driver is a provisional licence holder. You must make sure that all seatbelts (both front and rear) are in good working order.

Your ADI Certificate must be displayed if you are charging for the lesson. Even if you are not charging for the lesson you still need to take the certificate with you.

The rules about the type of car to be used are set out in detail in Chapter 3 (page 60).

If you normally use the back seat of the car as your 'office' with an accumulation of diaries, reference books, teaching aids and so on, make sure that it is reasonably tidy and that the examiner has sufficient room.

If the lesson is to be conducted in a pupil's car, make sure that it conforms to the test requirements.

The pupil

Your pupil can be either a learner driver or a full licence holder but they must not be another ADI or someone who has passed the first two parts of the ADI exams.

Some instructors make the mistake of selecting their 'favourite' pupil, or one whose driving is at a high standard. It is more important for you to use a pupil whose driving can be improved and worked on during the lesson.

Your examiner will ask you for some background information about the pupil, such as how many lessons they have had and what you've been working on recently.

You must demonstrate clearly to the examiner that the needs that you identify have been discussed and agreed with the pupil. You will then be asked to deliver a lesson in exactly the same way as you would normally do.

The examiner

At times, the examiner may be accompanied by a senior examiner. Whenever possible, you will be told in advance when this is going to happen. If you are not told before the assessment, five minutes is allowed for you to explain to the pupil what's happening. The lesson can include (if you wish) driving to the nearest garage or tyre centre to inflate the car's tyres to the recommended pressures for a heavier load.

You can be accompanied by your trainer/mentor, but that person can't take part in the lesson in any way.

At the start of the lesson you should discuss the lesson plan and agree it with the pupil. Where you have had little or no experience of working with the pupil you can suggest an assessment drive before finalizing a lesson plan. However, you should make sure you leave enough time for development and feedback during the lesson.

Assessment

During the Standards Check you will be assessed on the same competences as in the ADI Part 3. Details of these competencies and how to apply them are shown in Chapter 5, and they are listed again at the end of this chapter.

You will be given a grade based on the following marking criteria:

Table 6.1

85% or over	Grade A	indicates an overall high standard of instruction
60%–84%	Grade B	a sufficient level of competence
Less than 60%	Fail	an unsatisfactory performance

To achieve a pass you must meet three specific criteria:

- score eight or more marks in the risk management section;
- manage critical incidents effectively;
- identify any significant weakness and give correct and sufficient information to ensure that safety critical situations do not occur.

The theme for the lesson may be one of those listed on the *Standards Check* form – or it can be something else.

Before the lesson starts, the examiner will ask you some questions about the pupil.

You should be able to indicate:

- roughly how any hours of tuition the pupil has had;
- whether the pupil is getting any other practice, for example, from parents or others;
- the pupil's strengths and areas for development.

You can show the examiner the pupil's driver's record (if they have one) before the start of the lesson to help explain their current progress in their agreed training programme.

The examiner may make some notes during the lesson to help them identify locations that they may not be familiar with, but those notes will be destroyed as soon as the Standards Check is complete.

If your trainer/mentor intends to accompany you and the Standards Check is also planned for supervision, the supervising examiner will decide whether or not the supervision goes ahead.

Figure 6.1 Standards Check form

INFORMATION			
Driver & Vehicle Standards Agency	Trainer Name	Location	Outcome
	PRN	Date / /	
		Dual Controls Yes No	
	Valid Certificate Yes No	Reg No.	
		Accompanied? QA Trainer Other	

ASSESSMENT	Competence
	0	1	2	3

Pupil: Beginner □ Partly Trained □ Trained □ FLH New □ FLH Experienced □

Lesson theme: Junctions □ Town & city driving □ Interacting with other road users □
Dual carriageway / faster moving roads □ Defensive driving □ Effective use of mirrors □
Independent driving □ Rural roads □ Motorways □ Eco-safe driving □
Recap a manoeuvre □ Commentary □ Recap emergency stop □ Other

Competence columns: 0 No evidence | 1 Demonstrated in a few elements | 2 Demonstrated in most elements | 3 Demonstrated in all elements

LESSON PLANNING

	0	1	2	3
Did the trainer identify the pupil's learning goals and needs?				
Was the agreed lesson structrue appropriate for the pupil's experience and ability?				
Were the practice areas suitable?				
Was the lesson plan adapted, when appropriate, to help the pupil work towards their learning goals?				
Score for lesson planning				

RISK MANAGEMENT

	0	1	2	3
Did the trainer ensure that the pupil fully understood how the responsibility for risk would be shared?				
Were directions and instructions given to the pupil clear and given in good time?				
Was the trainer aware of the surroundings and the pupil's actions?				
Was any verbal or physical intervention by the trainer timely and appropriate?				
Was sufficient feedback given to help the pupil understand any potential safety critical incidents?				
Score for risk management				

TEACHING & LEARNING STRATEGIES

	0	1	2	3
Was the teaching style suited to the pupil's learning style and current ability?				
Was the pupil encouraged to analyse problems and take responsibility for their learning?				
Were opportunities and examples used to clarify learning outcomes?				
Was the technical information given comprehensive, appropriate and accurate?				
Was the pupil given appropriate and timely feedback during the session?				
Were the pupil's queries followed up and answered?				
Did the trainer maintain an appropriate non-discriminatory manner throughout the session?				
At the end of the session - was the pupil encouraged to reflect on their own performance?				
Score for teaching and learning strategies				
Overall score				

REVIEW	YES	NO
Did the trainer score 7 or less on Risk Management? (A 'Yes' response to this question will result in an automatic Fail)		
At any point in the lesson, did the trainer behave in a way which put you, the pupil or any third party in immediate danger, so that you had to stop the lesson? (A 'Yes' response to this question will result in an automatic Fail)		
Was advice given to seek further development?		

Feedback offered to trainer

Examiner Name   Signature

The Standards Check will last for one hour and you should allow 15 minutes at the end of the lesson for a debrief with the examiner.

Presenting the lesson

When you pick up the pupil from the normal starting point for lessons, allow plenty of time to drive to the test centre or other meeting point for the check. It is important that you do the driving at this stage so that you start the lesson without a warm-up for the pupil and that there is a clear distinction between the previous lesson and this one.

The examiner will want to know something about the pupil before the start, so you could provide a brief written indication of previous lessons and standards achieved to avoid a lengthy verbal explanation.

The procedure for the Standards Check will then follow the same format as the ADI Part 3 test (see Chapter 5).

The format of the lesson should follow the same pattern as a normal lesson. The fact that it is a Standards Check should make very little difference. Following the initial introductions of pupil to examiner and explaining to the pupil the purpose of the Check, follow the basic routine:

- Recap on the previous session. At the beginning of the lesson, go over the main points from the previous lesson to establish a base line. This should be a two-way discussion, taking into account the pupil's comments and responses.

- Agree the goals for the lesson by discussing what the pupil's needs are and what they would like to achieve by the end of the lesson.

- Plan the route so that it is suitable for the pupil's ability and the goal they want to achieve.

- Agree the level of support and instruction needed and divide the responsibility for risk so that both of you know what you are responsible for. This might mean reminding the pupil that you have dual controls, which you will use if necessary. Often this is reassuring to the pupil because they can then focus on the task in hand.

- Pull up at the side of the road to give regular feedback to establish what is going well and what needs improving. Use your skills in identifying, analysing and remedying faults to ensure the pupil will be able to achieve the goal.

- End with a summary and a recap on what has been covered during the lesson. You should assess and discuss the level of achievement of the pupil and encourage the pupil to reflect on this achievement: what went well; what didn't go so well; what needs improving.

The lesson should finish with a discussion of what will be covered in the next lesson.

Summary

Once you have finished any reflective discussion with the pupil, the examiner will take a few minutes to review the assessment and then offer some feedback.

The purpose of feedback from the examiner is to help you understand where you might have failed to demonstrate full competence and where you might need to focus your efforts when undertaking further development.

The Standards Check form shows a 'profile' of your performance against the individual competences. This will help you to see where you have given a strong performance as well as where you may need development.

As with the ADI Part 3, the Standards Check assesses competence across 17 areas. A review by the DVSA has shown that the following areas contributed most frequently to failures:

- Was the lesson plan adapted, when appropriate, to help the pupil work towards their learning goals?
- Did the trainer ensure that the pupil fully understood how the responsibility of risk would be shared?
- Was the teaching style suited to the pupil's learning style and current ability?
- Was the pupil encouraged to analyse problems and take responsibility for their learning?
- Was the pupil given appropriate and timely feedback during the session?
- Was sufficient feedback given to help the pupil understand any safety-critical incidents?
- Was the pupil encouraged to reflect on their own performance?

Assessment structure

As previously indicated, the assessment is made against three broad or 'high' areas of competence:

- lesson planning;
- risk management;
- teaching and learning strategies.

The three 'high' areas of competence are broken down further into 17 'lower level' competences and a mark is given for each of these.

Lesson planning

- Did the trainer identify the pupil's learning goals and needs?
- Was the agreed lesson structure appropriate for the pupil's experience and ability?
- Were the practice areas appropriate?
- Was the lesson plan adapted, when appropriate, to help the pupil work towards their learning goals?

Risk management

- Did the trainer ensure that the pupil fully understood how the responsibility for risk would be shared?
- Were the directions and instructions given to the pupil clear and given in good time?
- Was the trainer aware of the surroundings and the pupil's actions?
- Was any verbal or physical intervention by the trainer timely and appropriate?
- Was sufficient feedback given to help the pupil understand any potential safety critical incidents?

Teaching and learning strategies

- Was the teaching style suited to the pupil's level of ability?
- Was the pupil encouraged to analyse problems and take responsibility for their learning?

- Were opportunities and examples used to clarify learning outcomes?

- Was the technical information given comprehensive, appropriate and accurate?

- Was the pupil given appropriate and timely feedback during the session?

- Were the pupil's queries followed up and answered?

- Did the trainer maintain an appropriate non-discriminatory manner throughout the session?

- At the end of the session, was the pupil encouraged to reflect on their own performance?

For each of these competences a mark is given on a scale of 0–3.

Table 6.2

Score	Criteria	Description
3	Competence demonstrated	Keep up the good work
2	Competence demonstrated in most elements	Acceptable – there are clear areas of improvement
1	Competence demonstrated in a few elements	Not acceptable – more work needed
0	No evidence of competence	Completely unacceptable

These marks are added together to give an overall mark and they will also provide a profile of the areas where you have any strengths and where you might need to do some more development work.

After completing the marking sheet the examiner will then review the training session.

You will fail the Standards Check if:

- You get a score of 7 or less for the 'Risk Management' category.

- The examiner stops the lesson because you have put yourself, the pupil, the examiner or someone else in immediate danger.

- You have a total score of 30 or less (out of a possible 51).

If you get a total score of 43 or more you will be given a Grade A.

With a total score of between 31 and 42 you will be given a Grade B.

Table 6.3

Total score	Grade	Description
0–30	Fail	Your performance is unsatisfactory
31–42	Grade B	You will stay on the register of ADIs
43–51	Grade A	You have shown a high standard of instruction, and will stay on the register

Note: If you do not reach an acceptable standard in three consecutive checks, the ADI Registrar will start the process of removing you from the register.

Driver training 07

For many years driving instruction involved simply 'instructing' – telling the pupil what to do and how to do it without much interaction or pupil involvement. In this method, there would have been an element of 'I'm the expert – do this, do that' and 'This is what you have to do to pass the test'. As a result, the teaching/learning process was very passive and seen as slightly dictatorial. This approach also has the effect of encouraging only short-term learning, understanding and retention.

Nowadays the emphasis is much more on 'client-centred learning' rather than purely instructing. This involves the pupils in any decision making about the learning process and in taking more responsibility for their own learning as early as possible in their training. It creates an equal partnership between the pupil and the trainer, with greater benefits, particularly relating to longer-term and retained learning. The pupil is put in an active role by encouraging them to identify for themselves obtainable goals and objectives. A more effective and efficient performance will normally be achieved by coaching methods as a result of greater participation and willingness on the part of the pupil.

Using effective client-centred methods means involving the pupil in an equal partnership and using a variety of skills including effective questioning, using non-judgemental verbal communication, active listening skills and having an open and honest working relationship with pupils.

The most successful instructors are those who have a concern for their students and are most sensitive to their individual learning requirements. The needs of the learner driver are as varied and complex as the differences between the students themselves. Avoid grouping people into preconceived categories such as young and old, or quick and slow to learn. Making this type of pre-judgement before you get to know pupils may prevent you from treating them as individuals, and might also prevent you from seeing them with 'open' and 'more sensitive' eyes.

One of your first priorities will be to create a good working relationship with your students. A good test of this will be the rapport that develops between you; and, perhaps more significantly, the level of communication. For example, if a good relationship develops:

- your pupils should feel they can readily admit their mistakes without the risk of feeling inadequate;
- they should be able to discuss freely with you their fears and anxieties about their progress;
- you should both be able to laugh together about silly mistakes.

In order to develop your pupils' ability and confidence, learning should be founded on mutual cooperation. You can encourage this by structuring the learning so that the pupil is asked to carry out only those tasks that can be achieved with a degree of success.

The basic requirements for any effective learning to take place are attention, activity and involvement.

Attention is not always a completely conscious activity. Long periods of undivided concentration are difficult to maintain without a break, or at least a change in the type of activity. Periods of concentration, therefore, will need to be shorter in the earlier stages of learning.

Activity and involvement are vital if the pupil is going to learn efficiently and effectively. Activity should not be thought of as simply the physical activity. For example, although learning to drive a car involves a large degree of physical activity, mental involvement is also necessary to initiate the physical responses.

There is a saying often used in general education, which is particularly relevant to driver training:

What I hear, I forget. What I see, I remember. What I do, I understand.

Keeping the novice driver actively involved in the learning experience will normally result in more being remembered. However, physical activity alone is not sufficient; learners should also be encouraged to think about what they are doing and why!

Teaching and learning

You will know from your own experiences that learning is an inconsistent process over which there is little reliable control. Teachers have no mystical power by which to pour knowledge into the minds of their learners, so whatever students learn (whether it is a psychomotor or an intellectual skill), they must learn for themselves. You will merely be providing the circumstances in which learning may occur.

Your role will essentially be one of establishing the quality of the teaching and of planning and organizing the conditions in which learning can take place. Teachers manage the learning experience by:

- preparing the material;
- organizing the material;
- presenting the experience to the student;
- creating opportunities to practise;
- observing the student's reactions;
- assessing progress.

No matter how carefully prepared and presented the lesson may be, success can be judged only by how much knowledge or skill the learner gains from it.

The complete experience in learning to drive involves the car and/or some other location, and the personality and teaching methods of the instructor. It will also be dependent on the attitude, knowledge and skill of the student. Whatever natural abilities and aptitude your pupils have, they will only gain the full benefit of learning if they are actively involved and are attentive.

Motivation is vital to students' willingness to learn. You must motivate your students and create an environment and situations from which they can learn.

The key to the successful management of learning will be your ability to present, adapt and adjust the same basic knowledge and skills for the wide range of learning abilities of the different pupils you will be teaching. You should not only be master of your craft and skills, but you should also be able to use the complete range of instructional techniques to call on as and when the situation, or your pupils' needs, demand it.

Transfer of learning

It is unusual these days for people to present themselves for driving lessons without having some of the basic knowledge or skills required. For example:

- all your pupils will have been pedestrians and have learnt how to cross busy roads successfully;
- most will have been passengers in cars;
- many of them will have ridden a bicycle;
- some will have had some experience on motorbikes or driving 'off-road'.

Most of them will therefore have developed some skills in the judgement of speed, distance and timing of traffic. As these are among the most essential skills involved in driving, you should be able to take advantage of this knowledge and transfer it to driving.

There are numerous other associations through which you will be able to help your learners relate or transfer existing skills and knowledge to driving.

Interference in learning

Previous learning can sometimes be a disadvantage and interfere with learning a new skill. For example, where people have been passengers over a number of years, they will have probably developed a 'partial sense of speed'. They will have subconsciously learnt an impression of the speed norm of experienced drivers, and this can cause problems if they try to copy them. By driving at what they have learnt to accept as the normal speed, this 'previous learning' can interfere with progress, as, in the early stages, the basic car control skills need to be carried out at slower than normal speeds.

Examples:

Always change up through the gears as soon as you have moved off.

Always change down progressively using all the gears when you are slowing down or stopping.

Always signal for moving off, passing parked cars and stopping.

If pupils have been previously indoctrinated with certain views, it is likely to cause conflict with the new information you are giving. You must recognize that your pupils are not learning in a vacuum, and will therefore be subject to all kinds of conflicting pressures from other people.

Where this type of interference occurs, you must be tolerant and show an understanding of your pupils' problems during any difficult periods of 'unlearning'. You must also try to avoid saying that the information they have been given is totally wrong.

More importantly, there is always the danger that the pupil will have subconsciously picked up many driving faults and habits from a parent, friend or family members. Many experienced instructors make the point that their pupils have often been exposed to poor driving for 17 or more years before they start with any professional training.

Motivation

This describes the personal needs and desires of the individual. The fact that pupils are prepared to pay for a course of lessons will normally show that they are motivated by a desire to learn. The student will normally be alert and keen at the beginning of the course, with a willingness to follow instructions in eager anticipation of the next session. This initial enthusiasm, however, may not always be enough to maintain full interest and attention throughout the entire course, particularly if difficult patches are experienced where only slow progress is achieved.

An important part of your work will be to try to maintain pupils' motivation. Help them over any difficult periods by maintaining your enthusiasm and showing that you are interested in their progress. Motivation and interest can be stimulated through success. Even small successes are important to a pupil who is finding the learning hard work.

By creating the right conditions, you can do much to ensure success. This can be done by properly grading the tuition in short, progressive steps. You should then try to maintain this interest by giving suitable encouragement and approval for effort.

Traditional one-to-one methods of driving instruction mean that pupils are learning in total isolation from others, and this can frequently cause problems for both the instructor and pupil. While 'individual' tuition is advantageous, it does limit contact and comparisons with other people. By not being involved in a group learning situation, pupils are not able to measure their progress against that of their peers. More importantly, if they have no means of assessing their own progress and improvement, they may often feel they are making no progress at all. This may be a result of their instructor not giving sufficient feedback on where improvements have taken place.

If students feel they are making slow progress, encouragement alone from the teacher may not be sufficient to allay their fears of inability. Emphasis needs to be placed on where progress has been achieved, and excess criticism in other areas should be avoided. An unsympathetic teacher may cause students to feel so discouraged, isolated and incompetent that they become completely demoralized and may even give up the idea of learning to drive.

If you set up easily attainable, intermediate targets, you will help to reinforce your students' feelings of achievement. Intermediate goals also help to organize the learning situation, and do much to prevent pupils from being 'thrown in at the deep end before they can swim'.

Everyone learns at a different rate. It is therefore important that pupils are allowed to develop at their own individual pace, and setting intermediate goals should ensure that they progress with confidence. This, in turn, will keep the motivation at a good level.

Client-centred learning

As previously indicated, client-centred learning involves using a variety of skills, including:

Effective questioning

Questions can be used to find out if the pupil knows or understands a particular topic, but there are other reasons for effective questioning. By asking appropriate questions at the right time you can raise the pupil's awareness and generate in them a feeling of responsibility. Quite often the important questions are those that the instructor does not know the answer to. For example: '*How did you feel about...?*' or '*Had you considered anything else...?*'

Note: The use of effective questioning and other important client-centred skills are explained in detail in *Practical Teaching Skills for Driving Instructors*.

Active listening

Listening carefully to the pupil's responses will give an indication of how to phrase the next set of questions or organize the next phase of learning. To make sure you are actively listening, repeating back or summarizing the answer can be effective ways of letting the pupil know that you have taken note of his or her response.

It is generally recognized that there are several levels of listening:

- Cosmetic – it seems like we're listening, but we're not really.
- Conversational – we're listening, but also talking and thinking about our own situation.
- Active – we are generally focused on what the other person is saying.
- Deep – we are much more focused, particularly on what the other person means.

In many situations these four different levels of listening can be reduced to just two – either 'active listening' or 'not really listening'.

Checklist for active listening

- Minimize as many external distractions as possible.
- If possible, turn to face the speaker and maintain eye contact.
- Focus on what the speaker is saying.
- Be open-minded.
- Be sincerely interested.
- Have sympathy, feel empathy.
- Assess the emotion, not the words.
- Respond appropriately.
- Minimize internal distractions (such as your own thoughts).
- Avoid 'me' stories; resist the temptation to relate your own stories.
- Don't be afraid of silence – this can provide valuable thinking time.
- If appropriate, take notes.
- Avoid having negative thoughts about what is being said.
- Check your understanding (reflect back, summarize, rephrase).
- Listen for meaning.
- Understand, interpret and evaluate what is being said.

Barriers to active listening

- Not realizing that it isn't taking place: you simply don't realize that you don't really listen to what is being said.
- Reluctance to get involved: subconsciously you don't really want to get involved in the other person's situation.
- Not listening properly because you think you already know the full story: may cause you to respond negatively.
- Lack of interest: simply not sufficiently interested!
- Your opinion of the speaker: may affect your level of interest in what they are saying.
- Your own feelings: active listening can be affected by how you are feeling at that moment.
- Wrong time/wrong place: time constraints/location not conducive.

Four basic components that allow active listening

- Acceptance: that the other person has a right to express themselves.
- Honesty: openness, frankness, being open about your reaction.

- Empathy: understanding the other person's situation.
- Specifics: deal in details, not generalities.

Active listening shows the speaker that what they have to say matters and that advice is at hand.

Neutral and non-judgemental communication

If we concentrate too much on fault-finding we can sometimes create a situation where the pupil will be over-defensive, which then becomes a barrier to learning. To overcome this, we should attempt to balance the positives with the negatives and avoid direct personal criticism of the pupil by using neutral language and by addressing the specific problem with non-judgemental questions such as '*What do you think?*'

Non-directive language

Client-centred learning involves the use of non-directive language – '*Could you tell me a bit more about how you felt about dealing with that...*'; '*Help me understand your thinking about...*'. Questions are designed to guide and influence, not control.

Using non-directive language means that:

- the relationship is based on equality, openness, trust; not 'expert to novice';
- the trainer is not claiming to have all the answers; the pupil feels that their input is valuable;
- the pupil accepts more responsibility and ownership of the task;
- if the result is not satisfactory, the pupil will be more willing to persevere.

Two-way communication

As a professional driver trainer you will develop different ways of communicating effectively with all types of pupil. This will involve varying and adapting your methods and terminology to suit the needs of each individual pupil, making sure that the pupil is involved in the discussion.

Practise 'client-centred' conversations in everyday life. In casual conversation, change the focus from your thoughts and experiences to theirs. Avoid things like, '*Oh yes, that happened to me...*'. Where possible, try to keep the focus on the other person completely – their opinions, thoughts, what they do/have done/are doing.

When putting this into practice, ask yourself:

- *Do I feel comfortable when I'm not putting my own ideas into the equation?*
- *Am I able to resist adding my own thoughts and what I know?*
- *If I concentrate solely on what the other person says, what effect does it have?*

Motivation skills

Most pupils are mainly concerned with the immediate benefit of passing the test and obtaining a full licence. Part of your role as an instructor is to use your skills to motivate the pupil and encourage longer-term skills and 'safe driving for life'.

An effective motivator:

- is open and honest;
- makes the other person feel that their feelings and opinions are worthwhile;
- keeps the conversation flowing, without it feeling unnatural;
- is able to focus on the key issues and does not get side-tracked;
- is impartial and objective;
- can clarify, summarize or reflect back the pupil's thoughts;
- is encouraging and challenging, but also realistic;
- generates a feeling of equality.

We all have a level of competence in all these skills in everyday situations. If we are able to bring all of them together, productive conversations will flow.

One of the key areas in using client-centred learning methods involves the 'GROW' technique.

This is a fairly straightforward but powerful framework for structuring the learning.

GROW – an overview

- *Goal:* What are we aiming to achieve (by the end of the training programme/during the lesson/during the next 10 minutes)?
- *Reality:* Where we are now (what can the pupil do/know well, not so well, not at all)?

- *Options:* What are our different options (how can we do it)?
- *Will:* How will we achieve it (our strategy/syllabus/agenda)?

One way to think of the GROW model is to imagine how you would plan a journey.

First of all you would consider where you want to go to (the Goal) and establish where you are currently (the Reality of your situation).

Your next step would be to consider the various ways of getting to your destination (the Options).

Having decided on the most appropriate option, you would then commit yourself to making the journey (the Will) and prepare for any obstacles that you might encounter on the way.

The GROW model assumes that you do not act as the expert talking down to a novice. Rather, you should act as a facilitator, helping the pupil select the best or most appropriate options but not offering too much advice or direction.

On the other hand, you will have a certain amount of expert knowledge to offer, which means that you can guide the discussion without directing or instructing.

GROW – practical application

Goal

First, establish the Goal. This will be a discussion in which you and the pupil agree the general topic and then decide on the goal – whether it is short term (for the immediate lesson) or for a longer series of lessons.

Goals should always be 'SMART' – they need to be Specific, Measurable, Attainable, Realistic and Time-specific.

Reality

Next, outline and discuss the current situation – the Reality. This is an important step. You both need to know and understand the starting point for any training. In particular, this part of the discussion will clarify for the pupil whether the agreed goal is realistic.

Options

Explore the Options. Once you have established the current situation you can then determine what is necessary to achieve the goal. This will include exploring all the possible options. At this stage the pupil should be doing most of the talking. You can guide the discussion, but without actually directing it or making decisions.

Will (or way forward)

By this time you will both have a clear idea of how the goal can be achieved. This final step involves the pupil in committing themselves to specific actions in order to move forward towards the agreed goal. This commitment helps with the pupil's motivation.

Skill training

The term 'skill' describes an activity in which the performance should be economical and effective in order to achieve a consistent and satisfactory result. Although it is relatively easy to recognize the skilled performance of an expert driver, it is considerably more difficult to define why it is so. It is even more difficult to analyse (and to give a valid explanation of) the many skills involved in the complete task.

As experienced drivers, we are often unaware of the numerous individual tasks we are putting into practice because, with experience, these have mostly become subconscious actions. As an instructor, you need to be able to analyse each of the skills in detail before being able to teach the complex tasks involved in the process of learning to drive.

As drivers, we obtain relevant information from the environment and process it. We then respond by making decisions and executing the appropriate car control skills. The driving task involves attending to, perceiving and responding safely to driving-related stimuli. The activities involved relate to three different areas:

- psychomotor (or physical) skills;
- cognitive (or knowledge-related) skills;
- affective skills (or attitude).

When driving, we allocate attention by using our senses to gather information about the performance of the vehicle and also the conditions of the road and traffic environment. As drivers, we process the information by comparing it with existing knowledge, memories and previous experiences. We then assess its relevance and either ignore it and do nothing, or decide on a particular response or course of action to be taken to maintain a safe environment.

As an instructor, you will have to recognize all these different aspects and teach your pupils how to drive safely.

To assist your pupils in the acquisition of new skills you need to be able to identify key learning points and to isolate any areas of weakness. To do this you will need to identify the elements of knowledge, attitude and skill involved in a particular learning task.

Essential elements

Knowledge

This describes what you know. It has been found that knowledge influences attitude and assists in the acquisition of skills. Driving involves considerable knowledge of *The Highway Code*, traffic law and the principles of safe procedures. Certain aspects can be learnt more effectively in a classroom or at home rather than in the hustle and bustle of today's road and traffic conditions.

Knowledge, however, is only a basis for 'real' learning. Although it may influence attitudes, in practice, knowledge alone is not always sufficient to ensure we have the will or skill needed to behave safely. For example, although most drivers know about speed limits, this doesn't always prevent them from driving at excessive or inappropriate speeds. Legislation and the consequences of being caught, however, place incentives on drivers not to break the law.

Other incentives include the consequences of accident involvement. This knowledge may also help influence our attitude towards alcohol and driving. On this basis, the more we know, the better equipped we are to make our decisions.

Attitude

This describes what we really think, and it usually influences our behaviour. Attitudes are formed over a lifetime of experience and learning. They will not normally be changed overnight!

Unsympathetic attitudes towards others, and towards the established principles of road safety, can be contributory factors in causing many road accidents.

You can encourage your pupils to develop safe attitudes towards other road users. You can do this by constantly persuading and providing them with good examples.

In addition to knowledge, an attitude has motivational and emotional elements that influence behaviour. These elements can be so powerful that we may sometimes lose control of our actions. Uncontrolled aggression and love are two extreme examples of this.

Attitude and behaviour

Attitudes are normally formed through personal experiences from an early age. A driver's attitude will normally influence their behaviour; reckless or unsafe driver behaviour is frequently attributed to negative attitudes. These are often inherent in the person who has always 'done his own thing' without a thought for the consequences on other people, or who has been influenced by sitting for many years next to an inconsiderate driver.

Pupils who have a positive attitude, and who have learnt to be more thoughtful towards other road users, will normally respond more favourably; their understanding of correct behaviour and of the consequences of bad driving develops. For example, the person who drives at 30 mph in a busy road, where there are parked vehicles on both sides and a high volume of pedestrian activity, has a negative attitude. Someone who doesn't understand the risks involved, or simply does not care, may drive in this unsafe manner.

Knowing and understanding the risks may still not have the effect of slowing the driver down if a negative attitude is present. The driver with a positive attitude, however, will normally listen to your reasoning, analyse the effects of the reckless behaviour and work on correcting it.

It will be your responsibility to try to change negative attitudes. This can be done by:

- discussing the risks involved in any given situation;
- persuading the driver to act safely in order to protect other road users as well as him or herself;
- setting a personal example.

You may find that some of your pupils will resent your efforts to change their views, remaining subjective and even offering excuses for not complying. Pupils who have a positive attitude will, however, normally listen to reasoning and become more objective and flexible when they understand for themselves the consequences of their actions.

You should recognize that all human beings have their limitations. Try to remember that a driver who is normally patient and tolerant may sometimes, for a variety of personal reasons, such as emotional problems, become hostile. Discuss how conflict with others can be avoided if a little time is taken to relax and regain composure.

At the end of their course of training, new drivers should be able to:

- recognize features in the road and traffic environment where accidents are most likely to occur;

- identify the causes of accidents and assess their personal risk of becoming involved in them;

- recognize their own capabilities and limitations;

- apply defensive techniques to minimize the risk of becoming involved in potentially dangerous situations.

Skill

This describes what we can do! There are two main types of skill: *manipulative skills* are physical actions such as turning the steering wheel, pressing the footbrake or operating the clutch pedal; *perceptive skills* are skills associated with awareness, thinking, reasoning and making decisions. They are the predominant skills used in the overall driving task, and rely heavily on visual sense. They include the judgement of:

- reductions in speed caused by differing amounts of braking pressure;

- detecting changes in direction when steering;

- awareness – the general state of mind involving hazard recognition and comparisons with previous experience;

- assessing and predicting risk and making decisions.

Making the driving effective involves:

- attention – staying alert and concentrating;

- visual search – a systematic scanning of the road and traffic scene;

- responding to situations and taking the appropriate action to control the car;

- using the car's controls smoothly and efficiently.

To make the learning and the driving effective, organize lessons into short progressive steps and let your pupils work through them at their own pace. As aptitudes and abilities vary, you will need to adapt the pace of your instruction to the ability of each individual.

Build on what the pupil already knows and can do, then move on one step at a time. Before attempting a new skill, the pupil will require some basic knowledge upon which to build.

At the beginning of each session, revise and reinforce the points learnt in the previous lesson before moving on to the new subject matter.

Some pupils may become very good at following instructions, but when left to carry out a skill unaided they are unable to do so. Others who find it more difficult to follow individual instructions are often far more advanced when they are allowed to work on their own initiative. While controlled practice is an essential part of basic training in new skills, it should gradually be phased out when you feel pupils can cope for themselves. Some pupils will require a lot of encouragement to act and think for themselves.

Prompting, where required, is perhaps the natural progression from the controlled practice or talk-through. The amount of prompting required will largely depend on the ability and willingness of pupils to make decisions for themselves. The type of decision required is also significant. For example, if the conditions become too busy for the pupils' ability, there will be a tendency for them to refrain from making any decisions at all. Where these situations arise, you must be prepared to prompt as required. The ultimate objective is to get pupils to carry out all the skills under normal traffic conditions without any prompting at all.

Revision is important and it requires continuous consideration, particularly in the early stages of establishing a new skill. A true and wholly accurate assessment cannot be made of the driving skill where it is still necessary to prompt.

The use of detailed instructions should be reduced as the pupil's ability increases. Remember that a simple cue is often sufficient to bring back a whole sequence of complicated actions without further instruction. If capable, the pupil needs to be given the opportunity of achieving some success independently.

Practice will be required to build consistency and stamina, and to reduce the time taken to complete any sequence. When the skill becomes consistent and is carried out in a reasonable length of time, you can introduce other important aspects, with more emphasis on the visual search and timing.

Skills must be applied and practised progressively in more difficult traffic situations: for example, moving off from junctions and traffic lights; moving off and maintaining low-speed control in conjunction with steering.

Transferred responsibility

The responsibility for making their own decisions and acting on them is transferred to the pupil as early as possible in the learning process. As the pupil's control skills develop and confidence grows, you should place more emphasis on the development of perceptive and hazard recognition skills. Find out whether the pupil knows and understands what they should be looking for and where to expect it. Discuss the dangers involved and why particular responses are called for.

Encourage pupils to think and to make decisions. Get them to look for information, and encourage them to use their knowledge of the rules and previous experience in order to assess each situation. Build the confidence they need in order to make decisions and to act for themselves.

The use of appropriate questions is very useful in this stage of training. By asking questions relevant to the traffic situation, you can find out what pupils are thinking. How they respond will give you an indication of areas where misunderstandings are occurring and you can then make the necessary corrections.

Distributed practice

No matter what skills are being learnt, there is no substitute for practice and this should be organized sensibly. 'Cramming' everything into a few marathon sessions is not an efficient way of learning. 'A little and often' is a more effective strategy.

Carefully distributed practice, divided evenly over several weeks, is more efficient than working for the same amount of hours during an intensive period.

The general learning curve

You will be able to see the manipulative aspects of the driving task improving by simply watching your pupils execute them. However, prompts and verbal guidance during the early stages of learning will still be necessary. When the skill is sufficiently developed, hints and reassurance should be all that is required. Pupils' progress will vary depending on the type of skill being learnt.

With the learning of some skills, pupils often reach a stage that is referred to as 'the plateau of learning' and progress appears to come to a halt. However, this is not normally the limit of their potential and is usually very short-lived. After a brief while, most pupils will overcome the problem and progress to their own personal limits.

Structuring the learning

There are nine main principles involved in structuring any course of training or instruction. As there is a good deal of common sense involved in teaching a practical skill, most good instructors follow these principles intuitively.

1 The aims and objectives of a course of lessons, and each part of it, should be agreed in advance in terms of observable behaviour

Objectives are statements that describe what your pupil expects to be able to do at the completion of a lesson or a course of lessons. They are normally phrased in terms of observable behaviour. Pupils should be made aware of the new skills they are expected to be able to carry out, or what knowledge they are expected to have gained by the end of the session or each section of learning.

The DVSA has published a comprehensive set of objectives in its syllabus for learning to drive, but you will probably want to produce your own supplementary objectives – particularly for the earlier stages of learning.

2 The subject matter to be learnt, and the training routes used, should be appropriate to achieving the specified aims and objectives

The content of each lesson, together with your support materials and the training routes used, should ensure that the aims and objectives are achievable by the pupil. You should classify the matter to be learnt in order of importance:

- *essential material* – what the learner *must* cover in order to achieve the course objectives;
- *desirable material* – what the learner *should* cover, but is not absolutely essential to achieve the objectives;
- *useful material* – what the learner *could* cover, but is not completely relevant to the objectives.

3 The course content, and individual lessons, should be organized in short progressive steps that follow a logical sequence

Intermediate targets will help to stimulate interest and progress. They can help to reinforce learning by providing positive evidence of progress through each section and also organize the learning situation.

Considered as a whole, driving is a complex task. It is made up of many sub-skills such as moving off, steering and stopping. The whole should be analysed and organized into short progressive units of instruction taking the acquisition of these sub-skills into consideration.

A course of driving lessons should be structured to proceed from:

- the known to the unknown;
- the simple to the complex;
- basic rules to the variations;
- concrete observations to abstract reasoning.

Once pupils have grasped the basic rules and concepts, it becomes easier for them to develop new skills and understand the variables.

4 The content of lessons, and the routes selected, should be graded in difficulty so that your pupils will make as few mistakes as possible, especially in the early stages

Make sure your students experience success during the early stages of their training. To do this, avoid setting standards that are too high or using training routes that are too difficult or complex. Be prepared to accept some technical inaccuracies and deficiencies until they have developed more confidence in their ability. Initial failure may deter pupils and inhibit progress. Build confidence and understanding on a firm foundation of practical skills.

Progress from what the student knows and can do by working up to the unknown and the new. Simple skills should be taught before complex procedures are introduced. For example, it is unreasonable to expect pupils to deal with right turns at busy traffic light-controlled junctions before they can control the vehicle properly.

5 People should be introduced to new materials and skills at a level of difficulty that relates to their ability, previous experience and attainments

There are considerable variations in the rate at which students learn. This should cause few problems when giving one-to-one tuition because the course can be tailored to suit the needs of each individual. Pupils should be allowed to work through each unit of learning at their own pace. New skills and techniques can then be introduced at a level that is suited to the individual person's ability, knowledge and achievement.

One of your first tasks when meeting new students is to find out what previous experience they may have had, and how much they know and can do. In order to plan the level of training, it is necessary to establish the pupils' current knowledge and ability. Use appropriate questions with pupils to find out what they already know, then encourage them to take some responsibility for the decisions you will be making together.

As skills develop, and mastery of the controls is attained, keep pupils informed of what they are doing and why. They should never be left confused or in doubt. However, some of the basic skills may need to be taught as simple conditioned reflex procedures. Initially, it is more important for pupils to respond correctly to an emergency than to understand why the particular response was required.

6 Pupils should be allowed to proceed through the course at their own pace

The amount of time devoted to each element of training will vary from one pupil to another. Learning is more efficient when pupils are allowed to proceed at their own pace, as slowly or as quickly as they are able. This allows the learning to be most effective.

7 Keep pupils 'actively' involved in the learning process

Keep your pupils physically and/or mentally involved in the learning experience. Whatever the task under instruction, learning can only be achieved by pupils thinking and doing things for themselves. Activity will help to hold pupils' attention.

Observing the physical activity of the pupil is relatively straightforward. Recognizing what the pupil is thinking, however, is a rather more difficult problem. An active mind on the part of the pupil is essential to learning and is an important part of driving.

For example, driving at 40 mph along a quiet road with relatively little traffic requires little physical activity other than controlling the steering. The problem in this situation is that there is very little to occupy the mind, so it may not be involved in the driving at all. These situations provide ideal conditions for you to develop the pupil's visual search and observational skills and to relate them to the decisions of an experienced driver.

In the earlier stages of learning a task, keep the pupil's mind active – ask questions about the relevant road features, or of any intended actions. For example, if you see a bus with a left signal on, you could ask what the pupil expects it to do. However, when using this technique, make sure the questions are not too technical and likely to distract the pupil's concentration.

8 Give your pupils continuous feedback of progress

Learning should be reinforced through feedback of progress, helpful comments and a balance of constructive criticism and encouragement. Active involvement facilitates learning. However, this does not ensure that the learning is of the right kind, or that the pupil is making progress towards the final performance as stated in the objectives.

Make sure that pupils are not just correcting existing faults. Reinforce learning and improve performance by giving continuous information on progress. Feedback should occur as soon as possible after an event, or between each step in an exercise or manoeuvre. This will help prevent further faults appearing. Comments such as 'good' or 'well done' may be useful as an indication of progress where there is insufficient time to give more detailed information. These comments do not, however, tell the pupil anything about the actual performance. Comments that give information on the actual performance are usually generally more helpful:

> *Our position was a little wide on the approach to the turn. How far from the kerb do you think we should be?*

> *The gear change was left a little late. What would be the effect if we changed gear earlier?*

> *The approach speed needs to be a little slower. How do you think we can best achieve this?*

Short comments and corrections made on the move will be of great value in improving your pupil's performance. However, avoid giving detailed verbal corrections on the move. When they are required, give them as soon as practicable after the incident when a suitable parking position is found.

9 Pupils should master each skill and section of the course before you go on to the next stage

There is sometimes confusion over what is meant by 'complete mastery', and some instructors argue that this cannot be attained until a very advanced stage is reached. Do not expect 'total mastery of the full task' during the intermediate stages. Reduce the demands placed on your pupils by setting properly structured objectives and choosing your routes carefully.

If a course is properly structured, mastery can, and should, be attained in each sub-skill, technique or procedure before introducing new and progressively more complicated variables.

Consistency is an essential feature of good driving. To achieve it, each skill or task should be 'over-learnt' before proceeding to the next. Progress based on mastery of each phase of learning will do much to develop a sense of achievement and confidence. Staging the course into a number of progressive learning units also helps to increase pupils' motivation to learn by sustaining a continuous sense of urgency.

Route planning

Route planning is an essential element of lesson preparation. It requires a thorough knowledge of local geography and traffic conditions. When planning routes you must take into consideration any specific driving skill or procedure that is to be practised. An inappropriate route can have disastrous consequences when novices are unnecessarily exposed to conditions with which they are unable to cope. In extreme cases, and with particularly nervous pupils, it may even make them give up the idea of learning to drive at all.

Ideally, a fairly wide selection of planned routes containing various types of traffic hazards and conditions will be required. You should not consider them as being rigidly fixed routes from which there must be no deviation.

Flexibility is an important consideration when planning a route, because it allows for changes to be made midway through a lesson. This may become necessary to allow more time to be spent on an area of driving which may be proving unexpectedly troublesome, and yet still allow the lesson to be completed in time for your next appointment.

Excessive repetition over the same routes will often prove counterproductive. It frequently leads to a reduction in the pupil's interest. This in turn may result in boredom and slow progress. Some repetition, however, can be helpful at times when carried out deliberately for a specific purpose relevant to the lesson. For example, practising control skills on the approach to uphill junctions might need to be restricted to a localized area where the same junctions might have to be used several times. This will give pupils more opportunity to practise their skills.

Training routes

Training routes and areas fall loosely into three groups:

- nursery routes;
- intermediate;
- advanced.

There is no definite dividing line between these groups, and there may frequently be considerable overlap between them. On occasions, there is justification for incorporating all kinds of route in one lesson; for instance, when making an initial assessment of a new client with previous driving experience.

Starting with the nursery routes, introduce new traffic situations at a controlled rate that is sensitive to the needs of your pupil and sympathetic to their ability. However, in reality, the nature of traffic conditions can be very erratic. Even the most carefully planned route may suddenly prove unsuitable, and the pupil may be faced with new situations he or she cannot yet cope with. Route preparation will, however, help keep these incidents down to a fairly isolated and acceptable level.

Training routes are often a compromise between the ideal and the reality of local geography and traffic conditions. In general, instructors working near the centre of a large city may experience difficulty in finding suitable nursery routes. However, their counterparts, operating in isolated rural areas, may experience problems in finding suitably varied conditions for the advanced routes. Extending the length of some lessons may be a satisfactory answer in both instances, by allowing more travelling time to training areas that are more suitable to the needs of the pupil.

Nursery routes

Various kinds of roads are required, but in general, 'nursery' routes should avoid areas with a high proportion of turns and junctions. Remember too, that apart from not wanting to worry your pupil, you are your own best advert – select routes to allow minimum interference with the flow of traffic and inconvenience to other drivers.

You should progressively use routes that incorporate:

- fairly straight, wide roads that are long enough to allow uninterrupted progression through the gears;
- quiet, fairly wide roads on up/down/level gradients on which to practise the manipulative skills;
- roads containing right-/left-hand bends, allowing practice at slowing down, using the gears and steering;
- simple left turns from main into side roads;
- simple left turns into main roads;
- right turns from main into side roads and right turns into main roads.

Some routes containing parked vehicles will be necessary towards the end of the initial stages.

As far as possible avoid:

- busy roads;
- areas where there are lots of parked vehicles;
- pedestrian crossings;
- traffic lights;
- busy roundabouts.

Intermediate routes

There will be some overlap between these routes and the more advanced nursery routes. They should include:

- junctions with 'Give way' and 'Stop' controls;
- all types of basic rule crossroads;
- uphill 'Give way' junctions at which to practise first gear hold and control;
- traffic light-controlled junctions;
- roundabouts that conform to basic rules.

Roads selected for the initial practice of the turn in the road and reversing exercises should be reasonably traffic-free, and roadside furniture such as post boxes and telegraph poles should be avoided.

Routes should, wherever possible, be planned to avoid:

- dual carriageways;
- multi-lane roads;

- one-way streets;
- junctions that do not conform to basic rules;
- right turns on to very busy main roads;
- any other particularly difficult situations;
- driving test routes.

Because of the length of the tuition periods, you should take into account any special features of local geography and road design. If complicated situations cannot be avoided, you may either have to drive pupils to more suitable areas, or give them full instruction and talk-through.

Advanced routes

These will incorporate most of the intermediate routes. They should be progressively extended to include as many variations to the basic rules as possible. Where possible include:

- dual carriageways;
- multi-lane roads;
- one-way streets;
- level crossings;
- busy shopping streets;
- all types of pedestrian crossing;
- rural roads providing an opportunity to practise overtaking.

Advanced routes will provide an opportunity for you to conduct 'mock' tests in conditions similar to those used for the driving test. It is stressed, however, that you should avoid actual test routes.

Giving route directions

The quality of a pupil's performance will be affected if you give late or unclear directions. You must give pupils sufficient time to interpret and respond to any request. You should also bear in mind that inexperienced pupils will take longer to react to your instructions.

Instructions must be given clearly and concisely. Most directional instructions contain three basic ingredients:

- Alert – draw your pupil's attention to the imminent request.
- Direct – the instruction to turn or pull up.
- Identify – confirm where the instruction is to be carried out.

Examples:

Alert:	I would like you to ...
Direct:	... turn left ...
Identify:	... at the junction ahead.

Alert:	Would you ...
Direct:	... take the second road on the right ...
Identify:	... this one being the first.

Alert:	At the roundabout, I'd like you to ...
Direct:	... take the road leading off to the right ...
Identify:	... that is, the third exit.

Alert:	I'd like you to...
Direct:	... take the next road on the left, please.
Identify:	It's the one where the post box is.

Confirmation can be given where required by adding further information such as 'It's just out of sight around the bend' or 'It's just before the telephone box/bus stop'.

Instructions and terminology

General instructions

Be consistent and standardize your instructions. If you use terminology similar to that used by driving test examiners, your pupils will be familiar with it when they take their test. The following are examples of general instructions for normal driving and special manoeuvre exercises:

General route brief

I'd like you to follow the road ahead unless otherwise directed by road signs or markings.

When I want you to turn, I will ask you in good time.

Drive on when you are ready, please.

Stopping – parking – angled start – moving off

Would you pull up and park on the left at the next convenient place, please.

I'd like you to pull up just behind the stationary vehicle, but leaving yourself sufficient room to move out again.

Drive on when you are ready.

Reverse parking

Pull up on the left in a convenient place, please. Will you drive forward and stop alongside the vehicle ahead. Then reverse in and park reasonably close to, and parallel with, the kerb. Try to complete the exercise within about two car lengths from the vehicle.

Route confirmation

When confirming a straight-ahead direction, use the phrase, 'Follow the road ahead' at a junction or roundabout. Avoid terms such as 'Go straight on' or 'Carry straight on' as they may be taken literally, resulting in the pupil ignoring traffic signs, give-way markings, or stop rules.

Directional errors

Giving clear directions in good time may not always guarantee the correct response. People are often confused between left and right, particularly when under stress, and this problem can be embarrassing for them. Providing no danger or inconvenience is caused to other road users, if a pupil is not going where you have asked, it may be advisable to let him or her continue in the chosen direction – as long as he or she is signalling to go that way. Try not to over-emphasize the problem as this will only make the pupil feel more foolish.

Obviously, you should try to cure this problem as soon as possible. One way of helping a pupil who is right-handed is by saying, 'I write with my right and what's left is my left.'

Another is that most people wear their watch on the left wrist; similarly, wedding and engagement rings are worn on the left, so this could also be used as a point of reference.

Although candidates are not tested on their ability to distinguish between left and right, excessive errors of this nature could prove very difficult for the examiner.

When giving directional instructions to pupils who are near test standard, it is important that the instructions are as neutral as the circumstances allow. While they should always be clear and precise, guard against giving pupils too many reminders of what they should be observing for themselves. For example, telling an advanced pupil to turn left where there is a sign giving this order will not encourage independence, nor will it test his or her observation, knowledge or planning.

Extra information, however, may be justified in special circumstances at a particularly complex junction. In certain areas, it may be virtually impossible to ascertain which lane will subsequently be required without some knowledge of the area. Under such circumstances, you may have to tell your pupil which lane to select and give a reason for doing so.

Avoid using the word 'Stop', except in an emergency. This could result in the pupil stopping in a dangerous position. If you want the pupil to hold back, or avoid moving away unsafely, the word 'Wait' can be used quite effectively.

Avoid beginning an instruction with the words 'Turn' or 'Pull up'. You could get an immediate and incorrect response.

Try not to use the word 'right' for anything other than a directional change. For example, using the instruction 'Right, turn left at the crossroads please' could cause obvious confusion; as could saying 'That's right!' when in fact you mean 'That's correct!'

Instructions and terminology

Any instructions you give while the vehicle is in motion should be firm, concise and clearly understood. Your terminology should be consistent, particularly in the early stages of tuition. For example, if, after mostly referring to the 'holding point', you change your wording to the 'biting point', there is a possibility of confusion.

Similarly, if, after giving frequent instructions to 'signal' right or left, you change your terminology to 'indicate', it could lead to momentary hesitation, which could lead to serious consequences if there are other road users about. If you wish to instigate correct and immediate response, your pupils must be able to recognize and interpret your terminology.

The need for most instructional jargon is at its highest during the early stages of tuition. However, this is when pupils are least familiar with it. A new pupil should, however, in a short time, become accustomed to your style of terminology.

Prompts used to stimulate thought

New drivers, because of their inexperience, often fail to recognize or anticipate danger in many common 'high risk' situations. Short comments or questions, directed at drawing their attention to the danger, can help to improve anticipation and responses. Provided that the prompts are used in plenty of time for pupils to respond, this technique helps to make them think about and consider the consequences of their own inaction. For example:

Are you ready to move away when it's clear?

What's happening behind?

Is it safe to go yet?

Can you see properly?

How far can you see?

Is it clear?

Do you need to signal?

Do you know how much clearance you should give to a parked car?

Can you tell me what the normal driving position is?

What's the speed limit on this road?

Approaching a row of parked vehicles at an excessive speed, ask:

What will you do if a child runs out?

What will you do if a car moves out?

What will you do if a car door opens?

What will you do if the cyclist pulls out?

What will you do if the oncoming car keeps coming?

Approaching a pedestrian crossing at excessive speed, ask:

What will you do if that pedestrian steps onto the crossing?

Do you know what's behind us?

Driving too close to the vehicle ahead, ask:

What will you do if the car in front has to stop quickly?

Do you know how close the car behind is?

What is the stopping distance at x mph?

Approaching a bend or corner at excessive speed, ask:

What will you do if there is a car parked just around the bend?

What will you do if there is a pedestrian crossing the side road?

Corrections on the move

Under normal circumstances, detailed explanations should be avoided while the vehicle is in motion. This applies particularly if your pupil is concentrating on something else, such as when emerging from a junction or waiting at red traffic lights.

However, most incidents involving minor errors may not be recognized by the learner at the time they are committed and 10 minutes later, those that were recognized will have been forgotten. Some brief feedback, therefore, should be given at the time errors are committed, or as soon as possible afterwards. This will draw attention to them, making incidents easier to recall when later referred to and corrected in detail.

Serious errors, or repeated minor ones that appear to involve misunderstandings, should be corrected as soon as reasonably possible after they have occurred, when a suitable parking place has been found.

Intervention and dual controls

Because of their inexperience, new drivers lack anticipation and will fail to recognize or respond to potentially dangerous traffic situations. You should never completely trust them to follow your instructions or to do the correct thing.

Make sure they are aware of their legal responsibilities. Remember too that you could be jointly responsible for any offences committed by them. You must sometimes be firm and take whatever action necessary to protect your pupil, the car and other road users. Look, think and plan well ahead. Get to know individual pupils and watch them. You will soon learn to predict how they are likely to respond in given situations.

You must anticipate changes in the traffic situation and give instructions early enough for pupils to react. If anticipated early enough, most awkward situations can be avoided by giving verbal commands or, if it becomes necessary, taking action with the dual controls. Uncorrected errors will lead to the development of potentially dangerous and frightening situations.

There are four main reasons for intervening:

- to prevent risk of injury or damage to persons or property;
- to prevent an offence against the law;
- to prevent excessive stress to the learner in certain unplanned circumstances;
- to prevent mechanical damage to the vehicle.

A verbal command is often sufficient if given in time. However, if your pupil does not react to this, you will need to act. For example, you might:

- sound the horn;
- turn the wheel;
- switch off the engine;

- select a missed gear;
- release a partially engaged handbrake;
- prevent an unsympathetic gear change by covering the lever.

If it becomes necessary, you must be ready to use the dual controls. However, they should not be used as a matter of routine and when you do use them, you should discuss with the pupil the reasons why you took action.

Continual steering corrections and excessive use of the duals do little to build pupils' faith in their instructor. It could also lead to resentment, particularly if they do not understand why you used them.

There are various ways in which you can maintain a safe learning environment.

Verbal intervention

The verbal command is the most common form of intervention. It will usually work if you are concentrating properly, planning well ahead and giving instructions early enough for your pupil to respond. Commands range from a mild memory prompt to a more positive command for a specific and immediate action.

The prompt is usually associated more with the earlier lessons, but may be extended to more positive instructions such as:

Use the mirrors before changing direction.
Brake harder (or, Ease off the brake).
Clutch down (or, Hold the clutch still).
Increase the gas (or, Off the gas).

The more positive commands needed to relieve potentially dangerous traffic situations are usually those needed when you want your pupil to slow down earlier on the approach to hazards. 'Hold back' or 'Give way' are positive commands requiring a specific reaction, but these also leave the pupil with some freedom of judgement.

'Stop' is the final and absolute command. It should generally only be used in a situation that is fast getting out of control and/or where other instructions have been ignored or are unlikely to achieve the desired response.

Physical intervention

Physical intervention should normally be restricted to situations when it is necessary to avoid danger. This occurs when verbal intervention has not worked or where there is insufficient time to give it. The main methods of physical intervention are use of the dual footbrake, and steering corrections.

In any situation, you will need to consider the method of intervention best suited to correcting the problem. There are occasions when both steering and braking corrections may be required.

For example, you may need to control the steering wheel while using the dual footbrake. This is to resist the tendency the pupil may have to swing on the wheel. In order to generate more time for you to intervene and turn the wheel it may be necessary for you to control the speed of the car with the dual brake, particularly if the pupil has 'frozen' on the accelerator.

The dual clutch

Assisting pupils by using the dual clutch should be done sparingly. It should, of course, be used where there is potential danger or risk of damage, but try to avoid over-use as it can lead pupils to think that they have better control than they really do.

The dual clutch could also be used in relatively extreme circumstances when it is necessary to get away from a situation with which the pupil cannot cope. Covering the clutch so as to avoid an unexpected and potentially dangerous move off is one of the more important 'uses' of the dual clutch.

The dual accelerator

Dual accelerators are not normally fitted to driving instruction cars. If one is fitted, it must be removed while the vehicle is being used for a driving test. This is for safety reasons, so that the examiner does not use this pedal by mistake.

Its main use is to accelerate out of danger.

The horn

This should be used sensibly. It is better to remove a danger at source by giving a warning, than to find later that more drastic intervention has become necessary.

Dual eye mirrors

An extra rear-view mirror will help you to keep in constant touch with the all-round traffic situation, and a dual eye mirror, strategically placed and focused on the pupil's eyes, will enable you to monitor his or her mirror use.

Mirrors should be placed fairly high on the windscreen so as not to impede the pupil's view, but low enough to provide you with an adequate view to the rear. They should be correctly adjusted and perfectly directed for you to check just as you would adjust your driving mirror. They should give maximum vision with the minimum of movement.

Assessments and standards

To be able to judge how effective your teaching is, you will need to be able to properly assess your pupils' performance as they progress through the different stages of learning to drive.

You will be assessing the pupil's knowledge, skill and attitude.

As an instructor, you will mainly be concerned with assessing the practical skills involved in the driving task. However, because effective driving needs an understanding of the rules and regulations, you will also need to test your pupils' knowledge of *The Highway Code* and other relevant motoring matters, usually by asking relevant questions at regular intervals.

To assess the effectiveness of your training you will need to:

- ascertain the level of the pupil's ability at the start of the training;
- discuss what the pupil should know and be able to do at each stage, by agreeing objectives for each topic;
- assess the pupil's ability at the end of the course.

Driver's record

It is increasingly important to keep accurate records of pupils' progress and achievements in line with the industry code of practice. For this reason, the DVSA has introduced a 'Driver's Record' system. It has been designed and produced to help instructors and pupils keep a check on progress during a course of training, and to provide an accurate record of the pupil's level of ability.

The system is based on the official syllabus for learning to drive. It covers all the skills required for safe driving, and should be completed by instructor and pupil on each lesson. A personalized booklet for the pupil and a set of record sheets for the instructor are included. Additionally, the instructor is provided with a set of guidance notes and details of the competencies required for each item in the syllabus.

The Driver's Record is a way of helping both you and the pupil to identify areas where the pupil's skills and understanding need to be developed. It includes a list of 24 skills that are normally covered in the practical driving test and spaces for you to fill in as the pupil progresses through five levels of ability.

The five levels are defined as:

Level 1: the skill is introduced.

Level 2: it can be carried out under full instruction.

Level 3: it can be carried out correctly when prompted.

Level 4: it rarely needs to be prompted.

Level 5: the pupil can carry it out all the time without any prompting.

The record helps to remind the pupil about what they are trying to achieve, how to get there and how far they have got.

Copies of the complete system for both pupils and instructors can be downloaded from **www.gov.uk/government/publications/drivers-record-for-learner-drivers**. An integral part of the Record allows the pupil and instructor to monitor progress on each topic through the various stages of learning:

- topic introduced;
- pupil under full instruction;
- prompted practice;
- seldom prompted;
- independent.

The main advantages of a Driver's Record (or 'log book') include:

- It enables a structured approach to training and skill development through a written record.
- Both the instructor and the pupil are focused on the need to combine structured formal training and private practice where appropriate.
- Pupils and instructors are encouraged to expand on the learning process beyond the requirements of the 'L' test.
- Pupils are encouraged to gain experience in a wide variety of road and traffic conditions until each part of the syllabus has been achieved.
- The inclusion of a 'declaration of test readiness' raises the pupil's awareness of the need to be fully prepared before taking the test.
- A properly kept progress record will show where any distinct patterns of errors are developing that might otherwise not be so obvious.

Pass Plus

Pupils should be encouraged to take Pass Plus soon after passing the practical driving test.

The Pass Plus syllabus consists of six separate training modules covering:

- town driving;
- all-weather driving;
- driving out of town;
- night driving;
- driving on dual carriageways;
- driving on motorways.

Town driving

After an introduction to Pass Plus and an explanation of the aims and objectives of the course, you should include in the practical session:

- observations, judgement and awareness;
- eye contact;
- consideration for vulnerable road users;
- keeping space around your car.

All-weather driving

This section should include:

- correct speed;
- safe stopping distances;
- seeing and being seen in:
  - rain;
  - sleet, snow and ice;
  - mist and fog;
  - bright sunshine.
- skidding:
  - causes and prevention;
  - correcting slow-speed skids;

– braking on poor surfaces;

– aquaplaning.

Driving out of town

This module, which would be on country roads, will deal with the main differences between town and country driving including:

- observation of the road ahead;
- making progress safely;
- bends, hills, uneven roads, dead ground;
- keeping a safe distance from the vehicle ahead;
- overtaking safely;
- being aware of and showing consideration for:
  - pedestrians, horse riders and animals in the road;
  - farm entrances;
  - slow-moving vehicles.

Night driving

For this section of the syllabus, you need to cover the main aspects of driving at dawn and dusk, as well as in the dark, and in particular:

- the importance of the correct use of headlights;
- adjusting to dark conditions;
- judging speed and distances;
- correct use and care of lights;
- dealing with dazzle;
- road users who can be difficult to see;
- parking.

Driving on dual carriageways

Driving on this type of road requires particular skills:

- effective observations;
- use of mirrors and checking blind areas;
- judgement and planning well ahead;

- safe separation distances;
- joining and leaving dual carriageways;
- lane discipline;
- overtaking;
- correct use of speed.

Driving on motorways

Ideally, this module should be a practical session on a motorway. If this is not possible, then a theory lesson is acceptable, but the pupil should have a motorway drive as soon as practicable so as to put the theory into practice.

Either way, the training should include:

- planning journeys in advance;
- joining and leaving motorways;
- using slip roads properly and effectively;
- safe speeds for varying circumstances;
- effective all-round observations;
- signs, signals and markings;
- overtaking and lane discipline;
- courtesy towards other road users;
- motorway fatigue;
- breakdown procedures;
- use of lights and hazard warning lights;
- debris on the carriageway;
- crosswinds.

Pupils are allowed to take Pass Plus within a year of passing the driving test if they want to qualify for reduced rates of motor insurance from several companies.

'L' driver errors

Driving errors range from those with sometimes very simple causes, to those caused by the pressures and stress built up by driving in complex traffic conditions. Simple causes can range from unsuitable shoes being worn to an incorrect seating position. Both of these could make control of the pedals extremely difficult and result in loss of concentration. Make sure your pupils seat themselves correctly when they get into the car.

The tensions caused by driving in difficult conditions can sometimes result in unusual and possibly dangerous decisions or actions being taken. Avoiding road and traffic situations with which pupils are not yet able to cope should, in most cases, solve this problem.

Poorly developed perceptive skills frequently result in inexperienced drivers approaching hazards at excessive speed. This usually results in rushed actions when carrying out the manipulative skills, and this in turn will result in errors in vehicle control. This problem can be avoided by giving your instructions early enough for pupils to respond, and encouraging them to slow down sufficiently to maintain control.

The types of errors committed vary considerably according to the particular stage of learning reached. The aptitude and attitudes of pupils also influence the mistakes made. Most errors in the early stages of learning cannot seriously be considered as driving faults as they are usually caused through lack of knowledge or practice. However, unless nipped in the bud, they may well develop into driving faults.

A lack of understanding of new information may also cause errors. Many such problems are intensified by lack of sufficient practice in basic car control skills. This initial 'familiarization' should be carried out in relatively safe surroundings on suitably quiet routes.

You must remain acutely alert for any unusual, sudden or excessive movements with the steering or other controls, particularly during the initial stages of learning. Initially, most learners have difficulty in coordinating their hands, feet, steering and observations. You must allow for this and give full talk-through until these skills develop.

Some of the main causes of basic driver error include:

- lack of knowledge;
- conflicting knowledge;
- underdeveloped perceptive skills;
- lack of or inadequate observations and/or misinterpretation of visual information;
- deficiencies in the basic manipulative (car control) skills;
- deficiencies in behaviour caused by timidity or aggressive and irresponsible attitudes;
- poor health, fatigue, drink, drugs, emotional stress.

Note: the learner driver may often be subject to considerable pressure when having to interpret verbal directions while, at the same time, attempting to assimilate other instructions on the move. Do not overload the pupil with too much information, as this can result in lack of attention to the task in general.

General errors

Poor car control

Inadequate car control can usually be traced to insufficient practice at a basic skill, incorrect training and the interference of previous knowledge or practice, lack of knowledge, poor coordination, hurried movements, and excessive speed.

Persistent excessive use of speed

Excessive speed is often attributable to an unsafe attitude, incorrect use of the footbrake, lack of awareness of potential or actual danger, or poor perception of speed.

Lack of awareness of potential or actual danger

This fault is very common and generally caused by a lack of experience, knowledge, imagination or visual scanning. If a pupil is passively observing a traffic scene, it does not imply that he or she will take any action on a developing traffic hazard.

Indecision

This can be associated with lack of confidence, poor control skills, lack of knowledge, timidity or the conditions being too busy for the pupil's ability. Indecision and/or an unwillingness to give way, slow down or stop for a hazard is often caused because pupils lack confidence in their basic ability to move off again. They often fail to recognize that slowing down early will alleviate the situation by creating more time for it to clear, thereby often reducing the need to stop.

As a driving instructor, it is your responsibility to ensure that your pupils attain as high a standard as possible, taking into consideration their own individual abilities. You need to aim for a high standard of driving at all times and at all levels. Try to offer as wide a scope of driver education as possible. This will mean that your work is more interesting, varied and satisfying.

Assessing progress

To assess progress, you need to take pupils into traffic conditions appropriate to their experience and then observe their behaviour. This type of assessment is mainly of a visual nature and consists of watching the pupils' actions in the car. You need to constantly be monitoring their use of the controls, instrumentation, mirrors and ancillary equipment, and behaviour towards other road users.

You should guard against watching the pupil too intently, as this may result in your missing important changes in the situation to which your pupil should be responding; and against watching the road and traffic too intently, as you may miss faults of a physical nature inside the car, such as an incorrect signal being given, riding the clutch, poor mirror use, or attempting to select a gear with the clutch engaged.

You will need to divide your attention over a wide range of your pupil's activities in fairly rapid succession, and in order to maintain safety, you also need to be reading the road and traffic conditions.

There are some areas where prolonged observation of the pupil will be required so that a thorough assessment may be made. These are observation of his or her use of all mirrors, and the pupil's pattern of observations on the approach to, and emerging from, different types of road junctions. In order to limit the time required to check on mirror use, and also to leave you with more time to keep in touch with the all-round traffic situation, an additional mirror can be discreetly focused on to the pupil's eyes. This extra mirror does away with the need to look directly at pupils at appropriate times when a check would be required.

Looking at pupils often serves as a prompt for them to check mirrors or make some other form of visual check they might otherwise have forgotten to do. Reducing these prompts will allow you to make an entirely objective assessment. Similarly, unless they are intended to be prompts, you need to be extremely discreet with your observations of the road and traffic situation at junctions and during any of the manoeuvre exercises.

Intermediate assessments and tests of students' knowledge and ability are an integral part of a teacher's work, and a considerable amount of your time will be involved directly in this ongoing process.

Mock tests

An objective assessment is one that measures a learner's actual performance against a pre-fixed standard. For the ADI, this pre-fixed standard is the 'perfect driver'. It is a satisfactory yardstick by which any level of driving can be measured.

The perfect driver can be defined as someone who:

- is in complete harmony with the vehicle and traffic conditions;
- is always in the correct position on the road;
- is travelling at a safe speed for the conditions and visibility;
- has the ideal gear engaged to suit the varying speed and power requirements.

This 'perfect' driver is totally aware of the surroundings and shows consideration for the rights of other road users. Technically, anything that detracts from this perfection is an error. However, perfection to this degree is extremely rare, even in an experienced driver, and it would be unrealistic to expect an inexperienced learner to achieve this standard. It is therefore necessary to devise some means of grading faults whereby significantly more importance is attached to serious and dangerous faults than to those of a minor nature.

You should try not to class driving errors as either 'black' or 'white'. There are many shades of grey, and when assessing the seriousness of a fault, you need to bear in mind that an error can involve varying degrees of importance, and that some errors are of a more serious nature and can result in more severe consequences than others.

Continuous assessment

This type of assessment is more sensitive to the needs of the learner progressing through a course of lessons than is the more decisive objective assessment previously discussed. During the early stages of learning, it is unreasonable to compare the performance of the novice with the 'perfect driver'. Although assessments should be objective, they should also take account of previous experience, practice and general progress, as well as the learner's capability. They should take into consideration the reasons that faults may be occurring.

Continually look for ways to correct faults and encourage your pupils to have a greater understanding of their causes. If you do this, the pupils' overall knowledge and driving performance should improve.

When a learner makes a mistake, there is usually a valid reason for it; for instance there may be a basic misunderstanding of what is required. If there is a recurrence of errors, you will need to cure them at source rather than superficially treat the symptoms.

There are literally hundreds of different errors waiting to be committed by the learner. Their causes are fewer. If you concentrate therefore on curing the cause, improvement should result in other areas where similar mistakes may be occurring. For example, if a pupil is having difficulty steering around a corner because of lack of time, it is the speed on approach that needs to be worked on.

The 'halo effect'

It isn't possible to remove the human element from driver assessments! If you develop a particular regard for a pupil with whom you get on well, it's possible to subconsciously ignore minor errors. You may even gloss over those of a more serious nature. Without realizing it, you may even select an easier route for the pupil by avoiding some of the more difficult situations.

Acceptance that this phenomenon, known as the 'halo effect', exists is in most cases sufficient to guard against it. Try to remain objective, otherwise your pupils may suffer in the long term.

To a certain extent, the opposite can also occur with an unpopular client. In this case, you may subconsciously treat relatively minor errors as more serious ones, and perhaps fail to notice improvements in performance and give credit where it's due.

Summary – driver training

Structure

- Begin with what the learner already knows or can do and build on this.
- Structure the learning in short progressive steps.
- Move from simple to more complex tasks and skills.
- Make sure the pupil is fully involved and takes responsibility for their own learning.
- Be prepared to vary your methods of instruction.

Explanations and instructions

- Be consistent with your instructions and terminology.
- Make sure that your terminology is fully understood by the pupil.
- Keep explanations brief and to the point.
- Emphasize the key areas of learning and understanding.
- Give positive instructions – focus on what to do rather than what not to do.

Demonstration

- Explain the purpose of any demonstration before carrying it out.
- Carry out demonstrations at an appropriate level according to the ability of the learner.
- Review and discuss the outcome.

Practice

- Allow for plenty of practice – people learn by doing things for themselves.
- Stimulate interest and involvement – try to ensure that any initial practice is successful.

Route selection

- Select routes that will ensure, as far as possible, that the learner can cope with the conditions.

Feedback

- Give praise and encouragement to help stimulate progress – excessive criticism can inhibit motivation.
- Give continuous feedback of progress.
- Correct errors positively before they become habitual.
- Positive correction should be made to improve learners' performance.

Pupil's progress

- Reassure pupils that periods of slow learning are quite natural and common.

- Avoid comparing learners with other students.

- Setting achievable intermediate goals can help to promote progress.

- Allow pupils to learn and develop at their own pace.

Lesson topics 08

Controls lesson

The main objectives of a first driving lesson are to:

- allow you and your pupil to get to know each other;
- reassure the pupil and gain their confidence;
- explain the use and functions of the main driving controls;
- give the pupil some experience in moving off and stopping if time allows.

To establish the base line for the lesson ask a few questions to find out what the pupil already knows.

Confirm that your pupil has a valid driving licence and can read a number plate from the prescribed distance. It's normal, with pupils who have no experience, to drive them to a quiet training area with a stretch of reasonably straight road and very few hazards. During this drive, find out a little about the pupil and their reasons for learning to drive.

Lesson content

Consider how much information the pupil is likely to absorb. Avoid overloading your explanations with irrelevancies. For example, do you really need to include information about all the lights, gauges, dials and other equipment at this stage?

Timing your explanation

The time you spend on each of the key points should depend on whether the pupil has any previous knowledge or understanding. Most people have been passengers and will probably know about seat belts; others may already have an understanding of how the clutch works and the relationship between power requirements and gears. Many new pupils will also have ridden a bicycle or motorbike and will have an understanding of the use of gears and some road sense. Adapt your instruction to take this into consideration and in line with how your pupil responds.

Driver checks

Doors

Discuss the need for safety checks before opening any door, looking either for pedestrians on the pavement side or traffic in the road. Explain about the safety catch by opening it and demonstrating the light click when the door is not properly closed. Confirm the dangers of driving along with doors not properly closed and discuss how to open the doors safely in windy conditions.

Handbrake and neutral

Discuss how the extra weight of people getting into a car can affect stability, and the need to check the handbrake and neutral for security.

Seat adjustment

Make sure the pupil understands how to adjust the seat and back rake to ensure that all the controls can be reached comfortably and controlled effectively. The driver's left knee should be slightly bent when the clutch is fully depressed, and there should be a slight bend at the elbows when the hands are placed on the steering wheel in a balanced position. If your car has steering height adjustment, explain how it works, if appropriate.

Head restraints

Check that the pupil knows how to adjust the head restraints and explain their purpose: that is, to prevent neck and spinal injuries.

Mirrors

Discuss how to adjust the interior and door-mounted mirrors to give maximum vision to the rear and sides. Explain why they are made of different types of glass, confirming that all decisions must be made from the true image seen in the interior mirror.

Even with three mirrors, explain that there are still 'blind areas' around the car that can hide pedestrians, cyclists or other traffic.

Seat belts

Check that the pupil can put on and release the seat belt safely. Watch for any twists across the lap or chest. Remember, your pupil will probably have been a passenger and will therefore have some experience in using these; do not be patronizing.

Switching on the engine

Complete the 'cockpit drill' by getting the pupil to check the handbrake is on and neutral selected prior to switching on the engine.

The main controls

Accelerator, footbrake and clutch

Emphasize that it is more important to be able to stop the car than to make it go faster. Ask the pupil to position the right foot squarely over the brake pedal, with the heel acting as a pivot between it and the accelerator. Remember – be flexible. Although it is preferable to keep the heel on the floor, if it is not comfortable or possible (because of the pupil's height, for example) don't insist on it. Discomfort can be a distraction.

Find out if the pupil knows and understands the function of each of the foot controls. The accelerator works like a tap: the more the pedal is pushed down, the more fuel will flow into the engine to make it go faster. Releasing the pressure will slow down the flow of fuel, therefore slowing the car. It should be used gently and progressively. The brake works on all four wheels to slow the car down and eventually to stop it. Initial pressure should be light, gradually becoming firmer and then eased just prior to stopping in order to bring the car to a smooth stop. The mirrors should be used prior to use; the initial pressure on the brake will activate the brake lights to warn following drivers.

Outline some of the terminology you will be using, for example:

- 'gas' relating to the accelerator;
- set the gas;
- cover the brake;
- more gas/less gas;
- brake gently/brake firmly.

The clutch

Keep your explanation as uncomplicated as possible – use an illustration if you think it will help. The main purpose of the clutch is to connect and disconnect the power from the engine to the road wheels so that it is possible to make smooth gear changes.

Before turning on the engine, allow the pupil to cover and feel for the pedals without looking down. Explain how to use the ignition key and, to encourage good habits from the outset, remind the pupil to check the handbrake is on and the gear lever is in neutral before switching on. Allow some practice in:

- pivoting the right foot between the brake and gas pedals;
- setting the gas;
- checking the mirror before braking, explaining about the brake lights;
- listening and feeling for the range of the clutch.

The steering

Discuss the importance of positioning the hands in a 'balanced' position and of not holding the steering wheel too tightly. Describe how the hands will naturally follow the eyes, and emphasize the importance of looking well ahead to help maintain a straight course.

Indicators

Remember not to be patronizing – most people know something about cars. Ask the pupil to work out which stalk is the indicator, and also which way it's operated for signalling left and right. Relate this to the direction in which the wheel will be turned.

Let the pupil practise a couple of times by keeping the hand on the wheel and extending the fingers to switch the indicators on and off for left and right.

Horn

Check that the pupil knows the location of the horn, confirming that it should not normally be used while stationary. Ask a couple of questions about when not to use it.

Handbrake

Explain how this normally operates on the rear wheels. Discuss its purpose:

- it holds the car securely when stationary;
- it acts as a back-up system for securing the car;
- it allows the driver to hold the car on a slope when both feet are occupied with accelerator and clutch.

Give one or two examples of where to use the handbrake: pedestrian crossings and traffic lights or when stationary for more than a few seconds. Let the pupil practise releasing and applying the handbrake.

Gear lever

While the car is stationary, discuss the use of gears. Remember, a visual aid might help the pupil as well as serve as a memory jogger for you. If appropriate, explain about the power and speed requirements – for example, first gear would normally be used for moving off because it is the most powerful and has to get the weight of the car moving – and the spring-loaded mechanism on most new cars that allows the lever to come back to its natural position.

In order for the pupil to develop a feel for smooth and accurate gear selection, allow for plenty of practice. You might demonstrate with your right hand, showing how to 'cup' the lever in the direction it has to go. Explain the 'palming' method, relating the position of the first four forward gears to that of the road wheels on the car. Allow practice at changing up and down in sequence, and then show the pupil how to use the 'block-changing' method. Finally, ensure the pupil looks ahead through the windscreen while moving the gear lever.

Moving off and stopping

The main purposes of this lesson are for you to help the pupil to understand the principles behind the M–S–M routine and develop basic car control skills in order to:

- move off safely and under control;
- stop smoothly and parallel with the kerb;
- understand why we need to stop in safe places.

Lesson structure

Following the initial introductions, you need to establish the base line for the lesson. Use questions to recap what was covered in the previous session.

The point at which you start the lesson will depend on the pupil's answers. You would normally drive to a reasonably quiet training area and use the time to establish any prior knowledge.

If the pupil has moved off and stopped before, you will need to ask a few questions such as:

Can you reach all the controls comfortably?

Have you made all your driver checks?

What can you see in the mirrors?

What can you tell me about the blind areas?

What do you understand about the M–S–M routine? Can you explain the main points?

If the pupil has no previous experience of moving off, you will need to:

- discuss the M–S–M routine;
- allow the pupil to practise using the foot controls and selecting gears as necessary while stationary;
- give a limited amount of talk-through of, and practice in:
  - moving off and stopping (level, uphill and downhill, if circumstances allow);
  - moving off, building up speed and changing gear;
  - driving along and checking the mirrors;
  - slowing down and changing down;
  - stopping smoothly in safe places.
- give feedback and encouragement.

Mirrors

Decisions should be taken on what is seen in all mirrors. To confirm why this is so, ask the pupil to compare the images between the three mirrors. Confirm what the blind areas consist of and the importance of checking there are no road users in them prior to moving off.

Emphasize that the M–S–M routine should be applied when any change in speed or direction is intended. That is, that the routine needs to be used for:

- signalling;
- moving off;
- changing direction (passing parked vehicles, overtaking, turning corners);
- slowing down and stopping.

Confirm that no decisions should be taken before assessing what effect any actions may have on other road users.

Signals

Discuss the purpose and use of signals and relate them to *The Highway Code*. Introduce discrimination at this stage in order to develop the pupil's 'look, assess and decide' processes. Before moving away, you could ask, 'Is there anyone around who would benefit from a signal?'

Precautions before moving off

Discuss the blind areas. While the car is stationary, pick out an object on the offside pavement that will be in the blind area. Check whether the object can be seen without turning round. Confirm what could happen if we moved off when a cyclist was emerging from a driveway in that blind area.

Alternatively, get the pupil to watch in the mirror for a vehicle approaching from behind. Then follow it in the offside mirror and keep watching until it disappears into the blind area.

Before moving off, discuss how the M–S–M routine will be applied when stopping. After moving off for the first time and driving for a short distance, prepare the pupil for stopping. To encourage early development of mirror use, ask if there is anyone behind. Give the instruction to apply the left signal if needed. Be ready to help if necessary.

If appropriate, use direct instruction to ensure a smooth and safe stop. This could include saying: 'Cover the brake and the clutch. Brake gently. Clutch down, brake gently to a stop.' Give the instruction: 'Keep both feet still. Put the handbrake on and the gear lever into neutral. Now, rest your feet.' This will assist in building the pupil's confidence in his or her ability.

Normal stop position

Introduce *The Highway Code* rules relating to stopping. Ask the pupil for a couple of examples of where and why it would not be safe or legal to stop. For example:

> *Can you suggest some places where we shouldn't stop or park?*
>
> *Why should we not stop near a bend or the brow of a hill?*
>
> *What problems would it cause if we stopped too near or opposite a bus stop?*

Try to time your initial instructions to coincide with safe stopping places. If, however, the pupil stops somewhere unsafe or inconvenient, ask, 'Why do you think this is not a good place for stopping?'

Practice should now be given at:

- moving off;
- building up speed;

- changing through the gears to make progress;
- stopping.

It is vital that your pupil's confidence is built up through the car's response. Remember to time your instruction so that it sounds and feels smooth. For example, after moving off and building up a little speed you will need to ensure the change to second gear is smooth. Your instructions should allow for the pupil being a little slow and the car losing some momentum. You can compensate for this by allowing a little more speed to be built up than is necessary, particularly if driving uphill, and preparing the pupil for the change by saying, 'Can you hear the engine getting louder? We're going to change to the next gear.'

The pupil's left hand should be on the gear lever, palm towards you, before you add the instructions:

Off the gas and clutch down.

Gear lever straight back to second.

Ease up the clutch and back to the gas.

Hand back on the wheel, check the mirrors and gently accelerate.

Encourage the pupil to build up speed and progress through the gears following the above instructions, changing the wording to suit whichever gear is being selected. Encourage use of the mirror while driving along. This will help pupils develop the habit of regularly checking on the situation to the rear. This, in turn, should result in a more natural application of the M–S–M routine for dealing with hazards.

Discuss the differences between moving off on the level, uphill and down-hill and the effects of different gradients on the power requirements (uphill) or the use of the footbrake (downhill).

Using the mirrors

Making sure that the pupil understands the importance of using the mirrors effectively should be part of an ongoing programme. During the early stages of the pupil's learning you should be introducing an element of hazard perception and anticipation by pointing out possible problems and explaining how to respond.

Check whether the pupil has understood all the correct routines and procedures and is putting them into practice. Give feedback confirming the importance of using the mirrors correctly and being aware of the all-round situation.

Establish the base line for the lesson by confirming the pupil's previous knowledge. This means that you should:

- check that the pupil is in the correct seating position and has adjusted all the mirrors so that they can be checked without an exaggerated head movement;
- confirm the reason for checking blind areas and make sure that these checks are made properly;
- ask a few questions about when mirrors should be checked in relation to moving off/speeding up and slowing down/changing direction/passing parked cars/overtaking/M–S–M routine.

Fault analysis

Watch closely to make sure that the pupil is making regular checks of the appropriate mirrors. Assess the pupil's understanding through their actions: that is, checking the mirrors regularly before moving off, changing speed or direction, signalling or stopping; and reacting properly to what is seen in the mirrors, putting into practice the M–S–M routine by:

- deciding whether or not a signal is required;
- deciding how actions may affect any following driver;
- delaying signals if necessary;
- signalling earlier and braking more gently if appropriate before turning and when stopping;
- keeping a safe distance from the vehicle ahead if someone is following too closely.

Use of signals

The main objectives:

- establishing what the pupil already knows about the use of different methods of signalling;
- assessing whether the pupil understands and can correctly apply the M–S–M routine;

- how to approach and deal safely with pedestrian crossings;
- identifying and analysing faults;
- giving remedial advice;
- creating opportunities to practise the correct routines.

Lesson structure

Establish the base line for the lesson by finding out what your pupil already knows. At this stage the pupil should have a reasonable level of car control skills and an understanding of the basic driving routines. These skills include knowledge of the M–S–M routine, and the use of signals.

At this stage the pupil should be able to:

- check the mirrors regularly;
- be aware of the all-round situation;
- decide whether or not a signal is required;
- use the signals:
    - correctly;
    - when necessary;
    - at the appropriate time.
- respond safely to signals given by others.

Confirm the M–S–M routine by asking a few relevant questions. Ask for examples of the different methods of signalling. These should include:

- using the brake lights;
- indicators;
- reversing lights;
- early road positioning;
- the appropriate use of arm signals.

Arm signals

Although they are seldom used, arm signals can be helpful to other road users in some situations. For example, they might be used on the approach to a pedestrian crossing, to reinforce an indicator signal or if the indicators fail.

Approaching junctions to turn left and right

It is important to gradually build up pupils' skills and confidence by introducing topics in a logical manner. When the pupil has attained a reasonable level of skill in moving off and stopping, introduce basic junction routines. Beginning with simple left turns, it is normal to teach pupils how to turn into a side road and continue to the next left turn, which might be another side road on the left, or involve emerging onto a main road. Practise until a sound routine is established, then transfer this knowledge into dealing with right turns, following a similar pattern and introducing the differing elements.

The main objectives of the lesson are to:

- establish what the pupil already knows about the M–S–M routine and how this system is applied at junctions;
- introduce the pupil to dealing safely with junctions;
- identify and analyse faults;
- give remedial advice and create opportunities to practise the correct routines.

Establish the base line for the lesson by asking a few questions and assessing what the pupil already knows and can do.

The main element of the lesson is the correct application of the M–S–M routine, breaking this down as follows.

Mirrors:

- checking early to see what is happening;
- working out how any other road user may be affected by the manoeuvre;
- deciding if and when to signal.

Signal:

- to warn or inform other road users at the correct time, and so as not to confuse.

Manoeuvre:

- position: early to confirm the signal; appropriately for the direction, the width of the road, any obstructions, vision;
- speed: appropriate for vision, the required gear, obstructions, oncoming traffic, pedestrians;
- look: all around prior to turning for obstructions, other road users, pedestrians.

Set the base line by checking on the pupil's previous knowledge or experience at dealing with turning left and right. You may need to give an explanation of the routines. Use a visual aid if you think it will help. Questions can be used, either during your explanation or during the practical part of the lesson:

Why is it important to check the mirrors, and what are you looking for?

If a pedestrian is crossing the road you are turning into, who has priority?

Whose priority is it when you're turning right, yours or the oncoming driver's?

How will you be able to work out whether it's safe to turn right when there's an oncoming car?

Why would it be dangerous to cut the corner?

Fault assessment

Whatever the standard of the pupil, positive correction is better than negative or retrospective correction. If you can see a problem developing ahead and the pupil appears not to be responding, give some positive prompt to encourage some action. This is far safer, and more effective, than allowing a potentially dangerous situation to arise, particularly where other road users are involved.

During any drive, assess whether your pupil is putting all the established routines into practice. Identify and analyse any problems. Give advice on how to improve, and give your reasons.

Common faults

- A lack of understanding of the M–S–M routine.
- Not checking the mirrors effectively.
- Signalling at the same time as checking the mirror.
- Signalling too early or too late.
- Not positioning correctly according to the circumstances.
- Not using the brakes effectively to slow down in good time.
- Making unnecessary gear changes or changing down too early or late.
- Coasting around corners.
- Approaching too fast and swinging out on left turns.

- Lack of awareness of pedestrians and the need to give priority.
- Crossing approaching traffic.
- Not looking effectively into the new road.
- Cutting corners.

Stopping in an emergency

By definition, the word 'emergency' means 'a situation of a serious and often dangerous nature, developing suddenly and unexpectedly, and demanding immediate action'. Emergencies cannot therefore be planned for, so one could happen at any time. You need to know that your pupil will be able to cope. Introducing this exercise during the early stages, as an extension of braking and stopping exercises, will help develop the pupil's control skills and confidence.

The main objectives:

- teach the pupil how to stop promptly and under control;
- give basic advice on how to correct a skid.

How to avoid emergencies

Emphasis should be placed on the fact that good drivers plan well ahead, taking into consideration what is happening. They also anticipate what might happen where they can see a possible hazard developing, or where they cannot see at all. For example, no one can see around a bend, so how can a driver know what may be there? What you cannot see, you don't know.

Quick reactions

In an emergency, the priority is to react promptly and stop the car quickly and safely. Referring to the stopping distances in *The Highway Code*, relate these to the road and weather conditions, and explain how these will dictate the safe amount of pressure to apply to the brakes. Explain that progressive, firm pressure is required as harsh braking may result in a skid and this will only create further risk. Allow the pupil to practise the pivot between the accelerator and footbrake.

Ask your pupil where the driver's hands should be when braking. Confirm that a firmer hold than usual is necessary since more than normal braking pressure is being applied. This should also help to keep the car travelling in a straight line. Remind the pupil that engine braking can help to slow down the car more quickly. Confirm what the clutch is used for when stopping the car, and ask the pupil whether it will be different in an emergency situation.

Stopping the car is the priority, not necessarily keeping the engine running. Reassure the pupil that stalling is not a serious error as long as the necessary precautions are taken before restarting the engine. Explain about securing the car after stopping and confirm that this is even more important in an emergency, as the all-round situation needs to be checked before moving off again. Also confirm that, because the car was stopped in an unusual (a driving) position, checks of blind areas all around the car's sides will need to be made prior to moving off again.

Skidding

This part of the lesson should include a discussion on what can cause the most common types of skid, and to reassure the pupil of what to do if the brakes are applied too harshly and the car skids. Discuss the causes of skidding, and confirm that these normally only occur when a driver is not responding properly to the road and weather conditions. Harsh braking can cause a skid, and the most common type is the rear-wheel skid.

Make sure that the pupil understands the need to remove the cause of the skid, in this case by releasing the brake pedal, and apply and release the brakes until they take effect again. Then discuss how to steer into the skid by straightening up the front of the car. Use a model car, or show an illustration to clarify what you mean by 'steering into the skid'.

Maintaining safety

Explain the signal you will be giving when you want the pupil to stop. Once on the move, sit still and try not to make any movements that may distract the pupil into stopping prematurely. Remember, that you are responsible for the safety of yourself, your passenger, your vehicle and other road users. Make sure that you carry out this exercise in complete safety. Ideally this should be:

- not too near to any parked vehicles;
- where there are no nearby pedestrians;
- clear of junctions.

Check to the rear, and only give your stopping signal when there is no one close behind. After stopping, make sure that the car is secured. Get your pupil to check on the position in the road, and ask what blind areas will need to be checked before moving away. Practise the exercise two or three times, giving any necessary remedial advice on the pupil's reactions and use of the controls.

T-junctions – emerging

It is clear that you cannot keep turning into roads without eventually coming to the end of one. Most instructors therefore initially deal with 'emerging' in conjunction with turning into side roads. The main objectives are to:

- establish what the pupil already knows about the M–S–M routine and its application at T-junctions;
- introduce the pupil to approaching and emerging safely;
- identify and analyse faults;
- give remedial advice and create opportunities to practise the correct routines.

Establish the base line for the lesson by finding out what the pupil already knows and understands about junctions. The main elements of the lesson are to:

- confirm the application of the M–S–M routine;
- explain about 'Give Way' and 'Stop' junctions;
- emphasize the importance of taking effective observations;
- encourage safe decisions to proceed or hold back according to sightlines;
- outline correct position according to circumstances:
  - turning left or right;
  - wide or narrow roads;
  - obstructions;
  - one-way streets;
  - pedestrian activity.

As always, set the base line for the lesson. Confirm previous experience by asking a few questions on the M–S–M routine and its application when turning left and right into side roads. Find out what the pupil knows about 'emerging' from junctions.

Although 'emerging' may be a new topic, the pupil should already have turned left and right into side roads. You now need to build on this knowledge and transfer it to the new circumstances by including:

- the different types of junction, 'Give Way' or 'Stop' – ask the pupil to describe the signs and markings and to tell you their different meanings;
- positioning on the approach, depending on:
  - the direction to be taken;
  - the width of the road.
- vision:
  - restricted sightlines in one or both directions;
  - good vision in one direction only;
  - good vision all around;
  - emerging safely without affecting others, including pedestrians.

Practice

You may feel that it would be appropriate to give a limited amount of talk-through instruction until the pupil's understanding and control skills begin to develop. Gradually reduce the amount of instruction as the pupil's skills develop. However, be ready to give more help when necessary, and to intervene to prevent a pupil from emerging unsafely.

Assess how your pupil is responding to the all-round traffic situation. Do not allow a potentially unsafe situation to arise. For example, if you feel the pupil is about to emerge unsafely before being able to see properly in all directions, you should give some positive command, such as 'Wait!' Follow this up with, 'Have you checked both ways?', 'How far can you see?' or 'What if something is approaching out of the blind area at 40 mph?'

It may be appropriate, when convenient, to pull in to discuss sightlines and the importance of being able to see properly before emerging.

Common faults

- A lack of understanding of the M–S–M routine.
- Ineffective application of the M–S–M routine.
- A failure to identify or respond to the type of junction, 'Give Way' or 'Stop'.

- Not taking into consideration restrictions to sightlines.
- Not looking early enough at 'open' junctions.
- Stopping unnecessarily when safe to proceed.
- Not looking effectively in all directions.
- Not responding to pedestrians.
- Emerging unsafely.

Manoeuvres

The main purposes of any manoeuvring exercises are to:

- develop the pupil's car control skills;
- improve car control skills and confidence;
- develop an awareness of the importance of observations;
- teach the pupil how to respond to other road users.

Lesson structure

Establish the base line by asking a few questions about what the pupil has learnt previously and understands about clutch control. All the manoeuvring exercises are based on coordination between:

- clutch;
- accelerator;
- footbrake;
- steering;
- observations.

Safe and smooth control can be affected by something as basic as sitting too close or too far from the pedals. You should therefore confirm, at the beginning of the lesson, that the correct 'cockpit drill' is carried out and the controls can be reached comfortably.

Confirm prior understanding by asking how to control the car at low speed. For example:

How do you hold the car steady when moving off up a hill?

How do you creep slowly forwards to get a better view at junctions?

Which pedals would you use to control the car on a downhill slope?

Lesson content

Put into practice the general teaching principle of 'explanation/demonstra-tion/practice'. Confirm that it is a safe, legal and convenient place to carry out the exercise. Relate this to the rules in *The Highway Code* and ask a few questions, for example:

> *Are there any signs or road markings that would make the manoeuvre illegal?*
>
> *Do you think we will be inconveniencing other road users?*
>
> *Are there any parked vehicles or obstructions nearby that could affect us?*

If the pupil has previous experience, discuss the procedures with them. Listen carefully, and add any information or clarification you feel is neces-sary. Allow the pupil to practise the exercise so that you can make your assessment. Be ready to give help if the pupil is experiencing difficulty.

If the pupil has not carried out the particular manoeuvre previously, give some reassurance by confirming that it involves coordinating the skills previously learnt: that is, combining the use of the foot controls to keep the speed low, which in turn will give more time to work on the steering and make the observations.

Explanation

Use a visual aid if you think it will help the pupil understand the main prin-ciples. Your explanation should include:

- The importance of good all-round vision. For reversing to the left this will involve turning round in the seat, removing the seat belt where necessary.

- Confirming the position of reverse gear and letting the pupil practise selecting it while stationary.

- Describing each element of the exercise, including:
  - the control of speed with either the clutch and gas, or the footbrake if downhill;
  - steering;
  - observations: that is, where to look and how to respond;
  - checking for safety and convenience prior to the exercise.

- Confirm that control is of major importance and accuracy will come with practice.

Demonstration

Offer a demonstration if you think the pupil will benefit. You might consider combining a demonstration with your explanation. Do this by changing seats and talking yourself through the exercise. This could benefit you in two ways: the more anxious pupil will see the exercise is easier than it sounds, and it will take less time than giving the explanation and demonstration separately.

Practice

One of your main aims when teaching a new topic should be for the pupil to achieve a reasonable degree of success. To build up the pupil's confidence, therefore, you should ensure that your initial briefing and discussion is effective and that you respond promptly if the pupil is having difficulty.

Give advice or assistance where appropriate to encourage success and confidence. If after a couple of attempts you can see the pupil's skill developing, ease off on the level of instruction. Be ready, however, to give more help if necessary.

Observations and safety

As discussed several times previously, you are responsible for the safety of yourself, your pupil and other road users! Because at this stage pupils' observations are likely to be very superficial, you must remain fully aware of what is happening all around you, all the time. If you see other vehicles approaching, draw the pupil's attention to their presence by telling him or her to pause, then ask: 'Have you seen that other car? Let's wait and let it pass.'

At this early stage, the pupil does not need the extra pressure of knowing that another driver is being held up. As long as it is safe – and you have checked all around – avoid this pressure by encouraging the other driver to proceed. Confirm that other road users should be given priority. As your pupil's confidence increases you will be able to encourage him or her to respond to others according to the circumstances – for example, if it's obvious that another driver is being considerate and has decided to wait. On these occasions, you must emphasize that observations should also be made in the other directions to check that it's safe before proceeding.

Giving feedback

Praise goes a long way in building confidence. Confirm where progress and improvement have taken place. Discuss any weaknesses; confirm that more practice will be given. Encourage revision of the main points before the next lesson.

Common faults

- Not putting into practice the M–S–M routine prior to the exercise.
- Lack of consideration of the gradient or camber, resulting in incorrect use of the controls.
- Lack of coordination of the controls.
- Not looking in the direction of travel.
- Under- or over-steering.
- Not keeping a check on the all-round traffic situation.
- Not responding to other road users.
- Finishing in an unsafe position.

Meeting, crossing the path of, and overtaking other traffic

Allowing adequate clearance to other road users and anticipation

To develop safe attitudes in your pupils, anticipation should be introduced during the early stages of learning. There are so many vehicles parked on our roads that it is almost impossible for a new driver not to encounter some of them. It is important, therefore, that you take advantage of situations that arise to teach your pupils how to:

- read the road ahead and to the sides;
- consider the all-round situation;
- think about priorities;
- anticipate what others might do;
- work out the safest way to respond.

The main objectives are to:

- establish how much experience the pupil has in dealing with other traffic;
- make sure the pupil can deal with priorities when:
  - passing parked vehicles;
  - turning right;
  - dealing with pedestrians and cyclists.
- assess the trained pupil on all the above aspects of driving;
- explain how to overtake safely;
- identify and analyse faults;
- give remedial advice and create opportunities to practise the correct routines.

Establish the base line for the lesson by finding out what the pupil already knows about the topics. Confirm the M–S–M routine for approaching all hazards and then focus on those subjects that need either teaching or reinforcing.

Meeting other traffic, allowing adequate clearances

Key elements:

- Looking and planning ahead for parked vehicles.
- Deciding on priorities by acting on available information:
  - obstruction on the left side of the road;
  - obstruction on the right side of the road;
  - speed, position and size of oncoming traffic;
  - uphill or downhill situation.
- Applying the M–S–M routine and waiting in the hold-back position, to:
  - maintain a view of the road ahead;
  - be able to steer through in a straight line when safe.
- Allowing clearances for parked vehicles relative to:
  - the volume of traffic;
  - pedestrian activity.
- Adjusting the speed to suit the available space: the narrower the gap, the lower the speed to give more time to respond.

- Clearances for cyclists.

Crossing other traffic

Key elements:

- Priorities when turning right:
    - speed and distance of oncoming traffic;
    - if there's time to walk across, there should be time to turn safely;
    - is it safe to turn? What is happening in the new road?
    - is there time to turn without cutting the corner?
- Selecting lanes in good time to avoid cutting across the path of others.

Overtaking

Key elements:

- Safe. Is there an adequate view of the road ahead? Consider vision:
    - bends/brows of hills/dead ground;
    - any junctions ahead.
- Legal (refer to *The Highway Code*):
    - Are there any pedestrian crossings ahead?
    - What road markings are there?
    - Are there any signs that would make overtaking illegal or dangerous?
    - What is the speed limit and will it have to be exceeded to complete the manoeuvre?
- Necessary:
    - At what speed is the vehicle ahead travelling in relation to the speed limit?
    - Will we be turning off soon?
    - Do we need to get by to make progress?

Following at a safe distance

Explain that this is not only to allow sufficient braking distance, but also to give a better view of the road ahead.

Mirrors–position–speed–look (MPSL), M–S–M:

- Mirrors/Position – by moving out or in to obtain a better view.

- Mirrors/Speed – select a lower gear if appropriate.
- Look – check all around again.
- Mirrors – check that it is safe to carry out the manoeuvre.
- Signal – if appropriate – to let other drivers know of your intended manoeuvre.
- Manoeuvre – quickly and efficiently.
- Mirrors – check before returning to the left without cutting in.
- Accelerate away.

Anticipation

Teaching anticipation is an ongoing process that should start from day one of a pupil's driving career.

Key elements:

- Looking for other vehicles whose drivers may:
  - emerge from junctions;
  - open doors or move off without warning;
  - take priority when they should be giving way.
- Looking and planning ahead for any pedestrian activity:
  - expecting them to walk into the road;
  - at junctions between parked cars/behind buses/at crossings – in fact, anywhere.
- Looking and planning ahead for cyclists, expecting them to:
  - ride into the road without warning;
  - change position or turn at junctions without signals;
  - cycle around obstructions without checking;
  - ride alongside near crossings, at junctions and in traffic lanes.

Establish prior knowledge and driving experience. Using a visual aid if appropriate, explain how to approach and deal with the different types of hazard. If the pupil has very little experience of driving in busier areas, give sufficient talk-through to ensure both safety and confidence. Look and plan well ahead and describe what you can see happening, and encourage the pupil to respond early enough to avoid problems.

Even where the pupil has previously driven in busier areas, be ready to assist when necessary to avoid uncomfortable or unsafe situations developing. Identify any weaknesses in the pupil's general driving and explain how improvements can be made. Remember, when you suggest alternative action, you need to give a valid reason for it. Give encouragement where the pupil carries out the routines correctly and safely.

Common faults

- Failing to anticipate hazards or potential risk situations.
- Taking priority when it should have been given.
- Not applying the M–S–M routine when approaching hazards.
- Shaving parked vehicles on the left.
- Shaving parked vehicles on the right on narrow roads.
- Moving out too far and meeting oncoming traffic dangerously.
- Not allowing for the actions of pedestrians, cyclists or other drivers.
- Turning right across the path of approaching traffic.
- Showing an unsafe attitude and general lack of consideration.

Crossroads and roundabouts

Having previously dealt with turning into and out of T-junctions, you can then transfer this knowledge and develop the pupil's skill at dealing with the differences that apply at crossroads.

Establish the base line for the lesson by finding out what the pupil already knows and understands about different types of junction. Confirm that the M–S–M routine also applies at crossroads, emphasizing that more observations are needed in all directions.

The main elements of the lesson are to explain or confirm:

- the application of the M–S–M routine at crossroads;
- priorities at junctions with different markings;
- the requirement for extra all-round observations, regardless of the direction being taken;
- positioning for turning right, offside and nearside;
- observations and priorities when turning right.

Use a visual aid if you think it will help to explain the need for the extra all-round observations at crossroads, no matter who has priority. Explain how to respond to other road users and be willing to give way if unsure, particularly when turning right.

While allowing the pupil to drive and put into practice what they already know about junctions, be ready to help or give advice on the approach to crossroads. This applies particularly to the observations. Make sure that the correct routines are applied as opportunities arise when:

- driving through crossroads with the priority;

- approaching uncontrolled crossroads;

- emerging from 'Give Way' or 'Stop' lines;

- dealing with traffic lights.

Watch carefully to ensure that the pupil is making effective observations in all directions at crossroads, no matter who has priority. Confirm that the pupil should be looking for anyone who may be emerging or crossing.

If the local road layout dictates that you have to deal with traffic light-controlled or busier junctions, you may need to discuss how to turn nearside-to-nearside and offside-to-offside. Remember the level of ability of your pupil – you will probably have to give some verbal assistance to build up confidence.

By this stage, the pupil should have had experience in driving on most types of urban road. The procedures for dealing with crossroads should, therefore, merely need confirming with a few relevant questions. Listen carefully for any weaknesses in knowledge or understanding. Confirm what the main dangers are when turning right at crossroads, and what the pupil should be looking for.

Once on the move, assess how the pupil is responding in all situations. Look and plan well ahead. If you feel that the pupil is not reacting early enough to any situation, try to instigate the correct action by prompting with a question or suggestion, particularly where lane changes are necessary. Be careful, however, not to over-instruct. Avoid giving definite instructions unless you can see a potentially serious situation developing.

You will usually be able to deal with minor or one-off errors 'on the move', as long as this will not distract the pupil. However, if more serious faults or repeated errors occur it may be necessary to stop to discuss them.

Common faults at crossroads

When driving along main roads:

- proceeding through without adjusting speed or checking the side roads;
- turning left and/or right without checking in all directions;
- turning left and/or right without applying the correct M–S–M routine;
- cutting corners.

Approaching 'Give Way' or 'Stop'-controlled crossroads:

- failure to apply the correct routine on the approach;
- lack of awareness of the type of junction being approached;
- lack of effective all-round observations before emerging;
- incorrect response to other road users;
- failing to stop at 'Stop' signs.

Traffic light-controlled junctions:

- lack of forward planning and anticipation;
- incorrect application of the M–S–M routine on the approach;
- incorrect positioning for:
  - the type of junction;
  - road markings;
  - presence of other drivers.
- proceeding before it's safe;
- crossing closely approaching traffic;
- failing to look in all directions before turning.

Roundabouts

Roundabouts are junctions designed to improve traffic flow. You will need to teach your pupils how to deal effectively with the different types.

Although the previous sections dealt with the general approach to different types of junctions, for roundabouts you should include information and practice on:

- forward planning and anticipation;
- reading signs and markings;

- application of the M–S–M routine;
- emphasizing the use of all mirrors on multi-lane roads;
- lane selection and discipline;
- the 'give way' rule;
- looking in all directions to anticipate gaps in the traffic and maintain road position;
- making progress by taking opportunities to proceed;
- mirrors and signal before leaving;
- position in the new road.

Introduce this subject by including 'basic rule' roundabouts, progressing to more complex ones as the pupil's skills increase. If possible, and of course depending on local road layouts, begin with left turns, progressing to following the road ahead, then introduce taking roads to the right.

To build up skills and confidence, as with any new subject, you will need to give full talk-through instruction until the pupil can cope. Give as much help as you can to assist with this building of confidence.

Entering a large roundabout for the first time can be very confusing to the pupil and all the exits may look similar. You will need to identify the exit road quite clearly. For example, if you want your pupil to take the road to the right, which is the third exit, you can identify this by using similar wording to this:

At the roundabout, I'd like you to take the road to the right – it's the third exit.

It's the one where (for example) there's a pelican crossing.

I'd like you to take the road ahead – signposted Brighton.

The pupil should be encouraged to use the directional signs on the approach to visualize the correct exits. You can then give further assistance as you proceed through the roundabout by adding as you pass the first two exits:

This is the first exit.

This is the second.

We're taking the next exit so check your mirror and signal left for leaving.

During the later stages of training, try to create opportunities for practice on as many different types of roundabout as your area will allow. If necessary, plan for longer lessons to drive to different areas for this purpose. If this is not possible, then encourage pupils to sign up for further training under the Pass Plus scheme.

Common faults at roundabouts

- Lack of planning and anticipation.
- Failure to read signs and markings.
- Incorrect application of the M–S–M routine.
- Late mirror use resulting in unsafe lane changes.
- Failure to look in all directions resulting in:
  - missing gaps in the traffic;
  - an incorrect course being followed through the junction.
- Lack of anticipation of other vehicles taking an incorrect course.
- Driving in the blind areas of larger vehicles.
- Lack of mirror use before changing lanes, resulting in:
  - a lack of awareness of drivers to the rear and sides;
  - leaving in the wrong lane for the circumstances.

Pedestrian crossings

Your pupils will all have used pedestrian crossings – do not be patronizing. By asking a few relevant questions, you should be able to confirm whether they understand the basic rules relating to the different types of crossing. Ask how many types of crossing they can think of. The list should include:

- zebra;
- pelican;
- puffin;
- toucan;
- pegasus (equestrian);
- school crossings.

Sample questions:

What sort of sign might you see on the approach to a pedestrian crossing?

What markings would you see on the road?

What do the zigzag lines mean?

How would a pedestrian claim priority at a zebra crossing?

What is the sequence of the lights at a pelican crossing?

What is the difference at a puffin crossing?

Who is a toucan crossing for?

How is the pegasus (equestrian) crossing different?

The key elements to be emphasized are:

- looking ahead for signs and markings;
- anticipating and planning for pedestrian activity;
- the effective application of the M–S–M routine;
- approaching at the correct speed to allow a safe stop if necessary;
- planning for the lights to change at controlled crossings;
- using all signals safely and correctly.

You may need to offer some direct instruction to encourage forward planning, the correct application of the M–S–M routine, and to build up confidence. As skill improves, gradually reduce the level of tuition and transfer the responsibility by asking the pupil to tell you how far ahead they are looking and what they are planning to do. Remember – always be ready to give further assistance if required, particularly if safety is at risk.

Fault assessment

No matter what the standard of the pupil is, positive correction is better than negative or retrospective correction. If your pupil is not responding to a developing hazard, give a positive prompt to encourage them to take some form of action. This is far safer and more effective than allowing a potentially dangerous situation to arise, particularly where pedestrians are involved.

Try to include as many crossings as possible. During the drive, assess whether the pupil is putting all the established routines into practice. Identify and analyse problems. Give advice on how to improve, and when you make a correction, remember to give a good reason for it.

Common faults

- Lack of planning and anticipation.
- Incorrect application of the M–S–M routine.

- Signals:
  - given incorrectly;
  - given unnecessarily;
  - badly timed.

- Not reinstating signals that have cancelled themselves.
- Not cancelling signals after use.
- Misuse of the horn and/or flashing headlights.
- Inviting pedestrians or other road users to move forward.
- Approaching crossings too fast.
- Failure to respond to traffic lights.
- Failure to stop when necessary.
- Blocking crossings in traffic queues.
- Not securing the car when necessary.
- Moving off from crossings prematurely.
- Not responding safely to others' signals.

Judgement of speed, progress, hesitancy, road positioning

By the time your pupils are approaching test standard, their personal driving skills should be well developed. They should be applying all the correct routines and procedures for driving in different road and traffic situations. Your main objectives are to confirm knowledge of:

- the speed limits for different types of road;
- braking, following and stopping distances and the 'two-second rule';
- the factors that should influence the speed – for example the type of road/surface/weather conditions/volume of traffic/pedestrian activity;
- the need to make progress when safe;
- what effect driving too slowly for the conditions may have on other drivers.

At junctions, check that your pupils look for gaps in the traffic and that they have the car ready for moving off efficiently. When moving into a gap in traffic make sure that the speed is built up positively. Check that they position correctly for the type of road, direction to be taken, speed and position of other vehicles, and volume of pedestrian activity.

Discuss and set the objectives and establish the pupil's previous knowledge and understanding by asking a few questions. For example:

What's the speed limit in a built-up area?

What's the speed limit on a two-way road with a national speed limit sign?

What's the stopping distance at 30 mph?

Explain the 'two-second' rule to me.

Would you drive at 30 mph past a school at 3.30 in the afternoon?

What happens to your stopping distance on wet roads?

Dual carriageways are normally safer than single-carriageway roads, as the traffic on each carriageway is all travelling in the same direction. There are also fewer problems caused by traffic having to cross the path of other drivers. Make sure your pupils:

- look and plan well ahead for obstructions or junctions;
- use all the mirrors even more frequently;
- maintain lane discipline;
- read the signs and markings;
- anticipate early changes in direction;
- apply the M–S–M routine in good time to allow for safe lane changes;
- keep up to date with traffic to the rear and sides;
- avoid driving in other drivers' blind areas for prolonged distances;
- drive positively to suit the conditions.

Failure to make progress

If pupils are missing too many gaps at junctions, encourage them to:

- start making their observations earlier;
- work out when their gap is going to arrive;
- have the car ready to move promptly into the space;
- build up the speed and change up through the gears efficiently.

When pupils drive too slowly for the conditions, or miss opportunities to proceed, try talking through a few situations to demonstrate what you mean.

When pupils drive too fast for the conditions and without considering the possible dangers, you must be firm and get the speed under control. When this becomes necessary, you must give valid reasons. For example, if you are on a road where there is a lot of pedestrian activity, you will need to confirm what speed we should be driving at and explain what we should be looking for.

Positioning

Encourage correct positioning at all times. Ensure that your pupils:

- maintain the normal road position when driving along;
- position correctly at junctions, according to the type and width of the road;
- plan well ahead and select the correct lane in good time;
- maintain lane discipline.

Common faults

- Moving off slowly and not changing up through the gears efficiently.
- Driving too slowly on roads with higher speed limits.
- Breaking the speed limit.
- Driving too fast in unsafe conditions.
- Missing opportunities to proceed at junctions.
- Looking only to the right at roundabouts and getting out of position.
- Not using the mirrors regularly.
- Being unaware of drivers to the rear and sides.
- Lack of planning on dual carriageways resulting in becoming 'boxed in'.
- Positioning incorrectly on narrow roads or one-way streets.
- Driving too close to the kerb, or too far out.
- Incorrect positioning on bends.
- Not maintaining lane discipline.

The driving test 09

The 'L' test for new drivers is conducted in two parts – the theory test (including hazard perception), followed at a later date by the practical driving test. Candidates must pass the theory test before they can apply to take the practical driving test. After passing the theory test, the candidate has a maximum of two years in which to take and pass the practical test.

Theory and hazard perception test

The Theory and Hazard Perception Test is available at about 150 test centres throughout England, Scotland and Wales. The candidate can take the test at any of these centres. A list of centres is available at www.gov.uk/find-driving-test-centre.

In Northern Ireland, the theory test is conducted by the Driver and Vehicle Agency at six locations. For details see www.nidirect.gov.uk.

All test centres in Wales, and some in England, are equipped to conduct the test in Welsh. For candidates with special needs such as dyslexia or reading difficulties there is a facility to listen to the test being read in English or Welsh. For people who have learning difficulties, arrangements can be made for a showing of an 'on screen' video of the test in British Sign Language. Candidates with any other special needs can apply for more time to complete the multiple-choice part of the test.

Booking the test

The test can be booked online or by phone.

Online booking

Log on to **www.gov.uk/book-theory-test**. You will need the pupil's UK driving licence number and your credit or debit card details. To use this service, you must provide a valid e-mail address. Confirmation of the date and time of the test is available immediately.

By phone

Applications can be made by phone on 0300 200 1122. If you are ringing on behalf of a pupil, you will need to have his or her personal details and driver number. If you are using the pupil's card for payment, he or she must be present when you make the call.

Trainer booking

As a registered driving instructor you can make your pupils' test applications online. To do this, you need to register with the DVSA for an 'online profile', indicating which test centres you expect to use and which credit or debit cards you will be using for payment.

The website for bookings is available 24 hours, but you can only assign pupils to a test at times when their licence entitlement can be verified by the DVLA.

To register for this service, visit the DVSA website at **www.gov.uk/ register-book-driving-tests-trainer.**

One of the advantages of using this facility is that you can book slots up to three months ahead. You do not need to confirm details of the pupil at the time of booking. This can be done at a later stage and up to 4 pm a full working day before the test. You can also change or cancel a booking.

Test fees

The theory test fee is currently £23.

Cancelling tests

To cancel or postpone a theory test, the pupil needs to give at least three clear working days' notice. This period of notice does not include:

- the day of the test;
- the day that the notice of cancellation or postponement was made;
- Sundays;
- public holidays.

This means that you need to give more than six or seven days' notice if there are weekends and holidays involved.

A candidate who has to cancel their test at short notice is given a free re-booking if they:

- have a medical certificate of illness;
- have had a bereavement;
- have school exams;
- are called up for duty as a member of the armed forces.

Attending for the test

Your pupils must produce their photo-card driving licence as visual proof of identity. In the unlikely event that the pupil has an old-style paper licence instead of a photo-card licence, a valid passport (or some other form of visual identity) must be produced. Pupils should also take with them the appointment card or booking reference details.

Test format

The test involves multiple-choice questions, followed by a hazard perception test.

The multiple-choice questions

This part of the test involves answering 50 questions that are displayed on-screen. For each question a number of responses are shown, and the candidate makes a choice by using the touch screen. To pass, 43 questions must be answered correctly within 57 minutes.

Only one question appears on the screen at a time, and you can move backwards or forwards through the questions. This means that you can recheck or alter any answers. The system also alerts the candidate if any questions have not been answered.

There is no requirement for the pupil to be computer literate, as members of staff are on hand to assist with any queries or difficulties. A practice session of up to 15 minutes is allowed to enable candidates to familiarize themselves with the system before starting the actual test.

Pupils who have a 'Safe Road User Award' can take an 'abridged' version of the theory test. This version has only 35 questions instead of the usual 50, with a pass mark of 30.

The cost of the abridged version of the theory test is currently £18.

The Award, which was developed in conjunction with the DVSA, is available in schools across the UK.

The theory test syllabus

The pupil's knowledge of the following subjects is tested:

- *Alertness*: observation, anticipation, concentration, awareness, distraction.
- *Attitude*: consideration, safe distance, courtesy, priority.
- *Safety and the vehicle*: fault detection, defects, safety equipment, emissions, noise, vehicle security.
- *Safety margins*: stopping distances, road surfaces, skidding, weather conditions.
- *Hazard awareness*: anticipation, attention, speed and distance, reaction time, alcohol and drugs, tiredness.
- *Vulnerable road users*: pedestrians, children, elderly drivers, new drivers, people with disabilities, motorcyclists, cyclists, animals, horse riders.
- *Other types of vehicle*: motorcycles, lorries, buses, trams.
- *Vehicle handling*: weather conditions, road conditions, time of day, speed, traffic calming.
- *Motorway rules*: speed limits, lane discipline, stopping, lighting, parking.
- *Rules of the road*: speed limits, parking, lighting.
- *Road and traffic signs*: road signs, speed limits, road markings, regulations.
- *Documents*: licence, insurance, MOT certificate.
- *Accidents*: first aid, warning devices, reporting procedures, safety regulations.
- *Vehicle loading*: stability, towing.
- *Uninsured and unlicensed driving.*
- *Eco-driving and environmental issues.*
- *New motorway signage.*
- *First aid.*
- *Health and driver licensing.*

Case studies

Some of the multiple-choice questions are given as case studies. The subject matter of the case study focuses on real-life examples that drivers could come across in normal driving, with five separate questions based on that scenario.

Sample questions

Q   You are the driver of a car carrying two adults and two children, both of whom are under 14 years of age. Who is responsible for ensuring that the children wear seat belts?

(Select one answer)

a   the children

b   their parents

c   the driver

d   the front seat passenger

A   The correct answer is

c   the driver (*Highway Code*)

Q   You are driving towards a zebra crossing. Pedestrians are waiting to cross. You should:

(Select one answer)

a   slow down and prepare to stop

b   give way to the elderly and infirm only

c   use your headlamps to indicate that they can cross

d   wave at them to cross the road

A   The correct answer is:

a   slow down and prepare to stop (*Highway Code* and *The Official DVSA Guide to Driving – the essential skills*)

Q   On which three occasions must you stop your vehicle?

(Select three answers)

a   when involved in an accident

b   at a red traffic light

c   when signalled to do so by a police officer

d   at a junction with double broken white lines

e   at a pelican crossing when the amber light is flashing and no pedestrians are crossing

A   The correct answers are

a, b and c.

A practice theory test is available from gov.uk/take-practice-theory-test. This enables the pupil to use either 'practice view', which works on most phones or tablets or in 'test view', which is similar to the screen at the test centre.

Hazard perception test

After completing the multiple-choice questions, the candidate is given a short break before starting the hazard perception test. The test consists of 14 computer-generated clips featuring various types of hazard, with each clip lasting about a minute. The candidate has to respond to each hazard by clicking on a computer mouse as each hazard develops. Up to 5 marks can be scored for each hazard; the earlier a response is made, the higher the score. On this part of the test it is not possible to go back to change a response, as the object is to recognize hazards as early as possible.

This part of the test can be taken in English, Welsh or British Sign Language.

The hazards depicted are those that would need a response from the driver such as changing speed or direction, or by taking some other form of action.

Candidates are not penalized for clicking on insignificant hazards – they are only marked on the designated developing ones. However, if too many unnecessary responses are made in a very short space of time, a score of 0 might be allocated for that clip. This is to stop the candidate randomly clicking or guessing.

The pass mark for this part of the test is currently set at 44 out of a possible 75.

At the end of the test

Candidates are given the result of both parts of the test within a few minutes of completing the HPT test. Feedback is given on any incorrect answers.

Successful candidates are issued with a pass certificate that is valid for two years. The practical test must be passed within this two-year period, otherwise a further theory test needs to be taken.

If your pupil fails, they must wait at least three days before taking the test again. When applying for the practical test the theory pass certificate number should be quoted.

Test training

To prepare for both parts of the Theory and Hazard Perception Test your pupils will need to study:

The Highway Code.

The Official DVSA Guide to Driving – The essential skills.

The Official DVSA Guide to Learning to Drive.

The Official DVSA Theory Test for Car Drivers.

The Official DVSA Guide to the Hazard Perception Test – DVD.

For details of these books and other resource material see Appendix III. You need to have a thorough knowledge of the contents of all these books to prepare yourself for the ADI theory test. You also need to have an understanding of the syllabus and the various topics so that you can help your pupils prepare for their own theory test.

Your own knowledge and teaching skills will be even more relevant if you are dealing with pupils who have learning difficulties. In these circumstances, you will need to use plenty of encouragement, and might involve the pupil's family or friends to assist.

There are many books and CD-ROMs on the market to help with theory training. Some of these materials contain DVSA practice questions and can be used to aid the learning process. However, you will need to check, by the skilful use of your question and answer technique, your pupils' understanding of the rules and regulations if they are to be able to apply them to the on-the-road situation. Other CDs are aimed at the practical side of the ADI's job, and relate to hazard recognition and awareness.

The DVSA has produced programmes for all types of learner, including car, motorcycle, large goods vehicle (LGV) and passenger-carrying vehicle (PCV) drivers. Even if you do not have access to a computer, or the appropriate skills, you should make sure that you are able to offer the appropriate CDs to your pupils. Most of them will have these skills and be able to use a computer at home, school or college.

Good instructors will automatically be incorporating hazard perception into their practical training courses. This helps learners to understand how to apply the rules and procedures. For more information about both parts of the theory test, visit the website at **www.gov.uk/driving-theory-test** or phone the DVSA on 0300 200 1122.

Preparation for the theory test

The DVSA book, *The Official Theory Test for Car Drivers*, offers advice on how to prepare for the multiple-choice part of the theory test and recommends that pupils study the various books from which the questions are taken. You should also use the other resource materials as teaching and study aids. These include:

The Highway Code. Contains the laws that apply to all road users and up-to-date advice on road safety.

Know your Traffic Signs. Contains information and explanations of most signs and road markings.

The Official DVSA Guide to Driving – The essential skills. Explains the best driving practices in detail.

The Official DVSA Theory Test CD ROM for Car Drivers. Contains all the questions and allows your pupils to practise for the multiple-choice part of the theory test.

All of these books and materials can be obtained from The Stationery Office by telephoning 0870 600 5522 or at **www.tsoshop.co.uk**. Other suppliers of books and training materials are listed in Appendix II.

Remember that the theory test questions change from time to time. This can sometimes be as a result of revisions to legislation or because of customer feedback. Make sure that you and your pupils are using the most up-to-date versions of any publications.

Practical test

Driving tests are administered by the DVSA, which is an executive agency of the Department for Transport. About 1.6 million 'L' tests on cars and motor-cycles are conducted each year, as well as the vocational tests for LGV and PCV drivers. In Northern Ireland, driving tests are conducted by the Driver and Vehicle Agency.

To ensure uniformity in the conduct of practical driving tests, all driving examiners are trained at the DVSA training and development centre. They are monitored regularly and are sometimes accompanied on test by a senior member of staff.

Application

The practical test can be booked or changed online at **www.gov.uk/book-driving-test**. This service is available from 6 am to 11.40 pm. Alternatively, you can book by phone on 0300 200 1122 during normal working hours. The average waiting time for a test is about 6–7 weeks.

As a registered ADI you can book and manage your pupils' driving tests online. When you register as a 'trainer booker' you can book and pay for slots in advance and then nominate the individual pupil up to 4 pm at least one full working day before the test.

An application form for registering can be downloaded from **www.gov. uk/register-book-driving-tests-trainer** or by contacting the DVSA on 0300 200 1122.

The trainer booking system can be used for:

- viewing available test slots without giving the candidate's details;
- getting alerts for cancellations;
- booking several tests with one payment;
- swapping test appointments between candidates;
- managing your own availability for tests.

Practical test syllabus

You will find the test syllabus in full in *The Official DVSA Guide to Learning to Drive*, which is available from most good bookshops. Alternatively, it can be purchased in bulk from Desk Top Driving and other suppliers (see Appendix II) for selling on to pupils. The book describes in detail:

- the requirements of the test;
- the types of vehicle suitable;
- different categories of driver, such as those with disabilities, hearing and speech problems;
- general road procedures;
- the manoeuvring exercises;
- what the examiner will be looking for;
- the recommended syllabus for learning to drive.

Eyesight test

At the start of the test the examiner will ask your pupil to read a car number plate at the prescribed distance. The candidate must be able to read a number plate at 20 metres (for new-style 7-digit plates and 20.5 metres for the older-style 6-digit plate. If the pupil needs glasses or contact lenses for the eyesight check, they must wear them while driving. (To avoid any potential problems on the day of the test, make sure by checking that your pupils can do this a few weeks prior to the test and then again a couple of days before.)

Examiner's explanation:

"The test will last about 38 to 40 minutes and will include about 20 minutes of independent driving and various roads and traffic conditions. I will ask you to complete one manoeuvre and we may carry out an emergency stop. The sort of things you've been practising with your instructor or accompanying driver."

Vehicle safety questions

During the test the examiner will ask two 'vehicle safety' questions. One question will be a 'tell me' question and is asked at the start of the test before moving off. The other question, which will be asked while the pupil is driving, is a 'show me' question.

For a full list of possible questions, see page 226.

Safety precautions

Driver checks are carried out, including doors, seat, mirrors, seat belts and head restraint. The pupil should adjust these so that he or she is comfortable and can easily reach all driving controls. Before starting the engine, the doors should be shut properly, the handbrake should be on and the gear lever or selector in neutral.

Controls

Throughout the test all the main controls should be handled smoothly and at the correct time. This includes use of the accelerator, clutch, gears, footbrake, handbrake and steering.

Moving away

Moving away safely, under full control, on the level, from behind a parked car and, where practicable, on a slope, with correct observations.

Controlled stop

On some tests the candidate may be asked to do an 'emergency stop'. In this exercise the candidate is required to stop the vehicle in good time and under full control as if in an emergency. Even and progressive braking is required, avoiding locking the wheels. In wet weather, pupils should be aware that it could take twice as long to stop. The emergency stop exercise is conducted randomly on about one test in three.

Manoeuvres

The pupil is asked to do one of three possible manoeuvres:

- Parallel park at the side of the road.
- Park in a bay – either by driving in and reversing out, or reversing in and driving out.

- Pull up on the right-hand side of the road, reverse for two car lengths and then re-join the traffic.

Use of mirrors

The pupil should use mirrors effectively, acting appropriately on what is seen and being aware of what may be in the blind spots. Early use of mirrors should be made before signalling; changing direction and/or speed; and as part of the mirror–signal–manoeuvre routine.

Signalling

Give signals clearly and in good time to warn other road users of intentions in accordance with The Highway Code.

Response to signs and signals

Understand and be able to react to all traffic signs and road markings; check when proceeding through green lights; and respond to signals given by police officers, traffic wardens, school crossing patrols and all other road users. Watch out for signals by other road users and respond appropriately.

Use of speed

Safe and reasonable progress should be made according to the road, weather and traffic conditions, the road signs and speed limits. Candidates should always be able to stop within the distance they can see is clear.

Following distance

Maintaining a safe distance from the vehicle ahead in all conditions, including when stopping in traffic queues. Leave sufficient space when stopping in traffic queues.

Maintaining progress

Driving at appropriate speeds for the type of road and the speed limit; the type and density of traffic; the weather and visibility. A safe approach to all hazards should be demonstrated without being over-cautious. All safe opportunities to proceed at junctions should be taken promptly – driving too slowly can be frustrating for other drivers.

Junctions

Apply the correct procedure to all types of junctions, including applying the mirror–signal–manoeuvre routine and using the correct lanes. Good all-round observations should be made and safe response to other road users demonstrated. Be extra careful in poor light or bad weather conditions, particularly in relation to vulnerable road users such as cyclists and pedestrians.

Judgement

Correct responses when dealing with other road users including overtaking, meeting oncoming traffic and turning across traffic. Other road users should not be made to slow down, swerve or stop. Make sure you understand the intentions of other road users.

Positioning

Maintain correct positioning at all times according to the type of road, the direction being taken and the presence of parked vehicles. Look for, and be guided by, road signs and markings. Other road users may judge your intentions by where you are positioned.

Clearance of obstructions

Allow plenty of room when passing stationary vehicles and other obstructions that may be obscuring pedestrians.

Pedestrian crossings

Recognize and respond correctly and safely to the different types of crossing. Reduce speed and time the approach so as to stop safely if needed without causing inconvenience or danger to other road users.

Position for normal stops

Choose safe and legal places to stop without causing inconvenience or obstruction to others. Avoid blocking the road or creating a hazard.

Awareness and planning

Think and plan ahead and anticipate the actions of other road users. Act in good time rather than reacting at the last moment. Demonstrate safe attitudes, particularly when dealing with vulnerable road users such as pedestrians, cyclists, motorcyclists and horse riders.

Ancillary controls

Understand the function of all the controls and switches, especially those that have a bearing on road safety. Keep proper control of the vehicle when using secondary controls. Appropriate use of indicators, lights, windscreen wipers, demisters and heaters.

Eco-safe driving

During the test the examiner assesses candidates on their ability to drive in a way that shows eco-safe driving techniques. In particular, the examiner assesses control and planning and gives feedback on the efficiency of the driving at the end of the test. This is purely for guidance and does not form part of the criteria for a pass or fail. The examiner will, however, give guidance and feedback if there are any areas for improvement.

Two main areas are assessed. First, control: using all the vehicle controls as smoothly as possible, particularly when starting and moving away, accelerating, using gears and driving at an appropriate speed. Second, planning: anticipating road and traffic conditions and acting in good time, particularly when approaching potential hazards; making use of engine braking when appropriate; and switching off the engine during lengthy stops.

Applying for the practical test

When you feel your pupils have reached a fairly consistent standard, you will need to advise them on applying for their driving test. It is important that you make the decision and the application jointly. This avoids problems arising such as pupils:

- applying independently before they are ready;
- not informing you of the date until it is too late to be postponed;
- being reluctant to delay the test once they have an appointment;
- obtaining an appointment at a time when you may already have another test booked.

Whether or not to apply for the test is one of the most difficult and subjective decisions you may have to make. There are many reasons for this:

From a business point of view, you may feel obliged to apply for tests early on during their training to encourage the pupil to carry on with their lessons.

Because of pupils' wishes, you may often be put under pressure to apply too soon.

If there is a particularly long waiting list for test appointments in your area, a combination of this with the above two reasons may also affect your decision. However, sometimes an early application might act as an incentive and increased motivation for the pupil.

Where none of these pressures exist to any significant degree, your decision may still not be easy. You must be fair to pupils and not impose standards so high as to absolutely guarantee a pass. It could well mean that pupils feel you are delaying the decision for purely monetary reasons. Apart from this, you can never actually guarantee they will pass!

Pupils will make varying rates of progress at different stages of their training. For example, some make very rapid progress in the early stages, and later, when a higher degree of understanding is required, progress may slow down considerably. Others make very slow progress at first, then make very rapid headway after better understanding is achieved.

Although the DVSA try to ensure that tests are usually available within six weeks, the waiting time is occasionally unpredictable in its length. Sometimes, for example if a new examiner is appointed to a centre, you may receive an appointment much more quickly than you anticipated. To ensure that you do not arrange one before the pupil is ready, make sure you specify an earliest date on the application.

It is as well to remember that if you apply for tests too early:

- The test may subsequently have to be postponed. This means extra administration, expense, time and possible ill-feeling, since pupils generally do not like having tests deferred.

- The pupil may not be ready and will probably fail. This may reflect back on you since you were saying, in effect, that when you applied you considered that the pupil was ready for the test.

- Your efficiency record of passes and failures on the DVSA statistics will be affected.

If you are applying for a test where there is a long waiting list, you should emphasize to the pupil that the booking is made on the assumption that a reasonable rate of progress will be maintained and that his or her driving will have reached a suitable standard.

Having taken all of this into consideration you can make the application by phone or online. Make sure you give your driving school number as this will avoid problems with double-booked appointments. Most pupils and instructors these days prefer to book online, as it is now possible to use a 'trainer booking' facility and the opportunity to book, cancel or change a booking.

The current cost of a practical car test is £62 (for a weekday test) or £75 for evenings, weekends and Bank Holidays.

In Northern Ireland the test fee is £45.50 for a weekday test and £62.50 for evening and weekend tests.

It is important to keep a record of test applications. Make sure pupils inform you immediately they receive appointments so that the date and time can be entered in your diary and the school car reserved accordingly.

When the appointment card is received you should reserve the time in your diary. It is usual to give pupils a lesson immediately prior to the test. Ensure that on the day they know that payment normally has to cover both the lesson and use of the school car for the test. Some pupils may think that payment of the test application fee also includes your fees.

The same application form is used when applying for tests for people with disabilities and for drivers who have been ordered to take extended tests. It should be noted that the time for extended tests is double the length of the 'L' test and the fees charged are higher.

For more information on how to apply for tests for people with disabilities, see Chapter 12.

Driving test times

Practical tests are normally available at most test centres from about 7.30 am to 4 pm Monday to Friday. The application form allows you to request preferred days of the week and morning or afternoon appointments. If you apply for an evening or weekend test, make sure that your pupil understands that there is a higher fee.

Cancelling and postponing tests

The DVSA require at least three working days' notice for a cancellation, otherwise the test fee is lost. The only exceptions to this rule are if the pupil:

- has a medical certificate of illness;
- has a bereavement;
- has a school exam;
- is called up for duty as a member of the Armed Forces.

If you feel that the pupil is not yet ready to take their test, make sure they understand that it is in their own interests as well as those of other road users that you postpone it. Remember, though, that the booking is a contract between the pupil and the DVSA – you should not cancel without the pupil's agreement.

If the pupil is not ready to take the test you should advise them of the need to cancel at least two weeks before the day of the test and certainly not less than 10 days before.

The pupil may offer resistance to your advice. Be sympathetic and tactful, but firm. Be objective and give the pupil a realistic 'mock test'. This will usually convince even the most adamant that you are acting in their best interests. If the pupil still insists on going against your advice, then all you are entitled to do is withhold the use of your car.

It should be noted that driving examiners may not use the dual controls to avoid an accident unless there is a risk of danger – and then it may only be a last-second decision. Your car may be at risk! The school car is the 'tool of your trade'. It is imperative, therefore, that it is not off the road for unnecessary repairs because you let someone attend for a test too soon.

There are also other considerations. You are depriving other candidates of an appointment and, more importantly, your reputation could be at risk if you regularly present candidates for test when they are not up to standard.

When you and your pupil have come to a joint decision to postpone a test, you will need to give three working days' notice to avoid forfeit of the fee. Remember that this period of notice does not include Sundays, public holidays, the day of the test or the day of the cancellation. In practice this usually means that more than a week's notice has to be given – especially if any public holidays are involved. You may simply defer the test to a later date or you may cancel it. If a cancellation is made by telephone and a further appointment is not required, it must be followed up with a request in writing for a refund of the fee. The fee will be withheld pending receipt of this request, which should be made within one week of the cancellation.

Driving test cancellations: the DVSA's Compensation Code

Occasionally tests have to be cancelled by the DVSA at short notice: this means less than three clear working days. The DVSA will refund the fee or another test will be arranged at no further cost if the test:

- is cancelled by the DVSA;
- is cancelled by the candidate and the above amount of notice is given;
- is cancelled by the candidate for medical reasons and a doctor's letter or certificate is provided;
- does not take place or is not finished for a reason other than the candidate's fault, or the fault of the vehicle, for example bad weather conditions.

Certain expenses incurred on the day of the test will also be refunded to the candidate if the DVSA cancel at short notice, unless it is for bad weather or poor light conditions. Reasonable claims for the following will be considered:

- any standard pay or earnings lost through taking unpaid leave (usually for half a day);
- the cost of travelling to and from the test centre if a theory test is involved, or the cost of hiring a vehicle for the test, including travelling to and from the test centre if a practical test is involved (generally up to one and a half hours of vehicle hire).

The DVSA will not pay for the cost of driving lessons arranged prior to a particular test appointment, or for extra lessons taken while waiting for a rescheduled appointment.

Application forms, giving full details of the above and how to apply for compensation, are available from the DVSA at www.gov.uk/practical-driving-test.

Attending for the test

To ensure that everything goes smoothly on your pupil's test day:

- Check that the pupil has a valid, signed driving licence, his or her Theory and Hazard Perception Test pass certificate and some form of photographic identity if necessary.
- Take the test appointment card in case any errors have been made.
- Make sure your car is clean and tidy and has sufficient fuel.
- Clean the windows, leaving one slightly open if there is a risk of condensation.
- Make sure that the pupil knows where the ancillary controls are and how they work.
- Make sure that your car is:
  - roadworthy and has a current MOT certificate if applicable;
  - fitted with front and rear seat belts in working order, and adjustable head restraints;
  - fully insured for the pupil to drive while on the test;
  - properly taxed with the disc displayed in the correct position;
  - displaying 'L' plates clearly visible to the front and rear;
  - fitted with a rear-view mirror for the driving examiner.

The car must meet the minimum test vehicle requirements. For a car first registered after 1 October 2003, this means that it must be capable of reaching 100 kph (62 mph).

If any of these points are overlooked, the test may be cancelled and the pupil will lose the fee. As these requirements are your professional responsibility, you will then be obliged to pay for another appointment.

At the test centre

Take your pupil into the waiting room a few minutes prior to the time of the appointment, making allowances for toilet requirements. Try to maintain a relaxed atmosphere by chatting to your pupil.

Documents

The examiner will come in to the waiting room and ask for your pupil by name, request some form of identification and ask the candidate to sign the DVSA 'Driving Test Report' form. This signature will serve as a declaration that the vehicle presented for test carries valid motor insurance in accordance with the Road Traffic Act.

A reminder is given to candidates about motor insurance responsibilities on their test appointment card. However, it is sensible to remind your pupils, before they go into the waiting room, that this formality will take place. Confirm with them that your car is properly insured. If, for any reason, the candidate does not sign the declaration, the examiner will refuse to conduct the test and the fee will be forfeited.

Observer on test

At the start of the test the examiner will ask the pupil if he or she would like his or her instructor (or another observer) to sit in on the test. As well as accompanying the pupil on the practical part of the test, the observer can listen in to the examiner's feedback at the end of the test. It is purely the candidate's decision whether to have an observer with them.

The opportunity to go along on a test as an observer gives you, particularly if you are new to the job, a clearer idea of what is required by examiners.

Introduction

Examiners are trained to use their discretion about introducing themselves either on the way to, or in, the car. They will also decide whether or not it is appropriate to use first names. Driving test examiners are sympathetic towards candidates. They understand 'test nerves'. You should realize, however, that while nerves are frequently used as an excuse for failing, they are rarely the real cause. Provided your pupils are properly prepared, and know what to expect, nerves should not be too much of a problem. Conducting a realistic 'mock test', to give pupils an insight into what will happen, can do much to allay these fears.

Eyesight

The eyesight test will be conducted outside the test centre. The legal requirement is for the candidate to be able to read, in good daylight, a car number plate from a distance of 20 metres (or 20.5m for the old-style plates). If the candidate fails this, the test will not be conducted.

Vehicle safety questions

Before starting the 'on-road' part of the test the examiner will ask a 'tell me' question about the vehicle or other matters relating to vehicle safety.

The pupil is not expected to physically check fluid levels, or to touch a hot engine, but may be required to open the bonnet to show the location of the various items.

Example questions:

1 *Tell me how you'd check that the brakes are working before starting a journey.*
   Brakes should not feel spongy or slack. Brakes should be tested as you set off. Vehicle should not pull to one side.

2 *Tell me where you'd find the information for the recommended tyre pressures for this car and how tyre pressures should be checked.*
   Manufacturer's guide, use a reliable pressure gauge, check and adjust pressures when tyres are cold, don't forget spare tyre, remember to refit valve caps.

3 *Tell me how you make sure your head restraint is correctly adjusted so it provides the best protection in the event of a crash.*
   The head restraint should be adjusted so the rigid part of the head restraint is at least as high as the eye or top of the ears, and as close to the back of the head as is comfortable. Note: Some restraints might not be adjustable.

4 *Tell me how you'd check the tyres to ensure that they have sufficient tread depth and that their general condition is safe to use on the road.*

No cuts and bulges, 1.6mm of tread depth across the central three-quarters of the breadth of the tyre, and around the entire outer circumference of the tyre.

5 *Tell me how you'd check that the headlights and tail lights are working. You don't need to exit the vehicle.*
Explain you'd operate the switch (turn on ignition if necessary), then walk round vehicle (as this is a 'tell me' question, you don't need to physically check the lights).

6 *Tell me how you'd know if there was a problem with your anti-lock braking system.*
Warning light should illuminate if there is a fault with the anti-lock braking system.

7 *Tell me how you'd check the direction indicators are working. You don't need to exit the vehicle.*
Explain you'd operate the switch (turn on ignition if necessary), and then walk round vehicle (as this is a 'tell me' question, you don't need to physically check the lights).

8 *Tell me how you'd check the brake lights are working on this car.*
Explain you'd operate the brake pedal, make use of reflections in windows or doors, or ask someone to help.

9 *Tell me how you'd check the power-assisted steering is working before starting a journey.*
If the steering becomes heavy, the system may not be working properly. Before starting a journey, two simple checks can be made.
Gentle pressure on the steering wheel, maintained while the engine is started, should result in a slight but noticeable movement as the system begins to operate. Alternatively turning the steering wheel just after moving off will give an immediate indication that the power assistance is functioning.

10 *Tell me how you'd switch on the rear fog light(s) and explain when you'd use it/them. You don't need to exit the vehicle.*
Operate switch (turn on dipped headlights and ignition if necessary). Check warning light is on. Explain use.

11 *Tell me how you switch your headlight from dipped to main beam and explain how you'd know the main beam is on.*
Operate switch (with ignition or engine on if necessary), check with main beam warning light.

12 *Open the bonnet and tell me how you'd check that the engine has sufficient oil.*

Identify dipstick/oil level indicator, describe check of oil level against the minimum and maximum markers.

13 *Open the bonnet and tell me how you'd check that the engine has sufficient engine coolant.*
Identify high and low level markings on header tank where fitted or radiator filler cap, and describe how to top up to correct level.

14 *Open the bonnet and tell me how you'd check that you have a safe level of hydraulic brake fluid.*
Identify reservoir, check level against high and low markings.

Another vehicle safety question ('show me') will be asked while the pupil is driving. The question can be asked at any time during the test, including during the independent driving part. If the pupil is not sure about how to do the check, the examiner will ask them to pull in when it's safe and appropriate, and then ask them to find the control.

Example questions:

When it's safe to do so can you show me:
- how you wash and clean the front windscreen?
- how you'd switch on your dipped headlights?
- how you'd set the rear demister?
- how you'd operate the horn?
- how you'd demist the front windscreen?
- how you'd open and close the side window?

Directional instructions

At the start of the test the examiner will explain to the candidate that they should 'follow the road ahead unless directed otherwise'. Any instructions to turn off to the left or right will be given in plenty of time.

The directions and instructions described in Chapter 7 are general guidelines, and examiners may use slightly different terminology where appropriate to suit a particular candidate.

Independent driving

For this phase, candidates are asked to drive for about 20 minutes or so without any specific turn-by-turn instructions from the examiner. On most tests, the candidate is asked to follow directions from a sat nav. The sat nav equipment is provided by the examiner, who will set it up using a stored route. The pupil does not need to set a route – they are simply required to show that they can follow route directions effectively. You are not allowed to use your own equipment; it must be the one used by the examiner – a TomTom 52.

On one in five tests the pupil will follow directions from traffic signs.

If the candidate goes off-route it will not affect the result of the test as long as there are no actual driving faults.

If the pupil has special needs the examiner uses an appropriate method of directions, taking into account the particular needs of the individual candidate.

For candidates who speak little or no English, the examiner will use diagrams and/or written place names so that the driver can visualize the route to be taken.

Independent driving is designed to test the candidate's ability to drive unsupervised and to make decisions without guidance.

Manoeuvres

All manoeuvres need to be carried out under full control and with reasonable accuracy. Effective all-round observations and the correct response to other road users are both essential elements of the exercise. The pupil should also know and understand what factors to consider when looking for a safe, legal and convenient place to stop.

Parallel park

In normal driving this involves reversing into a space between two other vehicles – usually with about one and a half to two car lengths between them. On the driving test the exercise is carried out where there is only one other vehicle involved.

The candidate is required to reverse into the space, finishing close to the kerb.

Bay parking

The pupil is asked to park in a bay – either by driving in and reversing out, or reversing in and driving out. The examiner will decide which one is required.

Driving in forwards and reversing out may be carried out in any car park, including at the test centre. Reversing and driving out is only used in a driving test centre car park.

Pull up on the right

This manoeuvre involves pulling up on the righthand side of the road, reversing for about two car lengths and then re-joining the traffic.

If another vehicle pulls in behind and stops the pupil from reversing, the exercise is abandoned and another manoeuvre will be carried out later in the test.

If a vehicle pulls up in front, the exercise will continue. If the other vehicle blocks the pupil's view, the examiner will control the situation and give appropriate advice.

Marking system

Driving examiners are trained to look for the 'perfect driver'. At the moment of getting into the car every test candidate is considered to be perfect. Any deviations from this perfection are graded into three categories of fault: driving, serious and dangerous.

Faults are graded and recorded on the Driving Test Report form (DL25C), as they occur. Before any minor deviation from perfect is marked on the form, the examiner must consider its significance to the overall performance.

Fault categories

Faults committed during driving tests are assessed under the following categories:

- *Dangerous fault*: recorded when a fault is assessed as having caused actual danger during the test. A single fault in this category will result in failure.

- *Serious fault*: recorded when a fault is assessed as potentially dangerous. A habitual driving fault can also be assessed as serious when it indicates a serious weakness in a candidate's driving. A single serious fault is an automatic failure.

- *Driving fault*: a less serious fault, which is assessed as such because of the circumstances at that particular time. Driving faults only amount to a failure when there is an accumulation of 15 or more.

There is an obvious need for a degree of standardization between the consistency of assessments made in training and those used for the driving test. It is essential therefore that you become familiar with this grading system.

There are, of course, other types of errors that you will be dealing with during a pupil's training. These include marginal errors that could develop into more serious faults or that could lead to bad habits being formed.

Driving test faults

Driving fault

The pupil is approaching a junction to turn right into a fairly wide side road. Visibility into the road is good and, after ensuring it is safe to turn and the side road is free of traffic movement, the learner turns into the side road, cutting the corner very slightly. No potential danger was caused to other road users because the pupil had checked the situation before turning. On a driving test this would be recorded as a driving fault. It would not result in failure.

Serious fault

This time visibility into the side road is severely restricted by parked vehicles, making it impossible for the pupil to see whether or not there is traffic approaching the end of the new road. The pupil blatantly cuts the corner into this unknown situation. No actual danger occurred because no other road user appeared from the side road. This, however, was purely good luck and not an assessed judgement. The incident involved potential danger and the learner would fail the test.

Dangerous fault

In exactly the same circumstances as the example above, the learner cuts the corner. This time, another vehicle appears approaching the end of the side road. The other driver has to brake to avoid a collision. This incident involved actual danger and, of course, the learner would fail the test.

Driving, serious or dangerous?

It is not necessary for you to be able to grade errors exactly to DVSA Driving Test criteria. While some degree of standardization is desirable, it is not absolutely essential to get it right all the time, and you need not worry unduly over this matter. In any event, the difference between serious and dangerous is purely academic, because in both instances the result is the same – failure.

The difference between a driving fault and a serious fault in this situation, however, could mean the difference between pass and fail. Using again the above examples for comparison, we can define the errors in a different way. The essential difference between the two incidents is that the driver committing the driving fault in the first example was able to see that the new road was clear. In the second example the fault was a serious fault because the driver was unable to see if the new road was clear, but was prepared to take a risk or was completely unaware of any risk.

The fault really is not a difference between two people cutting a corner with one of them getting away with it. One of them was able to see and might well have acted differently had the visibility been restricted; the other proved to be totally unaware of the danger caused by the parked vehicles. It is only possible to assess the actions of a driver in the light of the prevailing situation.

Summary of 'L' driver faults

According to *The Official DVSA Guide to Learning to Drive*, some of the most common causes for driving test failure are:

- **Eyesight test**: unable to read a vehicle number plate at 20 m (or 20.5 m for an old-style plate).

- **Highway Code**: knowledge of the Highway Code (and application of it during the drive) weak or wrong.

- **Precautions before starting engine**: handbrake not applied, neutral not selected, when starting or restarting the engine.

- **Make proper use of**:
  - **accelerator**: erratic, fierce or jerky use; poor coordination with clutch;
  - **clutch**: not depressed far enough, causing noisy changing or stalling; poor coordination with accelerator;
  - **footbrake**: not used when needed; used late, harshly or erratically;
  - **gears**: incorrect selection; coasting; not in neutral when needed; harsh control of the gear lever; looking at lever; reluctant to change; incorrect use of selector on automatic;
  - **handbrake**: not applied when required; not released when moving; used before stopping;
  - **steering** (position of hands on wheel): one hand off; both hands off; hands on spokes, rim or centre; hands crossed unnecessarily; elbow on window ledge;

- steering (oversteer): erratic control of steering; wandering on wheel; late correction; over- or understeering; jerky or fiddling movements.

- **Moving off – angle, hill, level, straight**: not done smoothly; not safe; not controlled; causing inconvenience or danger to others; not using mirrors; not looking round or not acting sensibly on what is seen; not signalling when needed; incorrect gear; lack of coordination of controls.

- **Emergency stop**: slow reactions; like a normal stop; footbrake/clutch used in a manner likely to cause a skid; handbrake used before stopping; both hands off the wheel.

- **Manoeuvres**: rushed; poor coordination of controls; too wide or too close to other vehicles; lack of observation before or during the manoeuvre; poor response to other road users; not acting on what is seen.

- **Reverse park**: rushed; poor coordination of controls; incorrect course; too wide or too close to parked car; lack of effective observations before/during exercise; poor response to other road users; not using handbrake; not finishing exercise correctly.

- **Effective use of mirrors**: not looking in good time; not acting on what is seen; omitted or used too late; used as or after movement is commenced; not used effectively before signalling, changing direction, slowing or stopping; omitting final look when necessary.

- **Give signals correctly**: signals omitted; given wrongly, or given late; too short to be of value; not cancelled after use; not repeated when needed; arm signal not given when needed.

- **Prompt action on signals**: failing to comply with signals or signs – stop, keep left, no entry, traffic lights, police signals, school crossing wardens, signals given by other road users.

- **Use of speed**: not exercising proper care in use of speed; too fast for conditions or speed limits; too close to vehicle in front in view of speed, weather, road conditions.

- **Making progress**: not making normal progress; too low speed for conditions; crawling in low gear; no speed build-up between gears; speed not maintained; undue hesitation at junctions; over-cautious to the point of being a nuisance.

- **Crossroads and junctions**: incorrect regulation of speed on approach; late appreciation of, or reaction to, junctions or crossroads; not taking effective observation before emerging at a crossroad or junction; not being sure it is safe to emerge before doing so; incorrect assessment of speed and distance of other vehicles, including cyclists; incorrect positioning for right turns, at or on approach; position taken late, too far from centre, wrong position out of narrow road, or from one-way street, wandering, wrong position at end of right turn; incorrect positioning for left turns, at or on approach; too far from near kerb; swinging out before turning; striking or running over kerb; swinging out after turn; cutting right turns when entering or leaving.

- **Overtaking/meeting/crossing other traffic**: overtaking unsafely; wrong time or place; causing danger or inconvenience to others; too close or cutting in afterwards; inadequate clearance for oncoming traffic, causing vehicles to swerve or brake; turning right across oncoming traffic unsafely.

- **Normal position**: unnecessarily far out from kerb.

- **Adequate clearance**: passing too close to cyclists, pedestrians or stationary vehicles.

- **Pedestrian crossings**: approaching too fast; not stopping when necessary, or preparing to stop if pedestrian waiting; overtaking on approach; not signalling (by arm if necessary) when needed; giving dangerous signals to pedestrians.

- **Normal stops**: stopping unsafely or in inconvenient place; not parallel to kerb; too close to other vehicles or hazards, compounding hazards.

- **Awareness and anticipation**: lack of awareness or anticipation of others' actions. (This is marked when the result of bad planning or lack of foresight involves the test candidate in a situation resulting in late, hurried or muddled decisions.)

- **Use of ancillary controls**: not using equipment that is necessary for the conditions.

At the end of the test

During the test the examiner uses the Driving Test Report to record any driving errors (form DL25A – DL25A in Northern Ireland). Other information regarding the conduct of the test is also itemized. At the end of the test a copy of the marking sheet is given to the candidate. The examiner may also discuss the reasons for failure with the candidate and the instructor. The form lists the main subjects outlined in *The Official DVSA Guide to Learning to Drive*. It should be used as a guide for both you and your pupil.

Driving Test Report

DL25A
0408

I declare that:

- the use of the test vehicle for the purposes of the test is fully covered by a valid policy of insurance which satisfies the requirements of the relevant legislation.

- I normally live/have lived in the UK for at least 185 days in the last 12 months (except taxi/private hire). See note 30.

✗

Candidate

S D/C

Application Ref.

Date D D M M Y Y Time H H M M Dr./No.

DTC Code/Authority Reg. No.

Examiner: Staff/Ref. No.

	Auto	Ext
Cat. Type		

1 2 3 4 5 6 7 8 9 0 V

Instructor Reg Instructor Cert Sup ADI Int Other C

	Total	S	D
1a Eyesight			
1b H/Code/Safety			
2 Controlled Stop			
3 Reverse / Left Reverse with trailer — control			
— observation			
4 Reverse/ Right — control			
— observation			
5 Reverse Park — control			
R C — obs.			
6 Turn in road — control			
— observation			
7 Vehicle checks			
8 Forward park/ Taxi manoeuvre — control			
— observation			
9 Taxi wheelchair			
10 Uncouple/ recouple			
11 Precautions			
12 Control — accelerator			
— clutch			
— gears			
— footbrake			
— parking brake / MC front brake			
— steering			
— balance M/C			
— PCV door exercise			

	Total	S	D
13 Move off — safety			
— control			
14 Use of mirrors- M/C rear obs — signalling			
— change direction			
— change speed			
15 Signals — necessary			
— correctly			
— timed			
16 Clearance / obstructions			
17 Response to signs /signals — traffic signs			
— road markings			
— traffic lights			
— traffic controllers			
— other road users			
18 Use of speed			
19 Following distance			
20 Progress — appropriate speed			
— undue hesitation			
21 Junctions — approach speed			
— observation			
— turning right			
— turning left			
— cutting corners			
22 Judgement — overtaking			
— meeting			
— crossing			

	Total	S	D
23 Positioning — normal driving			
— lane discipline			
24 Pedestrian crossings			
25 Position/normal stops			
26 Awareness/ planning			
27 Ancillary controls			
28 Spare 1			
29 Spare 2			
30 Spare 3			
31 Spare 4			
32 Spare 5			

33 Wheelchair Pass Fail

Pass Fail None Total Faults Route No.

ETA V P D255

Survey A B C D E F G H

Eco Safe driving — Control Planning

Debrief Activity Code

I acknowledge receipt of Pass Certificate Number: Licence rec'd Yes

Wheelchair Cert. No: COA

No

There has been no change to my health: see note 29 overleaf.

✗

When your pupil passes

The examiner will record all driving faults on form DL25, and a duplicate is handed to the candidate. The examiner will discuss any relevant points and the instructor will be invited to listen to this explanation.

A Certificate of Competence to Drive (D10) will also be issued. This allows the candidate to drive unaccompanied on any type of road, without 'L' plates. You should advise your pupils to apply for a full licence as soon as possible, and in any case within two years, otherwise the D10 will become invalid.

In Northern Ireland the successful candidate receives a pass certificate that is sent, together with the provisional licence, to the licensing department for processing. For the first year after passing the test the driver is restricted to 45 mph and must display R plates on the front and rear of the vehicle.

If your pupil fails

As well as giving the pupil a copy of the Driving Test Report form, the examiner will give a verbal report on the reasons for failure. You may sit in and listen to this explanation if you wish – it may help you advise the pupil on any further training requirements. The reverse of the form gives an explanation of the markings, and an outline of the appeals procedure.

Application for a retest can be made immediately, but the test must not be taken within 10 working days. Book the pupil a lesson as soon as possible so that your analysis and correction of weaknesses is more valid. This also allows the current standard of driving to be maintained and improved where required.

After the test

Whether the pupil has passed or failed, it is usually appropriate and advisable for you to drive the car away from the test centre as soon as practicable.

There are several reasons for this:

- You can vacate the parking space for candidates who are preparing for the next test time.
- The pupil will be feeling very elated if he or she has passed and will not be able to concentrate properly on his or her driving.

- The pupil will be disappointed, angry or upset if he or she has failed — none of which is conducive to driving.
- The test centre is not the ideal place for carrying out a post-mortem.

Pass Plus

The 'Pass Plus' scheme was set up by the DVSA in an effort to encourage newly qualified drivers to undergo further training with an ADI in a wider variety of road and traffic conditions than is required for the 'L' test. You can encourage your pupils to take the extra training by emphasizing that many insurance companies offer substantial discounts to successful participants, usually equivalent to one year's no-claims bonus.

Pass Plus is designed to 'make newly qualified drivers better drivers'. For details of the Pass Plus syllabus, see pages 166–168. Training can be taken up to a year after passing the practical 'L' Test. The insurance discount can be deferred for a further two years if the participant is driving on someone else's insurance.

Although the number of drivers taking Pass Plus is slowly increasing, this is still a vastly untapped market with very few instructors taking advantage of its potential. When ADIs were asked by the DVSA for the secret behind successful promotion of Pass Plus, some of the tips given were to:

- mention the scheme when pupils first contact you for information;
- try to involve parents, getting them to recognize the added reassurance Pass Plus gives;
- give a reminder about the scheme before and after pupils take the practical test;
- inform pupils and parents of the statistics of newly qualified drivers being involved in accidents.

Since the major part of an ADI's work is teaching new drivers, the Pass Plus scheme adds a little more variety to the job.

To register, contact the DVSA for your instructor's starter pack. These packs include all the necessary course material and are available from the DVSA in Nottingham.

Car and trailer test

From time to time you may need to train a pupil in a car towing a trailer. This is because the current regulations allow a new driver to tow a trailer where the net weight of the car exceeds the gross weight of the trailer, and if the total weight of the outfit is under 3,500 kg. For heavier trailers, or where the trailer weighs more than the car (a horsebox, for example), an additional test will be needed for category B+E.

To take this test, the pupil must:

- already hold a full category B licence;
- be over 21;
- be accompanied by a person who has held (and still holds) a full licence for B+E for at least three years.

The vehicle must carry 'L' plates (or 'D' plates in Wales if you prefer).

Minimum test vehicles

The vehicle to be used for the test must conform to the minimum test vehicle requirements. For vehicles first registered before 1 October 2003 the vehicle must be capable of 100 kph (62 mph) and the trailer must be at least 1 tonne maximum authorized mass. (Test fee: £115; evenings/weekends: £141.) A vehicle used on a category B+E test must carry a minimum weight. The minimum real weight of the trailer must be 800 kg and the minimum load requirement is 600 kg of sand or a 1000 litre IBC (intermediate bulk container).

Test centre

Vehicle and trailer tests are conducted at LGV/PCV testing stations, where there are special facilities for manoeuvring and for braking exercises.

Safety questions

At the start of the test the examiner will ask five questions on vehicle safety. As with the car test, these questions are based on the 'show me'/'tell me' principle.

The subjects covered include:

- tyres and wheels;
- brakes;
- steering;
- engine oil and fluid levels;
- lights and reflectors;
- direction indicators;
- audible warning devices;
- loading;
- trailer body condition.

Sample questions include:

- '*Tell me* the main safety factors in loading this vehicle.'
  The trainee's explanation should include 'even distribution throughout the length of the vehicle', 'securely stowed, within the size and weight limits' and 'secured so that there is no danger of the load moving or falling off when cornering or braking'.

- '*Show me* how you would check for air leaks on this vehicle.'
  The pupil would need to show the examiner the location of the air tanks and how to check the gauges for a drop in pressure, and would need to walk round the vehicle to listen for obvious leaks.

Test syllabus

Reversing

This exercise is carried out at the test centre, using an area that is set according to the size of the vehicle and trailer combined. The candidate has to reverse to the right and then to the left between cones, finishing in a simulated loading bay. The manoeuvre must be done:

- under control and in reasonable time;
- with good observation;
- with reasonable accuracy;
- inside a clearly defined boundary.

The extreme rear of the trailer should finish within a yellow painted box area at the end of the marked bay.

Braking exercise

The braking exercise takes place on the special manoeuvring area rather than on the public roads. The examiner travels in the vehicle during the exercise. The candidate is asked to achieve about 20 mph in a distance of about 200 feet, and then stop the vehicle on reaching a set of markers. The vehicle should be stopped:

- as quickly as possible;
- under full control;
- as safely as possible;
- in a straight line.

The candidate should avoid:

- driving too slowly;
- braking too soon;
- taking too long to stop.

On the road

The test is about one hour long. Because the braking and reversing exercises are carried out at the test centre, the candidate is not required to do any other manoeuvres, such as turning in the road, reversing round a corner, or emergency stop. There is, however, a requirement to move off:

- at an angle;
- on an uphill gradient;
- on a downhill gradient.

The route includes dual carriageways, one-way systems and, where possible, motorways.

Uncoupling and recoupling

At the end of the test the candidate is expected to park the outfit and uncouple the trailer. The towing vehicle is then parked safely alongside the trailer before recoupling the trailer.

Some of the key points:

- Jockey wheel lowered correctly.
- Electric lines disconnected and stowed safely.
- Stabilizing equipment removed.

- Safety chain or coupling removed.
- Coupling removed and trailer moved clear of the towing hook.
- Check that the coupling is secure by using an appropriate method.
- Wheels, legs etc are raised.
- Operation of the lights and indicators.

The pupil should be able to uncouple and recouple the vehicle and trailer confidently and without any unnecessary delay.

Medium-sized goods vehicles (Category C1)

It is illegal to act as an accompanying driver in a Category C1 (medium-sized lorry), C1+E, D1 (minibus) or D1+E vehicle unless you have passed a driving test for the category of vehicle concerned.

A supervising driver in category C1 or D1 vehicles (including vehicle plus trailer combinations) must:

- hold a full (post-1997) licence for the category of vehicle that is being driven by the learner;
- have held that licence for the relevant period of time – usually three years.

Drivers who hold category C1, C1+E, D1 or D1+E entitlements that were obtained before 1997 ('implied rights') and who passed the appropriate driving test in one of those categories before 1 May 2010 are given 'credit' for the time they held implied rights entitlement. This means that they would have held the entitlement for long enough to be allowed to accompany a learner.

If you pass the relevant test from now on, you would have to wait until you have held the new entitlement for the relevant period, usually three years, before you would be able to act as an accompanying driver in a vehicle covered by that entitlement.

These arrangements apply to accompanying or instructing on these types of vehicle and do not affect your entitlement to drive a medium-sized lorry or a minibus.

Extended driving test

If a driver is convicted of an offence of dangerous driving the court will impose an Extended Driving Test as part of the disqualification process. Similarly, courts have discretion to order an Extended Test for other offences that involve obligatory disqualification.

The Extended Test is much longer than the ordinary test, lasting about 70 minutes, and is much more demanding. During the test a wide variety of different road and traffic conditions are covered, including dual carriageways. As the candidate will hold a provisional licence, motorways are not included. Because of the extra duration of the test a higher fee applies.

The test includes all the exercises that are part of the normal 'L' test, but with particular emphasis on whether the candidate is able to concentrate for the duration of the test and whether his or her attitude to other road users is satisfactory. The current cost of the extended test is £124 for a weekday test and £150 at weekends.

DVSA service standards

Full information about complaints is given in the DVSA's Service Standards leaflet, available from the Head Office in Nottingham. The contract for driving tests is between candidates and the DVSA. If you have a pupil who has a complaint to make about any of the following, they should write to or telephone the appropriate DVSA section:

- test cancellations;
- compensation;
- lost applications;
- delays in providing tests or results;
- theory test results;
- the conduct of a practical test.

The DVSA will forward the complaint to the appropriate area customer service unit. The complaint must be set out clearly, including any redress the client is seeking.

You should note that if a pupil has a complaint about the conduct of a practical driving test, the result of the test cannot be overturned. However, if it is felt that the test was not conducted according to the relevant regulations, the pupil should contact a magistrates' court, or sheriff's court if he or she lives in Scotland, which can order a retest.

The driver　　　　　　10

As a professional driver trainer, you should have a reasonable working knowledge of the regulations and procedures relating to driving licences. Just as importantly, you need to know where to obtain up-to-date, detailed official information about the law and current procedures. Your pupils will frequently need your advice and assistance with their licence applications and with the various licence entitlements.

This chapter deals mainly with a summary of the legal responsibilities of the driver and instructor in relation to:

- driving licence regulations;
- licence categories and minimum driving ages;
- health and eyesight requirements;
- vocational driving licences;
- traffic offences and penalty points;
- accident procedures;
- vehicle regulations and documents.

To make sure that you are completely up to date with your information you should regularly check some of the following useful points of contact:

- The DVSA and DVLA websites at **www.gov.uk/dvsa** and **www.gov.uk/ dvla**
- Register with the DVSA to receive regular updates by e-mail.
- Trade magazines published by the main national ADI organizations such as the Motor Schools Association of Great Britain (MSAGB) and the Driving Instructors Association (DIA).

Driver licensing

The DVLA at Swansea issues licences for all categories. The licence shows details of all categories for which the driver has entitlement, including lorries and buses. Any provisional entitlement is shown, together with any relevant restrictions such as maximum trailer weight or 'not for hire or reward'. Driving without the appropriate driving licence entitlement usually invalidates the insurance cover.

The licence has to be renewed after 10 years to keep the photographic likeness up to date. To avoid the necessity of sending off an important document such as your passport or birth certificate, an additional service is available at most main post offices whereby your details and documents can be checked and verified at the time. For this service there is an additional fee as well as the cost of the licence. To take advantage of this service you need to attend in person at a participating post office. Some form of personal identification such as a current UK passport must support your application.

All vehicle categories are shown on the back of the licence. If a particular category is applicable an expiry date is shown. You are not entitled to drive any category that has lines in place of a date.

Licences for categories C1, C, D1, D, C1E, CE, D1E and DE are issued for a maximum period of five years.

Provisional driving licences

In order to learn to drive and to take the official driving test, a provisional driving licence must be obtained before a vehicle can be taken out on the public roads. The holder of a provisional licence may drive a vehicle only when accompanied by, and under the supervision of, a driver who holds a full licence for that type of vehicle. The supervising driver must be over 21 years of age and have held a full driving licence for the type of vehicle being driven for at least three years. This rule, however, does not apply under certain circumstances and when driving certain vehicles, for example when taking a driving test or when riding a motorcycle.

Learner drivers are now allowed to use motorways, provided that they are accompanied by a fully qualified ADI in a car with dual controls.

To validate a provisional motorcycle licence the rider must also hold a valid certificate of basic training (CBT). Note that a provisional motorcycle licence holder must not carry any pillion passenger, even if that passenger is a qualified rider or driver.

In Northern Ireland, a vehicle displaying 'L' plates is restricted to a maximum speed of 45 mph.

Driving licence categories

Mopeds

Category AM

2-wheeled or 3-wheeled vehicles with a maximum design speed of over 25km/h (15.5mph) but not more than 45km/h (28mph).

This category also includes light quad bikes with:

- unladen mass of not more than 350kg (not including batteries if it's an electric vehicle);
- maximum design speed of over 25km/h (15.5mph) but not more than 45km/h (28mph).

Category P

2-wheeled vehicles with a maximum design speed of over 45km/h (28mph) but not more than 50km/h (31mph).

The engine size must not be more than 50cc if powered by an internal combustion engine.

Category Q

2-wheeled vehicles with:

- an engine size not more than 50cc if powered by an internal combustion engine;
- a maximum design speed of no more than 25km/h (15.5mph).

Motorcycles

Category A1

Light motorbikes with:

- an engine size up to 125cc;
- a power output of up to 11kW;
- a power to weight ratio not more than 0.1kW/kg.

This category also includes motor tricycles with power output up to 15kW.

Category A2

Motorbikes with a:

- power output up to 35kW;

- power to weight ratio not more than 0.2kW/kg.

The motorbike must also not be derived from a vehicle of more than double its power.

You can also drive motorbikes in category A1.

Category A

- Motorbikes with a power output more than 35kW or a power to weight ratio more than 0.2kW/kg.

- Motor tricycles with a power output more than 15kW.

You can also drive motorbikes in categories A1 and A2.

Light vehicles and quad bikes

Category B1

Motor vehicles with 4 wheels up to 400kg unladen or 550kg if they're designed for carrying goods.

Cars

Category B – if you passed your test before 1 January 1997

You're usually allowed to drive a vehicle and trailer combination up to 8,250kg maximum authorised mass (MAM). View your driving licence information to check.

You're also allowed to drive a minibus with a trailer over 750kg MAM.

Category B – if you passed your test on or after 1 January 1997

Vehicles up to 3,500kg MAM with up to 8 passenger seats (with a trailer up to 750kg).

You can also tow heavier trailers if the total MAM of the vehicle and trailer isn't more than 3,500kg.

You can drive motor tricycles with a power output higher than 15kW if you are over 21 years old.

Physically disabled drivers with provisional category B entitlement will also have provisional entitlement to ride category A1 or A motor tricycles.

Able-bodied drivers can no longer ride motor tricycles with a provisional category B licence.

Category B auto

Category B vehicle – but only an automatic one.

Category BE

Vehicle with a MAM of 3,500kg with a trailer.

The size of the trailer depends on the BE 'valid from' date shown on your licence. If the date is:

- before 19 January 2013, you can tow any size trailer;
- on or after 19 January 2013, you can tow a trailer with a MAM of up to 3,500kg.

Medium-sized vehicles

Category C1

Vehicles between 3,500 and 7,500kg MAM (with a trailer up to 750kg).

Category C1E

C1 category vehicles with a trailer over 750kg.

The combined MAM of both can't exceed 12,000kg.

Large vehicles

Category C

Vehicles over 3,500kg (with a trailer up to 750kg MAM).

Category CE

Category C vehicles with a trailer over 750kg.

Minibuses

Category D1

Vehicles with:

- no more than 16 passenger seats;
- a maximum length of 8 metres;
- a trailer up to 750kg.

Category D1E

D1 category vehicles with a trailer over 750kg MAM.
    The combined MAM of both can't exceed 12,000kg.
    Buses

Category D

A bus with more than 8 passenger seats (with a trailer up to 750kg MAM).

Category DE

You can drive D category vehicles with a trailer over 750kg.

Other categories

Category   Vehicle

f	Agricultural vehicle
G	Road roller
H	Tracked vehicle
k	Mowing machine or pedestrian-controlled vehicle
l	Electrically-propelled vehicle
M	Trolley vehicles
n	Exempt from duty

Full details of licence categories are at www.gov.uk/driving-licence-categories.

Driving licence categories are different in Northern Ireland

For details, see www.nidirect.gov.uk.
    The normal minimum age for driving is varied in the case of:

- drivers who receive Disability Living Allowance;
- members of the armed forces;
- trainees in the Young Driver scheme;
- drivers of minibuses and PCVs in limited circumstances.

Passing a driving test for a particular category may entitle you to drive vehicles of some other categories, and may also entitle you to use the licence as a provisional licence for other vehicles. There are also certain restrictions. For example:

- If you pass the test in a car with automatic transmission you are not entitled to drive a car with manual gears.
- Passing the test on a moped does not give you motorcycle entitlement.

Driving licence application

You may apply for a full licence if you have:

- passed the driving test and you exchange the pass certificate for a full licence within two years of the date of the test;
- held a full licence issued in the Channel Islands or the Isle of Man, valid within the last 10 years; or
- held a full British licence or a full licence issued in Northern Ireland granted on or after 1 January 1976.

You may also apply for a full licence if you have been resident in Great Britain for less than one year and you surrender a valid full licence issued in the EU or some other countries. Application may be made at any time up to two months prior to the date from which the licence is required, and should be made at least three weeks before the date of commencement of the licence. The appropriate forms are normally available from post offices and local vehicle licensing offices. The completed form should be sent to the Driver and Vehicle Licensing Agency, Swansea SA99 1AB. If you need to make an enquiry about your licence, you are advised to contact the Driver Enquiry Unit, DVLA, Swansea SA6 7JL (tel: 0300 790 6801) quoting your driver number. It is worth making a note of this number in case your licence is mislaid.

If you are disqualified from driving, you will normally have to pay £65 for a new licence (or £90 for some drink/drive offences). Licences are normally valid until the applicant's 70th birthday, at which time a new licence may be issued for one, two or three years at a time, depending on health and other factors. Renewal in these circumstances is free of charge.

A duplicate or exchange licence is valid for the period of the original licence. A replacement licence that is issued after a period of disqualification is charged at the same rate as a duplicate licence. A driver who is adding an extra category to an existing licence may require an exchange licence, which is also issued where motorcycle entitlement is required, or when a licence contains out-of-date endorsements. A Northern Ireland full licence may be exchanged for a GB licence for the appropriate fee.

Table 10.1 Driving licence fees (at January 2018)

Licence type	Fee	Online	By post
First provisional licence:			
– car, motorcycle, moped		£34	£43
– bus or lorry		Free	Free
Changing provisional for full licence		Free	Free
Duplicate licence:			
– licence lost, stolen, destroyed or defaced		£20	£20
Replacement:			
– change of name and/or address		Free	Free
Exchange:			
– removing expired endorsements (photo-card to photo-card)		N/A	£20
– paper licence to photo-card		£20	£20
Adding replacement photo	£	£14	£17
Adding a test pass to a full licence		N/A	Free
New licence after revocation under the New Drivers Act		N/A	£50
Renewing a licence:			
– car licence at age 70 or over		Free	Free
– full licence for medium/large goods vehicles, minibus/bus		N/A	Free
– provisional for medium/large vehicles, minibus/bus		N/A	Free
– for medical reasons		N/A	Free
Exchanging a licence from other countries:			
– full Northern Ireland licences		N/A	Free
– full EC/EEA or other foreign licence (including Channel Islands and Isle of Man)		N/A	£43
New licence after disqualification:			
– car, motorcycle		N/A	£65
– if disqualified for some drink/drive offences		N/A	£90 or £65

NOTE All vocational licences for buses and lorries are free of charge.

A duplicate licence is needed to replace a licence that has been lost, mislaid or defaced. Replacement of a licence following a change of address is made free of charge.

For driving licence fees in Northern Ireland, see www.nidirect.gov.uk/cost-driving-licence.

Driving licence information codes

When checking a pupil's licence details you will often find certain information codes adjacent to the entitlement section. These codes specify any particular restrictions that might apply to the individual driver for a variety of reasons. For details, see www.gov.uk/driving-licence-codes.

Health and eyesight

When applying for a licence the driver has to make various declarations regarding health and eyesight. You must declare, for example, any disability or illness that might affect your driving.

You must notify the DVLA if you have, or have ever had, any diagnosis from a long list of medical conditions. Details of these conditions are available from **www.gov.uk/health-conditions-and-driving** or from the DVLA, Swansea SA99 1TU, tel: 0300 790 6801.

It is not necessary to report any medical conditions that are not likely to last more than three months.

Epilepsy: under certain circumstances a licence may be issued to someone who has been free of attacks for one year.

Pacemakers: people who are subject to sudden fainting or giddiness have, in the past, not been issued with a licence. A licence may be granted if this disability is corrected by the fitting of a cardiac pacemaker and if other medical conditions are satisfied.

Disabilities: drivers who are physically and mentally capable of driving but are otherwise disabled may be issued with a licence which restricts them to driving a vehicle of special design or construction. This type of licence does not entitle the driver to use it as a provisional licence for other groups of vehicles. If the driver then wishes to learn to drive a vehicle of a different type, he or she must first apply for the appropriate provisional entitlement to be added to the original licence.

Eyesight: in order to conform to the law there is a minimum standard of eyesight which must be reached (with glasses or contact lenses if necessary). The requirement is to read a motor vehicle number plate in good daylight at a distance of 20 metres (65 ft) or 20.5 metres for the old-style plates with seven digits. In the case of the driver of a mowing machine or pedestrian-controlled vehicle the relevant distances are 45 feet and 40 feet. If you need glasses or contact lenses in order to attain these standards, you must wear them every time you drive. It is an offence to drive if your eyesight does not meet the required standard.

An applicant who declares a disability to the DVLA may be asked for permission to obtain a report from their doctor. A licence may be issued for a limited period so that the condition can be reviewed or the licence may be restricted to certain types of vehicles.

Medical assessment

When information about a disability is received, the applicant may be required to authorize his or her doctor to give information about the disability to the Medical Adviser at the DVLA. If the applicant or licence holder fails to do so, or if the information available from the doctor is not conclusive in relation to fitness to drive, the applicant may be required to have a medical examination by a nominated doctor.

Motorcycle licences

A full car licence usually acts as a provisional licence for motorcycles and as a full licence for mopeds. A new provisional motorcycle licence is issued for a maximum of two years. If a full licence is not obtained in this time it is not possible to renew the licence for a period of one year. The provisional licence entitles the rider to use a solo motorcycle with an engine capacity of up to 125 cc. Pillion passengers are not allowed to accompany a learner rider, even if the passenger has a full licence for that type of machine.

A Compulsory Basic Training (CBT) certificate is required for all riders of mopeds and motorcycles. The learner has to undergo a short course of off- and on-road training before riding unaccompanied on public roads. On successful completion of the course, the learner is issued with a certificate that validates the provisional licence. This applies to anyone riding a motorcycle or moped on 'L' plates, irrespective of when their licence was issued, and includes full Category B (car licence) holders who have not passed the motorcycle test.

After taking CBT the learner may ride on the road, but is limited to machines of up to 125 cc with a maximum power output of 11 kW. 'L' plates must be displayed and pillion passengers are not allowed on a solo motorbike. CBT certificates are valid for two years. To obtain a full licence, both the theory and practical tests have to be passed within a two-year period.

Motorcycle licence categories

There are different procedures to follow depending on whether you want to ride a moped, a 125 machine or a larger motorbike. There are also variations depending on what licence you already hold and your age at the time of applying for the new licence.

Details of all motorcycle licence requirements are available at **www.gov. uk/ride-motorcycle-moped**.

Direct Access

Direct Access is a means of achieving an unrestricted licence without waiting for two years. It is available only to those over the age of 21, and must be taken on a motorbike that exceeds 35 kW. Training and practice can only be undertaken under the direct supervision of a specially qualified instructor, with radio communication between instructor and pupil.

For full details, contact the DVSA on 0300 200 1122.

Licence application

Provisional licence entitlement for motorcycles is normally granted for a maximum of two years. Learners are not permitted to ride on the roads until they have successfully completed CBT. The only exception to this is when they are under the supervision of an authorized instructor during the training. Mopeds may be ridden at 16 years, subject to the CBT requirements.

A full car licence normally includes provisional entitlement for motorcycles but a CBT certificate is needed to validate the licence. A full car licence issued before 1 February 2001 includes full entitlement for mopeds, and CBT is not needed in those circumstances.

Vocational licences

The DVLA issues all licences, including those for large goods vehicles (LGVs) and passenger-carrying vehicles (PCVs). The entitlement is shown on the photocard licence, with provisional entitlements indicated on the paper counterpart.

A driver who passes the 'L' test is issued with a licence for driving vehicles up to 3,500 kg or with a maximum of eight passenger seats. For driving anything over these limits, a separate test is needed for each type of vehicle. For example, you need to hold a full licence for cars before obtaining a provisional licence for medium-sized goods vehicles, and a full rigid vehicle licence is required before you can drive an articulated vehicle or draw-bar combinations. There are also restrictions on the type of trailer that can be towed. For example, a separate test and licence entitlement would be needed to tow a large trailer behind a heavy motor car if the combined weight was more than 4,250 kg or if the gross weight of the trailer was more than the unladen weight of the towing vehicle.

Road traffic law

Drivers are affected by civil as well as criminal law, and an offence in a criminal court may well be followed by another case in a civil court. For example, someone who injures a pedestrian and is found guilty of dangerous driving might later find themselves being sued for damages in a civil court.

Most of the relevant motoring law is found in the Road Traffic Act (RTA) 1991. Apart from criminal law, the RTA 1991 gives the Secretary of State for Transport the power to make other regulations regarding various motoring matters. The most important of these are the Motor Vehicles (Construction and Use) Regulations.

Much of the civil law that affects motorists is not contained in special rules relating to the roads. It is a part of the general law of the land. For example, the law of negligence applies to anyone, whether driving or not. Motorists are most likely to encounter the civil law after they have been involved in a road accident in which there has been injury to a person or damage to property. In these cases, the law allows the person injured to claim against the other driver, or the insurance company. However, a motorist may be guilty of an offence under criminal law even if no accident has taken place. An offence may have been committed even if it was not intended; for example, driving without lights at night is an offence even though the driver checked the operation of the lights before starting his or her journey. There is also a certain amount of confusion regarding *The Highway Code*. Although the *Code* is based on the specific rules of the RTA, a breach of it is not necessarily a punishable offence. However, *The Highway Code* can be used as a reference in a court when assessing the actions of a driver. A breach of a particular part of *The Highway Code* may in some cases amount to a breach of a specific part of the RTA. Nevertheless, the offence will be found to be against a section of the RTA.

Driving offences

Offences that are covered by the 1991 RTA include:

- causing death by dangerous driving;
- dangerous driving;
- causing death by careless driving when under the influence of drink or drugs;
- causing danger to other road users.

These offences are based on the actual standard of driving. 'Dangerous driving' has to have two main features: the standard of driving falls far below that expected of a competent and careful driver, and the driving must involve actual or potential danger of physical injury or serious damage to property.

The standard of driving is judged in absolute terms and takes no account of factors such as inexperience, age or disability of the driver. It is not intended that the driver who merely makes a careless mistake, of a kind that any driver might make from time to time, should be regarded as falling far below the standard expected of a competent and careful driver.

The danger must be one that a competent and careful driver would have appreciated or observed. It means any danger of injury (however minor) to a person or of serious damage to property.

Careless and inconsiderate driving is defined in relation to 'a person driving a mechanically propelled vehicle on a road or other public place'. This means that non-motorized vehicles and offences on private property to which the public have access may be included. The main constituents in this offence are referred to in terms of 'driving without due care and attention, or without reasonable consideration for other road users'.

Offences of driving without a licence, without 'L' plates, without supervision, or under the age when a licence can be obtained, are now dealt with under the offence of 'driving otherwise than in accordance with a licence'. Penalty points for this offence vary from three to six depending on the circumstances and seriousness of the offence.

Offences incurring disqualification

The following offences carry automatic disqualification:

- manslaughter caused by the driver of a motor vehicle;
- causing death by dangerous driving;
- causing death by careless driving when unfit through drink;
- dangerous driving;
- motor racing on the highway;
- driving, or attempting to drive, when under the influence of drink or drugs, or with more than the permitted blood alcohol level;
- failure to provide a blood or urine sample.

The penalties for drink/drive offences are quite severe:

For driving (or attempting to drive) when above the legal limit, the maximum penalty is up to six months' imprisonment, an unlimited fine and a driving ban for at least one year (or three years for a second offence within 10 years). These penalties also apply for refusing to provide a specimen of breath, blood or urine.

For being in charge of a motor vehicle when over the legal limit, the penalties include maximum of three months in prison, a fine of up to £2,500 and/ or a possible driving disqualification.

Causing death by careless driving while under the influence of alcohol carries a maximum penalty of up to 14 years' imprisonment, an unlimited fine, disqualification from driving for at least two years and an extended driving test before the licence is renewed.

Drink/drive offences

The legal alcohol limits in England, Wales and Northern Ireland are:

- 35 micrograms of alcohol per 100 millilitres of breath;
- 80 milligrams of alcohol per 100 millilitres of blood;
- 107 milligrams of alcohol per 100 millilitres of urine.

The limits in Scotland are lower:

- 22 micrograms of alcohol per 100 millilitres of breath;
- 50 milligrams of alcohol per 100 millilitres of blood;
- 67 milligrams of alcohol per 100 millilitres of urine.

The minimum period of disqualification is 12 months, with a minimum of three years for a second offence within 10 years.

Driver rehabilitation scheme

Drivers who are convicted of a drink/drive offence and have been banned for 12 months or more are normally offered the opportunity to take a voluntary 'driver rehabilitation course'. This enables them to have a reduction of up to one quarter off the period of disqualification. Courses are usually organized at weekends and during the evening, with a total of about 16 hours' instruction. The cost of the course (typically about £150) has to be paid by the offender.

The extended driving test

Courts have the power, for some of the more serious offences, to order disqualification until an 'appropriate' driving test is passed. These offences include motor manslaughter, causing death by dangerous driving and dangerous driving. The test is longer and more rigorous than the normal 'L' test. It therefore provides scope for the driver to be tested in a greater variety of road and traffic conditions.

In determining whether to make such an order, the court must have regard to the safety of road users. For offences involving obligatory disqualification, the 'appropriate' test is the Extended Driving Test, and this might therefore apply to the driver who has been disqualified under the 'totting up' procedure, and who has been ordered by the court to retake the test. For offences involving obligatory endorsement (as opposed to obligatory disqualification), the appropriate test is the ordinary Test of Competence to Drive.

Penalty points for some offences are graded according to the seriousness of the offence (see Table 10.5). An accumulation of 12 points within three years means that the driver will automatically be disqualified from driving, although the courts are given powers not to disqualify in exceptional circumstances. The three-year period is measured backwards from the date of the latest offence. The period of disqualification as a result of an accumulation of penalty points is:

- six months, if there has been no disqualification in the past three years;
- one year, if there has been one disqualification in the past three years;
- two years, if there has been more than one disqualification in the past three years.

Disqualification may be imposed for a single offence if the court feels that the offence is serious enough.

The 'New Driver' Act

This Act affects any newly qualified driver who accumulates six or more penalty points within two years of passing their driving test. The accumulation of six or more points (whether arising from court convictions or from fixed penalty offences) means that the licence is automatically revoked by the DVLA and the driver has to revert to a provisional licence. Both the theory and practical tests will need to be retaken before a full licence can be issued. After passing the tests a new full licence will generally include all previous licence entitlements, but the points will carry forward, as these could count towards any future 'totting up'. Recent figures from the Driver and Vehicle Licensing Agency show that about 14,000 new drivers have their licences revoked each year.

Disqualification and the ADI

One of the requirements of ADI qualification is, 'will have held a full driving licence for four years'. An important point to be remembered by professional driving instructors is that any period of disqualification from driving will involve a further period of disqualification from the ADI Register. For example, a one-year disqualification for a driving offence is followed by a four-year disqualification from the official Register. The instructor would, therefore, be unable to work as an ADI for a total period of five years.

Fixed penalties

Traffic wardens and police officers are empowered to enforce the law in connection with various offences by use of the fixed penalty system. The relevant offences include waiting, parking, loading and obstruction as well as offences relating to vehicle tax, lights and reflectors. Driving offences such as making an unauthorized 'U' turn and driving the wrong way in a one-way street are also included. The ticket is given to the driver or is fixed to the vehicle. Payment must be made within 28 days or alternatively the offender may request a court hearing. If the driver who committed the offence cannot be identified or found, the registered owner of the vehicle is ultimately responsible for payment of the fine. However, in the case of hired vehicles, special rules apply and the person who hires the vehicle will become liable for any fines or excess charges.

The extended fixed penalty scheme covers various moving traffic offences including speeding, failure to comply with traffic directions and vehicle defect offences. The following categories are included in the scheme, and for these offences the issuing of the ticket is normally the responsibility of the police:

- Contravening a traffic regulation order.
- Breach of experimental traffic order.
- Breach of experimental traffic scheme regulation in Greater London.
- Using a vehicle in contravention of a temporary prohibition or restriction of traffic on a road, such as where a road is being repaired.
- Contravening motorway traffic regulations.
- Driving a vehicle in contravention of an order prohibiting or restricting driving vehicles on certain classes of roads.
- Breach of pedestrian crossing regulations.

- Contravention of a street playground order.

- Breach of a parking place order on a road.

- Breach of a provision of a parking place designation order and other offences committed in relation to it, except failing to pay an excess charge.

- Contravening a parking place designation order.

- Breach of a provision of a parking place designation order.

- Contravention of minimum speed limits.

- Speeding.

- Driving or keeping a vehicle without displaying a registration mark or hackney carriage sign.

- Driving or keeping a vehicle with the registration mark or hackney carriage sign obscured.

- Failure to comply with traffic directions or signs.

- Leaving vehicle in a dangerous position.

- Failing to wear a seat belt.

- Breach of restrictions on carrying children in the front of vehicles.

- Driving a vehicle elsewhere than on the road.

- Parking a vehicle on the path or verge.

- Breach of Construction and Use Regulations.

- Contravention of lighting restrictions on vehicles.

- Driving without a licence.

- Breach of provisional licence provisions.

- Failure to stop when required by constable in uniform.

- Obstruction of highway with vehicle.

Penalty tickets for endorsable offences are handed to the driver, as the driving licence will have to be surrendered for possible endorsement with the appropriate penalty points. If the licence shows an accumulation of points which, together with the current offence, would bring the total to 12 points or more, the fixed penalty ticket would not be issued. In those circumstances a prosecution for the offence would follow.

If the licence is not immediately available, it must be produced within seven days at a nominated police station. A receipt for the licence is then issued, and this is an accepted document if for any reason the licence has to be produced at a later date.

The fixed penalty fines of £30, £40 or £60 are payable within 28 days (or as specified in the notice). If payment is not received in time, the charge is increased by 50 per cent. A court hearing may be requested if the driver feels that the ticket was issued incorrectly or unfairly.

National driver improvement scheme

A driver who has been involved in a road traffic incident may be offered an opportunity to attend a driver improvement course as an alternative to prosecution for careless or inconsiderate driving. Attending a course means that you can avoid a fixed penalty fine and the possibility of penalty points on the licence.

Courses usually last about one and a half days and are mainly classroom-based. You can choose to attend at a venue that is convenient to you. There is no examination or end-test – all that is required is your attendance and willingness to take part in the programme.

You are only allowed to undertake one course within a three-year period; if you are involved in another incident that is deemed to be your fault within the three years, you will be given a fixed penalty or will have to attend court.

Driver identity

The 1991 Act defines the circumstances in which a person can be required to give information about the identity of a driver who is alleged to be guilty of a road traffic offence. This is particularly important in connection with the identification of drivers involved in speeding or other offences detected by automatic devices, including cameras.

A photograph, showing the registration number, is taken of the offending vehicle. It is not intended that the registered keeper of the vehicle should bear responsibility for the offence detected by the device if someone else was driving at the time of the offence. It is, therefore, necessary to trace the driver through the registered keeper. The penalty for not providing the information has been increased to three penalty points to provide an incentive to do so.

The existing fixed penalty system requires the vehicle and the person committing the offence to be present at the time the fixed penalty ticket is issued. However, under the provisions of the RTA 1991, a conditional fixed penalty offer is available for all fixed penalty offences, including those detected by automatic cameras and other devices. These provisions allow for the police to issue a notice to the alleged offender by post.

The notice is first issued to the registered keeper of the vehicle, requiring information about the identity of the driver. The conditional offer of a fixed penalty will then be issued to the person identified as the driver of the vehicle when the offence was detected. If the information about the driver is not given, the 'keeper' of the vehicle will have committed an offence, which is now endorsable.

If the driver wishes to take up the offer of the fixed penalty, the driving licence and payment are sent to the Fixed Penalty Office and the payment is accepted, so long as the licence shows that the driver would not be subject to a 'totting up' disqualification. In those circumstances, the payment and licence would be returned and a court summons would then be issued.

Speed limits

A speed limit of 30 mph normally applies to all vehicles on a road where street lamps are positioned at regular intervals. On occasions a higher speed is allowed on such a road, in which case appropriate signs show the higher limit.

Speed limits apply to roads and vehicles, and where there is a difference the lower limit applies. The maximum speed on motorways and dual carriageways is 70 mph and on single carriageways 60 mph. However, these limits apply to cars, car-derived vans and dual-purpose vehicles adapted to carry not more than eight passengers. A different set of speed limits applies to other types of vehicles.

Penalty points and offences

Most penalty points stay on the licence for four years from the date of the offence. These mainly include offences relating to accidents, licensing, construction and use, or careless driving. Other penalty points remain on the licence for four years from the date of conviction. These generally apply to the more serious offences such as reckless or dangerous driving and drugs.

Penalty points stay on the licence for a period of 11 years (from the date of conviction) for a range of serious offences, including drink/drive offences and driving while disqualified.

For full details of all driving offences and penalty points, see www.gov.uk/penalty-points-endorsements-and-penalty-points.

Disqualification

If you are disqualified for less than 56 days the court will stamp your licence and return it to you. The stamp shows the length of time of the disqualification. You don't need to renew the licence after the disqualification. The licence is valid from the day after the disqualification ends.

Table 10.3 Speed limits (mph)

Type of vehicle	Single	Dual carriageway	Motorway
Cars, motorcyles, car-derived vans and dual-purpose vehicles	60	70	70
Cars, motorcycles, car-derived vans and dual-purpose vehicles when towing trailers or caravans	50	60	60
Motorhomes or motor caravans (not more than 3.05 tonnes maximum unladen weight)	60	70	70
Motorhomes or motor caravans (more than 3.05 tonnes maximum unladen weight)	50	60	70
Buses, coaches and mini-buses (not more than 12 metres overall length)	50	60	70
Buses, coaches and mini-buses (more than 12 metres overall length)	50	60	60
Goods vehicles (not more than 7.5 tonnes maximum laden weight)	50	60	70 (60 if articulated or towing a trailer)
Goods vehicles (more than 7.5 tonnes maximum laden weight) in England and Wales	50	60	60
Goods vehicles (more than 7.5 tonnes maximum laden weight) in Scotland	40	50	60

NOTE 1 Most vans have a lower speed limit than cars and must follow the speed limits for goods vehicles of the same weight. Vehicles under 2 tonnes laden weight may qualify as a 'car-derived van' or 'dual-purpose vehicle'. These vehicles have the same speed limits as for cars.

2 Motorhomes or motor caravans are classed as goods vehicles if they:
- carry goods for exhibition and sale;
- are used as a workshop.

If you are disqualified for 56 days or more you must surrender your licence. You need to apply to have the licence renewed. DVLA will normally send a reminder about two months before the disqualification ends.

Drivers who are disqualified for more than two years can apply to have their licences reinstated after a specified amount of time:

- For disqualification between two and four years an application can be made after two years.
- For disqualification between four and ten years the application can be made after a period equal to half the driving ban.
- For disqualification for 10 years or more the application can be made after five years.

Speed awareness course

The national speed awareness scheme allows motorists who are caught speeding the opportunity to complete a course rather than face a £60 fine and three penalty points on their licence.

Eligible drivers for the scheme are usually those who have exceeded the speed limit but not by a large amount. Individual police forces decide what their margins are.

Courses usually last four to five hours at a cost to the individual of about £100, but this varies from one provider to another.

Once you have attended a speed awareness course you are not allowed to take another one for at least three years.

Mobile phones

It is illegal to use a hand-held mobile phone while driving. This includes situations such as waiting at traffic lights or level crossings and in queues of stationary traffic. To make a call or to answer the phone you should find a safe and suitable place to park. However, in a lengthy stoppage on a motorway it would be obvious that you were not 'driving' if the engine was switched off.

The only exemption from the regulations is for calls to 999 (or 112) in a genuine emergency where it would be unsafe or impractical to stop.

Using a hand-held phone while driving can incur a fixed penalty fine of £100 with three penalty points. This amount can increase to a maximum of £1,000 if the case goes to court. The regulations also apply to anyone supervising a learner driver. As an instructor, you should be concentrating on what your pupil is doing and not be using a phone.

Hands-free equipment is not covered by the regulations, provided that the phone can be used without actually holding it.

Motor vehicle insurance

Compulsory motor vehicle insurance was introduced in 1930. At that time it was decided that insurance was necessary to make sure that people who were injured in a road accident were not left uncompensated. Property damage should be included within the minimum insurance, and this cover is required by the RTA 1988.

Other types of insurance policies have been in operation for many years, as it is recognized that there is a need for more cover than the minimum requirements of the RTA.

Types of insurance

Compulsory insurance

Users of motor vehicles must be insured with an authorized insurer against third party risks. The cover must include compensation in respect of death, injury to another person and also the cost of any emergency medical treatment. All passengers must be covered and no 'own risks' agreements are allowed between passengers and the user of the vehicle. This type of insurance policy (which is very rare) is sometimes known as a 'road traffic only' policy, and leaves the user with a vast amount of risk. As an alternative to insurance, application may be made to the Secretary of State at the Department for Transport for a warrant to enable a deposit of £500,000 in cash or securities to be made with the Accountant-General.

A vehicle must be insured at all times unless the DVLA has been notified that the vehicle is being kept off-road.

Third party property damage is a compulsory requirement under the RTA 1988.

Third party insurance only

A 'third party' insurance policy usually requires at least the minimum cover as that described above.

This type of policy would normally cover:

- liability for injuries to other people (including passengers in your car);
- liability in respect of accidents caused by them (for example, causing injury to a passer-by, or damaging his or her property by opening a car door);
- liability for damage to other people's property (for example, damage to another vehicle may be paid in full or in part by your insurance company).

For an additional fee the policy may be extended to include the risks of fire and theft. An additional premium may be required if the car is not kept in a locked garage overnight.

A 'third party, fire and theft' policy offers slightly more than the bare minimum but still leaves a lot of risk with the driver/owner/operator.

Comprehensive insurance

In view of the heavy cost of repairs, car owners take out a 'comprehensive' insurance policy. However, the term 'comprehensive insurance' can be misleading, and care should be taken in reading the small print. The term 'comprehensive' as applied to motor insurance means that a variety and a great deal of protection is provided under one policy document, but does not mean that cover is provided against every conceivable contingency of whatever nature.

This type of insurance cover will normally include the risks for third party, fire and theft, together with cover for accidental damage to your own car, medical expenses, and loss of or damage to personal effects in the car.

The policy will specify the uses to which the car may be put. For instance, a policy restricting use to social, domestic and pleasure purposes will not provide cover for any business use (including use by a driving school). There may also be a restriction to cover driving by specified drivers only, or the policy may exclude driving by certain persons.

Other restrictions vary from one insurance company to another, but it is normal practice for the company to specify an 'excess' when a young or inexperienced driver is driving the car. The excess is the amount that you would normally have to pay towards the cost of repairing your vehicle in the event of a blameworthy accident. If the accident was the fault of another driver, you might need to recover this amount from that person. In the case of driving school vehicles, the excess can vary and might be up to £250 depending on who was driving the car (or who was in charge of it) at the time of the accident.

Policies are usually invalidated if the vehicle insured is not maintained in a safe and roadworthy condition. Proof that the vehicle is insured in accordance with the RTA is given by insurers in the form of a Certificate of Insurance. The certificate is quite distinct from the policy of insurance itself. It is the certificate that must be produced when renewing the car licence; it must also be produced to a police officer on request.

Driver's responsibilities

As a driver you must provide details of your insurance to the person who holds you responsible for an accident which results in damage to his or her property. The law also requires you to give insurance details following an injury accident.

For your own convenience you should be prepared to give your insurance details following an accident, or to a police officer, who can ask to see evidence of your insurance at any time. Therefore it is in your interest, as well as those of accident victims, to keep your insurance details to hand when driving. You are advised, however, not to leave them in the car in case they are stolen.

Even with the new insurance requirements, drivers and other road users can find themselves without a source of compensation. This can happen where the accident is nobody's fault, or where you yourself are in some measure to blame. It is for you, as a driver, to consider whether you take out additional insurance cover against such risks as injury to yourself or damage to your own car in these circumstances.

EU requirements

All UK motor insurance policies must include cover against any third-party liabilities that are compulsorily insurable in any other EU member state. The full cover provided under a comprehensive policy can be extended for travel in Europe, if required. A 'green card' is no longer legally necessary but it may be prudent to obtain the card from the insurance company in order to have much wider cover. Possession of the green card can also help to eliminate some of the problems of procedure and language.

Accident procedures

An 'accident' is generally and legally regarded as one that causes injury to another person or animal, or one that causes damage to another person's vehicle or property. If you are involved in an accident you must stop and give your name, address and vehicle registration details. If there is personal injury, your insurance details must be produced to anyone who has reasonable cause to see them. You must also give information about the ownership of the vehicle. If it is not possible to exchange these details at the time, the accident must be reported to the police as soon as possible, and in any case within 24 hours. A police officer may, in certain circumstances, ask for driver and vehicle details if it is thought that the driver may have been involved in an accident.

These responsibilities apply regardless of who is to blame for the accident. Even if you feel that the accident is relatively trivial or that it was

Figure 10.1 Accident procedure flowchart

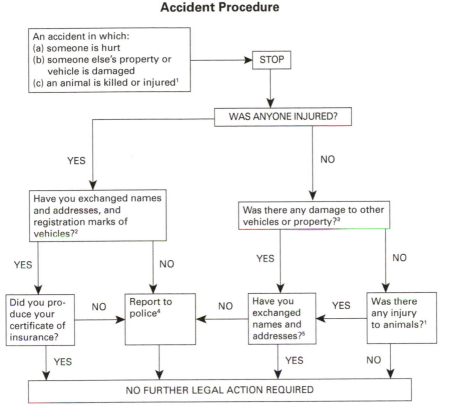

Accident Procedure

NOTE The chart shows the *minimum* legal requirements.
  1 An 'animal' is regarded as horse, cattle, ass, mule, sheep, goat, pig or dog.
  2 You must exchange details not only with the other driver, but also with any person who has reasonable grounds for asking for them.
  3 'Damage' includes roadside furniture, for example lamp posts and other fixtures.
  4 You must report an accident as soon as possible, and at least within 24 hours. Your insurance certificate must be produced at the time of reporting or within seven days.
  5 Your details must be given to the owner of the vehicle, property or animal.

not your fault, you still need to follow the procedure outlined in Figure 10.1. The figure and the notes give useful guidance for instructional purposes.

With regard to your responsibility as an instructor, it should be noted that the duty to carry out these procedures applies to a person accompanying the holder of a provisional licence and not only to the driver of the vehicle.

Legal obligations of a supervising driver

Anyone supervising a learner driver must have held a full GB licence for at least three years and be over 21 years of age. It is the learner's responsibility to check that anyone supervising his or her practice is covered by these regulations. An offence against the regulations carries a penalty of a fine, discretionary disqualification or two penalty points.

The tuition or practice vehicle must display regulation-size 'L' plates (or 'D' plates in Wales, if preferred) that are clearly visible within a reasonable distance from the front and rear of the vehicle. 'L' plates should be removed from the vehicle when a full licence holder is driving it, except in the case of driving school cars.

As well as all the legal obligations, any driver supervising a learner has certain moral obligations relating to the safety of passengers and other road users. If a driving instructor commits or aids and abets a traffic offence, the subsequent punishment resulting from a successful prosecution is likely to have disastrous effects. Even relatively minor offences will attract a disproportionate amount of bad publicity that not only causes disgrace and inconvenience, as well as possible loss of livelihood, but also stains the character of the driving school industry as a whole.

In addition to the responsibilities as driver, already covered in this chapter, the instructor has further responsibilities. Where a supervisor sees that the 'L' driver is about to commit an unlawful act, whether it is through ignorance or lack of skill, and takes no verbal or physical action to prevent it, a prosecution for aiding and abetting could ensue. For example, if a learner was about to ignore a red traffic light and the instructor allowed the car to be stopped after passing the solid line, an offence would have been committed by both persons – even though it was the instructor who finally brought the car to a stop.

You need to pay particular attention to ensure that the tuition vehicle is in a roadworthy condition and that it is taxed and adequately insured for driving instruction and driving test purposes. The vehicle must carry 'L' plates (either 'D' or 'L' plates in Wales) of the prescribed size, showing clearly to the front and rear of the vehicle.

Driving licence and eyesight

Before allowing pupils to drive your vehicle you should make sure that they have a current, valid, signed driving licence and that they can meet the eyesight requirements. You must check this even though the pupil may have signed a declaration to this effect on the licence application form. Where glasses or contact lenses are required to meet the minimum standard, they must be worn at all times while driving.

Tuition in client's vehicle

On occasions where clients may choose to provide their own car for their lessons, you must give special consideration to all the points previously mentioned, but in particular to the roadworthiness, MOT certificate and insurance cover of the vehicle.

Before agreeing to give tuition in a non-dual-controlled vehicle, you should give serious consideration to the standard, or estimated standard, the client has reached. This is particularly important if you have not had an opportunity to make a valid assessment (for example, a new client booking by telephone).

Consideration should also be given to the type of vehicle, to see if you can easily reach the handbrake (some cars have the handbrake on the right of the driver or under the dash).

Vehicle regulations

There are many laws that specify the way in which cars are to be manufactured, what equipment they must have and the condition of vehicles when used on the roads. Most of these are contained in the Motor Vehicles (Construction and Use) Regulations. Some of the rules apply only to cars first registered after a specified date; older vehicles may therefore not have to include some of the items of equipment mentioned.

Some of the basic rules apply to vehicles of any age. These include the strict rules relating to brakes and steering gear – each part of the braking system and all steering gear must be maintained in good and efficient working order at all times when the vehicle is being used on the road.

The car must be roadworthy. It is sometimes thought the MOT test certificate is a certificate of roadworthiness, but this is not so. The test system looks at the condition of certain main components, but does not necessarily consider the overall roadworthiness of the car.

The regulations contain rules about the dimensions of cars, and about the maximum overhang. The car must have wings or mudguards. The speedometer must work to within an accuracy of plus or minus 10 per cent. Driving mirrors must be fitted, and other compulsory items include safety glass, windscreen wipers, horn, silencer, seat belts and direction indicators.

Lighting

The regulations require that lights and reflectors be kept clean and in good working order. They must be maintained so that the vehicle may be driven during the hours of darkness without contravening the regulations.

Fog lamps are used as two front fog lamps (or one fog lamp and one headlamp) in darkness and fog, falling snow or conditions of poor visibility. The lights must be placed symmetrically and must be placed more than two feet from the ground unless they are to be used only in fog and falling snow.

Rear fog lamps are obligatory on cars first used on or after 1 April 1980. If one lamp is fitted it must be positioned on the offside of the car, and if two are fitted they must be symmetrical. Rear fog lamps may only be used during adverse weather conditions and when the vehicle is in motion, or during an enforced stoppage.

During the hours of darkness, a vehicle must display:

- two headlamps (when the vehicle is driven on unlit roads);
- two side lamps;
- two rear lamps; two red rear reflectors; one or two rear fog lamps (for vehicles first used after 1 April 1980).

Headlamps must be used when the vehicle is being driven on unlit roads (that is, roads where there are no street lights or where the street lamps are not at regular intervals). Headlamps must be switched off when the vehicle is stationary (except traffic stops). During daylight hours, headlamps must be used when travelling in conditions of poor visibility such as fog, smoke, heavy rain, spray or snow. If matching fog or spotlights are fitted, these may be used in the place of headlights.

Parking lights at night: a car or light goods vehicle may park at night without lights if the following conditions apply:

- the vehicle is parked on a road with a speed limit not exceeding 30 mph;

- no part of the vehicle is within 10 metres of a junction;

- the vehicle is parked with its nearside close to, and parallel with, the kerb, except in a one-way street.

The lighting regulations also permit a vehicle to park without lights in a recognized parking area, and within the confines of an area outlined by lamps or traffic signs. If these conditions are not met, lights must be shown (that is, side and rear lights).

Hazard warning lights may be used only when the vehicle is stationary for the purpose of warning other road users that the vehicle is temporarily causing an obstruction, or to warn following drivers on a motorway that there is a hazard ahead.

Parking

Common law states that a public highway is specifically for the free passage of the general public and vehicles, and there is no legal right to park on the road except in specially designated parking places or with the express permission of a police officer or traffic warden. There is no legal right even to park outside your own home. A stationary vehicle in the road or on the grass verge is technically an obstruction, even where no other road user is inconvenienced.

It is a more serious offence to park a vehicle in a position where it might constitute a danger to others (see *The Highway Code* for examples of what might be considered dangerous parking). Parking within the zigzag lines at a pedestrian crossing is an offence punishable by an endorsement. It is illegal to park on an urban clearway at the stipulated times, and on a rural clearway and motorway at any time.

Parking in controlled zones

A controlled parking zone is indicated by waiting restriction signs situated on all entrances, and is marked with yellow lines along the kerb. Restriction times vary from town to town and care should be taken always to read the signs. Parking meter zones are marked with the signs 'Meter zone' and 'Zone ends'. It is an offence to park at a meter without paying or to overstay the time paid for, or to feed the meter on return for an extended period.

Use of horn and flashing headlamps

Motor vehicles must be fitted with an instrument capable of giving audible warnings of approach. The tone of the horn must be continuous and uniform, with the exception of emergency service vehicles, which may use a two-tone horn, siren or bell. Some goods vehicles are permitted to use an instrument to announce goods for sale, but the vehicle must also carry the standard audible warning device.

The horn should be regarded as a warning instrument. It should not be used to assert a right of way, and should not be used aggressively. There are some legal responsibilities regarding the use of the horn. It must not be used when the vehicle is stationary on the road, except to avoid danger due to another vehicle moving, and may not be used in a built-up area between the hours of 11.30 pm and 7 am.

The flashing of headlamps has the same meaning as the horn. It is an indication of your presence to other road users. The lamps should not be used to tell other people what you intend to do, or to tell them what to do. Flashing headlamps can be useful in certain driving conditions – high-speed roads and where there is a high level of noise – but should not be regarded as an indication of another driver's intentions. The signal may be directed not to you but to someone else.

Seat belts

The law requires that seat belts are fitted to all the seats of new motor cars, that they should be maintained in good order, and that they conform to the regulations. The use of seat belts may be an important factor in the assessment of compensation by a court. Recent cases have shown a reduction in the amount of compensation awarded to non-users of seat belts.

Front seat belts are compulsory on cars and three-wheeled vehicles made after 30 June 1964 and first registered after 31 December 1964, and on light vans made after 31 August 1966 and first registered on or after 31 March 1967. Rear seat belts must also be used.

The use of seat belts, where fitted, by drivers and passengers is compulsory. The maximum penalty for failing to wear a seat belt is £500. Drivers are not responsible in law for the non-use of belts by adult passengers.

There are several exemptions provided in the regulations. For example, you do not have to wear one under the following circumstances:

- When driving and carrying out a manoeuvre that includes reversing.
- If you are the holder of a valid medical exemption certificate.
- When you are making a local delivery or collection round using a specially constructed or adapted vehicle.
- If a seat belt has become defective on a journey, or previously, and arrangements have been made for the belt to be repaired.

- If an inertia reel belt has temporarily locked because the vehicle is on, or has been on, a steep incline. The belt must be put on as soon as the mechanism has unlocked.
- If you are an instructor supervising a learner who is carrying out a manoeuvre including reversing.
- Driving test examiners need not wear a seat belt if they feel that the wearing of a belt would endanger them or someone else.
- When driving a taxi during normal taxi work, so long as the vehicle displays a plate showing it is licensed as a taxi.
- While driving a private hire vehicle displaying a plate showing it is licensed as such, or that it is licensed at the Hackney Carriage rate and while used for that purpose.
- If you are driving or riding a vehicle displaying trade plates and you are looking into or repairing a mechanical fault.

Other exemptions apply to people in special jobs and in certain circumstances, for example the police.

Child car seats

Children under the age of 14 travelling in the rear of cars should be restrained where an approved restraint is available. The essential point is that the seat belt or restraint should be appropriate for the age and weight of the child. The law does not require that all children in the rear of cars should be restrained, only that if an appropriate device is available it should be used. An appropriate child restraint is deemed available if carried in or on the vehicle, where there is space for it to be fitted without the aid of tools. Children can be exempt from the regulations on medical grounds.

Children up to three years old

The child must use the correct child seat. In the front seat, a child must not be carried in a rear-facing child seat where the seat is protected by an active frontal air bag. In the rear seat, children up to three years old must use the correct child restraint.

Children aged three and above.

Until they reach either their 12th birthday, or a height of 135cm, in the front seat, the child *must* use the correct child restraint. In the rear seats, the correct child restraint must be used where seat belts are fitted. There are only three exceptions to this:

In the rear seat of a licensed taxi or private hire vehicle.

If the child is travelling on a short journey in an unexpected necessity.

If there are two occupied child restraints in the rear that prevent the use or fitting of a third restraint.

Only if rear seat belts are not fitted may a child over three years old travel unrestrained. (ie in a vehicle that was originally made without seat belts).

Children over 1.35m in height or who are 12 or 13 years old

In both front and rear seats the adult seat belt must be worn if one is available.

Note: In all cases where a child under the age of 14 is involved, it is the responsibility of the *driver* to ensure that the child is correctly restrained.

Passengers over 14

When travelling in the front or rear seat, an adult seat belt must be worn. It is the responsibility of the individual passenger to ensure that he or she is wearing a seat belt.

Other vehicles

There are separate regulations covering the use of child restraints and seat belts in other vehicles (vans, buses, mini buses and goods vehicles). These details can be found at **www.childcarseats.org.uk**.

Mirrors

All new motor cars must be fitted with two rear view driving mirrors – one inside, the other mounted on the exterior offside. Most vehicles now also have a nearside door mirror. Interior mirrors must have protective edges to minimize the risk of injury in the event of an accident. This regulation also applies to the dual mirrors used by driving instructors.

Windscreen washers and wipers

The law requires that all windows are kept clean so that the driver has a clear and unobstructed view of the road. This includes keeping the windscreen free of stickers, novelties and mascots. There is a legal requirement for automatic windscreen wipers capable of efficiently cleaning the screen. The driver must have an adequate view of the road in front of the vehicle, and in front of the nearside and offside of the vehicle.

There must also be windscreen washers that work in conjunction with the wipers.

Vehicle defects

Under the Vehicle Defect Rectification Scheme (VDRS), some minor vehicle defects such as lights, wipers, speedometer and silencer may not result in a prosecution if the driver agrees to participate.

The vehicle fault must be fixed and the driver must provide proof that it has been fixed within 14 days.

Documents

Registration document

A motor vehicle must not be used on the road until it has been registered by the Driver and Vehicle Licensing Authority (DVLA). When a vehicle is first registered, a registration document (form V5 – occasionally called a 'log book') is issued, in which the appropriate details are listed. The DVLA will also issue a 'registration mark' for use on the number plates of the vehicle.

The document should normally be kept in a secure place away from the vehicle. The registration document is not in itself an indication of the owner-ship of the vehicle. It is issued to the 'registered keeper' of the vehicle. Should a registration document be accidentally lost, destroyed or defaced, a duplicate can be obtained from the DVLA, Swansea, for a fee of £25. Any alterations to the registered particulars of the vehicle should be notified immediately.

Vehicle excise licence

Application for vehicle excise licences can be made to the DVLA, Swansea, or to the local vehicle licensing office in whose area the vehicle is normally kept. Vehicles can be licensed for either 12 months or 6 months. A variable rate, based on carbon dioxide emissions, is now in place for newer vehicles. Renewals can be made online at **www.gov.uk/vehicle-tax**, by telephone on 0300 123 4321 or at a DVLA local office and most main post offices.

Duty must be paid if you 'keep' your vehicle on a highway, even if the car is never driven. If you do not tax your vehicle on time you will be liable to a financial penalty, which can rise to £1,000 if the vehicle continues to be driven on the roads. The DVLA now carries out regular checks on its computer for untaxed vehicles.

You must renew the licence before it expires. When applying for a new licence, in addition to the registration document and the appropriate fee you must provide a valid certificate of insurance and the Department of Transport test (MOT) certificate (if the car is more than three years old).

A vehicle must not be used or kept on the road after licence expiry unless an application was made before the expiry date of the old excise licence.

A licence may be surrendered for any complete months unexpired and must be posted to the DVLA before the beginning of the month for which the refund is being requested. There is no refund for parts of a month.

The keeper named on the Vehicle Registration Certificate is legally responsible for taxing the vehicle until the DVLA has been notified that it is off the road or has been sold, transferred, scrapped or exported. If you are the keeper of a vehicle but are not using or keeping it on public roads, you must make a statutory off-road notification (SORN). When you sell, transfer, scrap or export a vehicle, you must notify the DVLA. If you do not, you will continue to be liable for taxing the vehicle and for any other offences committed in the vehicle. When you notify the DVLA it will send confirmation that you are no longer responsible for the vehicle.

MOT test

Most small cars, small goods vehicles and passenger vehicles are subject to an annual test starting three years after the date of the original registration. The car may be taken for test within a month before a certificate is required. If a certificate has expired, the car may be driven to and from a test appointment without a certificate, provided it does not have a serious fault that would contravene the Construction and Use Regulations.

Testing is carried out at designated garages that display the sign of three white triangles on a blue background. The test requirements include brakes, lights, steering, stop lamps, tyres, seat belts (correct fitting, condition and anchorage points), direction indicators, windscreens, windscreen wipers and washers, exhaust systems, audible warning instruments, bodywork and suspension (in relation to braking and steering). A vehicle that passes the test is issued with a test certificate that is valid for one year.

A vehicle failing the annual test but that is left at the testing station for rectification of the faults does not incur a further fee for a re-test. A fee of half the original is charged when the vehicle is removed and then returned for the necessary repairs to be carried out within 14 days of the original examination.

The certificate must be produced, along with the other necessary documents, when applying for a vehicle licence, and on the request of a police officer.

Driving Syllabus 11

The *Car and Light Van Driving Syllabus* ('the Syllabus') is based on the DVSA's National Standard for Driving Cars and Light Vans, an evidence-based statement of the competences needed for safe and responsible driving. As a driver trainer you should also refer to the 'National Standard for Driver and Rider Training'. This Standard is explained in detail in *Practical Teaching Skills for Driving Instructors* and both documents are available at www.gov.uk/dvsa/driving-standards.

The Syllabus provides a structured approach for the driver to gain the skills, knowledge and understanding needed to be a safe and responsible road user.

As a result of using the Syllabus, drivers should be able to demonstrate:

- their knowledge and understanding of the theory of safe driving;
- their ability to apply their theoretical knowledge and understanding while driving;
- their ability to reflect on their own driving performance and to recognize the need to take remedial action if needed.

This Syllabus is intended to be used by both the learner (provisional or full licence holders) and the trainer.

The Syllabus is divided into four units:

- Prepare a vehicle and its occupants for a journey.
- Guide and control a vehicle.
- Drive a vehicle in accordance with *The Highway Code*.
- Drive safely and efficiently.

Each unit is broken down into several sections:

Unit aim – gives an indication of the areas to be covered and why this is important in the lifelong learning-to-drive process.

Learning outcomes – provides a brief overview of what the learning outcome will be as a result of studying the unit.

What you need to be able to do – to demonstrate that you have achieved the learning outcomes

What you need to know and understand – to enable you to demonstrate achievement of the learning outcomes

All driver and instructor training and testing (including the ADI Standards Check) is based on these National Standards and the Syllabus, so it is important that you are familiar with the requirements in preparation for the exams and for your work as a professional driver trainer.

1: Preparing a vehicle and its occupants for a journey

Aim

You should:

- be able to come to an informed judgement about whether you, your passengers and your vehicle are fit to undertake a particular journey;
- act appropriately on the basis of that judgement.

This unit is based on the understanding that:

- a driver's physical and emotional state;
- the physical and emotional state of any passengers;
- the roadworthiness of the vehicle

can all contribute to the cause of crashes. It aims to make sure that you have the knowledge to assess your own fitness, and your passenger's fitness, and that you can check that your vehicle is safe to drive.

The unit will help you understand the issues involved in carrying passengers, loads and animals safely and securely and how to reduce the risks that this can generate.

The final learning outcome focuses on the importance of planning a journey before setting off, taking account of road, traffic and weather conditions as well as the driver's own fitness and that of their passengers.

The underlying challenges of this unit are:

- to address the attitudes and misunderstandings that prevent drivers acting on the knowledge and understanding that they have;
- to help you recognize that the factors affecting your fitness to drive can change from day to day and over your driving lifetime.

Learning outcomes

On completion of this unit you will:

1 be able to understand when you are physically and mentally fit to drive, know when you are not fit to drive and make suitable decisions based on that understanding.

2 understand and act on a driver's responsibility to make sure that your vehicle is legally compliant.

3 be able to control the risks associated with carrying passengers, loads and animals.

4 be able to plan a journey using suitable transport.

OUTCOME 1

Be able to understand when you are physically and mentally fit to drive, know when you are not fit to drive and make suitable decisions based on that understanding

What you need to be able to do

a Actively review your fitness to drive before beginning any journey. Make alternative travel arrangements when your ability to drive safely and responsibly is affected.

b Assess whether your ability to drive safely and responsibly is affected by any drugs that you have taken.

c Assess whether your ability to drive safely and responsibly is affected by any alcohol you have consumed.

d Assess whether your ability to drive safely and responsibly will be impaired by how tired you are.

e Assess whether your ability to drive safely and responsibly will be impaired by your emotional state.

f Assess whether your ability to drive safely and responsibly will be impaired by your physical condition.

Assess whether you would benefit from having your vehicle fitted with an adaptation to help you overcome any physical impairment.

What you need to know and understand

a That your fitness to drive can be affected by various factors.

That these factors can vary from day to day and over your driving lifetime.

b How to recognize the symptoms of drug impairment.

The range of possible effects – from making you hyper-active and over confident to making you sluggish and slow in your responses – that illegal, over-the-counter and prescribed medication can have on your physical and mental ability.

The law on driving while under the influence of drugs.

That different drugs, which have no negative impact individually, can combine to produce negative effects.

That it is not always possible to predict when the effects of a drug will disappear from your system.

c Why the most desirable level of alcohol in your blood, when driving, is zero and the benefits of never drinking and driving.

That alcohol can have a range of effects, from making you more relaxed to more aggressive.

That the way you respond to alcohol may change in different circumstances but however you react it will have a negative impact on your ability to drive safely and responsibly.

That alcohol can affect men and women differently.

That alcohol can remain active in your system for a long time after you stop being aware of its effects.

What a unit of alcohol can 'look' like and how it is presented in different products such as 'alcopops', spirits or wine.

The legal limits that apply to driving with alcohol in your system. This is currently breath alcohol higher than $35\mu g/100ml$ (equivalent to blood alcohol level of $80mg/100ml$).

The penalties you will face if prosecuted.

d What can happen when you are suffering from extreme tiredness, such as falling asleep for periods of a few seconds or longer while on the move.

How to recognize symptoms of tiredness.

When you are at risk from tiredness while driving.

How factors such as poor posture and extremes of temperature can lead to tiredness.

What effective actions you can take to address tiredness when you are driving, and the limitations of some of the actions that people recommend.

e That your ability to make appropriate decisions can be impaired by the whole range of emotions, for example anger or excitement.

That emotional states can aggravate inappropriate behaviour in yourself and in other road users.

f That both long-term and temporary physical impairments, such as sports injuries and illnesses, may have an effect on your ability to drive safely and responsibly.

That the effects of physical impairment or illness that you deal with from day to day, or perhaps are not even aware of, may begin to present problems when you start to learn to drive.

That if you are affected by a physical impairment there is a range of ways in which you can be supported to overcome any problems you have.

How to recognize the effects of eyesight deterioration.

The issues involved in using light-sensitive or tinted lenses to manage eye conditions, particularly when driving in adverse weather conditions.

The effects of the physical and emotional changes associated with ageing, such as:

- slower response times;
- deterioration of vision and hearing;
- loss of muscle strength and flexibility;
- drowsiness due to medications;
- a reduction in the ability to focus or concentrate;
- lower tolerance for alcohol.

OUTCOME 2

Understand and act on a driver's responsibility to make sure that your vehicle is legally compliant

What you need to be able to do

a Make routine checks of vehicle roadworthiness in accordance with the vehicle handbook.

For example, check:

- tyres are in good condition, legally compliant and correctly inflated;
- lights are in good working order and legally compliant;
- engine oil level is correct;

- water coolant and washer reservoir levels are correct;

- there is no damage to the vehicle that would impair roadworthiness;

- windscreen and other areas of vision are clear;

- seat belts and any other safety devices are in working order and undamaged.

b If the vehicle is new to you, familiarize yourself with the layout of instruments and controls.

Make adjustments so that you can drive the vehicle in a safe and comfortable way, with good all-round visibility.

Check that there is enough fuel for your journey.

Make sure the vehicle has basic vehicle maintenance equipment, such as equipment for dealing with a puncture.

c Make sure all driver and vehicle documentation meets legal requirements by checking that:

- your driving licence is valid for the category of vehicle being driven;

- your driving licence is signed;

- you have valid insurance for the vehicle and for how you intend to use it;

- the vehicle road tax is up to date;

- the vehicle registration is updated if you change or sell the vehicle;

- the vehicle has a current MOT certificate (where applicable).

What you need to know and understand

a That different vehicles have different maintenance requirements.

The importance of regular checks (as set out in the handbook) for the vehicle you are using – including the need to make any seasonal adjustments.

How to find a copy of the handbook, or the information you need to carry out checks, if a copy is not available in the vehicle.

How to recognize early warning signs that need further investigation, such as abnormal wear on tyres or smoke in the exhaust.

The legal restrictions on damage to the windscreen and the risks associated with driving with a damaged windscreen.

How ignoring a roadworthiness issue can affect your ability to use your vehicle in a safe way, such as:

- the brakes not working properly;

- engine failure.

How failing to maintain the roadworthiness of your vehicle can affect your insurance status.

How failing to maintain your vehicle can have an adverse impact on the environment, such as:

- the effect of excessive exhaust emissions;
- excessive noise from a damaged silencer.

How to do routine maintenance tasks, such as topping up oil levels. If you cannot do them yourself, the importance of making arrangements for routine maintenance tasks to be completed by a competent person before you use your vehicle.

Your responsibilities to dispose of waste products (for example used oil, batteries and old tyres) appropriately, and the impact of failing to do so.

b How to use the handbook to check the layout and operation of instruments and controls each time you use a new vehicle.

How to adjust a new vehicle to suit your needs, such as by altering the position of:

- your seat (including the head restraint);
- the steering wheel;
- the mirrors.

How to identify:

- the fuel type for your vehicle;
- the tank capacity;
- whether there is a reserve tank from the handbook or from symbols on the filler cap.

That each vehicle you use may:

- have different gear ratios;
- be a different width, height or length;
- handle differently;
- have different systems and controls fitted and that you may need to take time to adjust to these differences.

Where basic maintenance equipment is located and how it can be accessed if the vehicle breaks down.

c That you must have a valid, signed driving licence and must be aware of and act on any restrictions that may apply, such as:

- provisional entitlement;
- rules on towing a trailer;
- wearing glasses or contact lenses when driving.

That you must display red L plates (red D plates in Wales) if you are a learner driver.

How to check the licence category entitlement and renewal date of your driving licence, which is separate from your entitlement end date.

That you must inform the DVLA if you change your name or address, and about certain changes to your health and how to find out which changes this applies to.

The importance of keeping the vehicle Registration Document up to date and the owner's responsibility to notify the DVLA of any change of ownership.

The operation of the Statutory Off-Road Notification (SORN) process.

How to apply for vehicle road tax.

When an MOT test certificate is required.

The requirement for a valid and legal insurance certificate covering at least third party liability.

The factors that affect the cost of insurance, such as:

- vehicle engine capacity and performance;
- age and driving record of the driver(s);
- the address where the vehicle is kept;
- the main purpose of driving.

That, if asked, you must be able to produce:

- your driving licence;
- a valid insurance certificate;
- a current MOT certificate (if applicable) either immediately, or within seven days to a police station.

OUTCOME 3

Be able to control the risks associated with carrying passengers, loads and animals

What you need to be able to do

a Make sure that your passengers do not affect:

- your ability to drive safely and responsibly;
- other road users.

b Make sure passengers are correctly and safely seated.

c Make sure loads are secure and evenly distributed.

d Allow for the way that carrying passengers or loads may affect the handling characteristics of your vehicle.
Manage the effect of extra weight and its distribution.
Manage the effect of reduced visibility.

e Make sure animals are secure and restrained in the vehicle.
Make sure that animals carried or left in the vehicle have enough air and are not too hot or too cold.

What you need to know and understand

a That a passenger who is:

- taking drugs;
- drunk;
- emotionally disturbed; or
- otherwise agitated

may affect your ability to drive safely and responsibly and may also affect other road users.
   That it is your responsibility to take suitable action to lessen that risk.
   That simply talking to your passengers is a risk if you allow it to distract you from what is happening on the road around you.
   That children as passengers can affect your ability to drive safely and responsibly because:

- they may be noisy or physically disruptive;
- your natural reaction to children's needs may override your ability to focus on the driving task.

b When you are legally responsible for passengers using their seatbelts.
The law on the use of booster seats, child seats and carry cots.
   How to fit booster seats, child seats and carry cots so that they are secure and do not interfere with the operation of controls or other safety devices such as airbags.
   The importance of head restraints and how to adjust them correctly.
   How many passengers your vehicle can carry safely and legally.
   The potential dangers of carrying too many passengers or seating them inappropriately.

c How to pack and transport loads safely.

The types of load-securing equipment that are available, such as roof racks and cycle carriers, and when to use them.

What might happen if you carry unsecured loads, for example if you are required to brake suddenly or take avoiding action.

That you must not allow any load to stick out dangerously from your vehicle.

The rules that apply to the carriage of hazardous goods, such as fuel.

d That the carriage of passengers or loads can affect vehicle handling when cornering, accelerating and braking.

That older vehicles may be more affected by carrying passengers or loads than newer vehicles fitted with stability control systems.

How to use the vehicle handbook to find out what adjustments you should make to your vehicle when carrying passengers or loads, such as re-aligning headlights and adjusting tyre pressures.

That your view may be restricted when you carry passengers or a load, and that you need to take active steps to maximize visibility in these situations.

e How to secure animals safely.

The particular risks that animals pose for drivers, such as:

- interfering with the control of the vehicle;
- causing distractions;
- being a physical hazard if you brake suddenly.

The conditions animals need when being carried in or left in a vehicle, such as fresh air and shade from the sun.

The rights that some authorities have, such as entering a vehicle to release an animal.

OUTCOME 4

Be able to plan a journey using suitable transport

What you need to be able to do

a Choose a suitable mode of transport based on your understanding of:

- your fitness and needs;
- the fitness and needs of any passengers;
- the environmental, economic and personal safety implications of different modes of transport.

b Plan a suitable route and calculate the time required for your journey. Choose roads that are:

- suitable for your vehicle;

- not badly affected by weather conditions, traffic volume or road works.

    Choose a suitable alternative route if appropriate.
    Choose locations for rest breaks and refuelling.
    Memorize key route references where necessary.

What you need to know and understand

a How any of the factors identified in LO1 above might affect your choice of transport.

How the factors that affect your choice of transport may change from day to day and over time.

The costs and benefits of different modes of transport such as walking, taking public transport or car sharing.

The environmental impact of different types of vehicle and engines, such as on climate change and air quality, and the benefits of making a suitable choice.

b The use and limitations of the range of tools available to help you plan your journey, such as:

- maps;

- the internet;

- weather reports;

- GPS facilities;

- hotlines.

The need to build in extra time to allow for unforeseen delays.

How particular road conditions, such as rush hour congestion, may affect your ability to drive safely and responsibly, given your vehicle and your level of experience.

How particular road conditions, such as rush hour congestion, may affect fuel consumption and the importance of planning refuelling locations.

The importance of taking regular breaks from driving.

The dangers of not recognizing the onset of dehydration and the effects of hunger.

The operation and impact of traffic-calming legislation, such as inner city congestion charges.

2: Guide and control a vehicle

Aim

This overall aim of this unit is that the driver should be able to guide and control their vehicle safely and responsibly, taking into account road, traffic and weather conditions.

This unit is based on the understanding that driving is a complex task; it involves taking in a large amount of information and responding to it appropriately. To be able to do this a driver must be able to constantly scan the world around them, understand what is happening and identify possible hazards and risks.

A key part of being able to manage this complexity is the ability to master basic driving skills, such as steering and coordinating the use of controls, so that the driver does not have to think about doing them.

Acquiring these skills will provide a driver with the basic blocks on which they can then build. It is important, therefore, that they work through any factors or issues that are getting in the way of their learning. It is also important that they get as much supervised practice as they reasonably can. Accompanying drivers can play a vital part in this process.

Although a learner may not experience towing a trailer or caravan while they are learning they will be able to do so when they pass their test (within the restrictions of the licence category). It is important, therefore, that they understand the principles.

Learning outcomes

On completion of this unit you will:

- treat learning to drive as an ongoing learning experience.
- be able to start, move off, stop and leave a vehicle safely and appropriately.
- be able to drive and manoeuvre a vehicle safely on different road surfaces and in different weather conditions.
- know the legal constraints that apply and the principles of towing a trailer or caravan safely and responsibly.

OUTCOME 1

Treat learning to drive as an ongoing learning experience

What you need to be able to do

Recognize and keep up to date with changes in the driving environment, such as:

- *The Highway Code* and other rules and regulations;
- vehicle and road technologies.

Recognize changes in yourself and your approach to driving that might happen, for example if you start to drive for work or become a parent.

Continuously evaluate your driving performance, in relation to any changes in yourself or the environment.

Take steps to improve or adjust your driving, including seeking additional training or development, so that you can continue to drive safely and responsibly.

What you need to know and understand

How to access the most up-to-date information on:

- rules and regulations relating to driving;
- the use of your vehicle;
- vehicle technologies;
- road technologies such as active traffic management systems (managed motorways).

Why it is important to remain up to date in relation to your responsibilities as a driver and as your life changes, for example if you:

- drive for work and are subject to time pressures;
- become a parent and carry your children as passengers.

That short-term changes to yourself or in your driving environment may require an adjustment in the way you are driving, for example driving in another country.

How to reflect on your overall ability to drive safely and responsibly and to identify and implement appropriate strategies for overcoming any problems or deficiencies that you identify.

That ongoing reflection on your ability to drive safely and responsibly will help you become and remain a better and safer driver.

The importance of ongoing driver development in supporting safe driving.

OUTCOME 2

Be able to start, move off, stop and leave a vehicle safely and appropriately

What you need to be able to do

a Carry out pre-start checks in line with the vehicle handbook and ensure the vehicle is secure and safe to start.
Consider the effects of starting the engine on other road users including vulnerable road users.

b Monitor instrumentation and gauges during engine start up.
Correctly react to instrumentation and gauges during engine start up.

c Start the engine using an appropriate method.

d Switch lights on, if required.

e Coordinate the use of controls to move off safely and under control in different situations.
Check brakes when first moving off.
Recover quickly and effectively if the vehicle stalls.
Only move off when it is safe to do so, taking all-round effective observations, including blind areas.
Move off safely and under control, at an angle, from behind a parked vehicle or obstruction.
Consider risks to vulnerable road users.

f Stop the vehicle in a safe, legal and convenient position.
Use the parking brake to secure the vehicle.
Switch off the engine and ancillary controls.
Make sure the correct lights are left on, where required.
If appropriate, select a gear to make sure the vehicle is safe when parked and the engine is turned off (including the park position for automatic transmission vehicles).
If appropriate, position the steer wheels of the vehicle to increase security when parked on a gradient.
Secure the vehicle against theft.

What you need to know and understand

a The importance of carrying out checks prior to starting the engine.
Why you should make sure the vehicle is secure and the transmission disengaged when starting the engine.

That starting your vehicle may be taken as a sign that you are about to move off.

That some groups of road users (such as pedestrians, cyclists or horse riders) may be startled when you start your engine when they are nearby.

b How to use the vehicle manual to identify the main visual aids on the instrument panel (such as oil warning light, rev counter, parking brake) and what they should do during start-up.

That dashboard displays will be set out differently in different vehicles.

What to do if any warning light stays on or fails to come on.

c Different methods for starting vehicles, such as key, push button or card.

d How to operate light switches in your vehicle, referring to the vehicle handbook if required. When to use the different vehicle lights, such as:

- dipped and full headlights;
- front and rear fog lights.

e How to use the 'biting point' to help you coordinate the use of the clutch and the accelerator.

The use of the footbrake when on a downward slope.

The importance of checking the operation of the brakes before moving off.

What causes an engine to stall and how to re-start safely and effectively.

How to make effective observations when moving off, including what 'blind spots' are and how to check they are clear.

The importance of using a safe and systematic routine when moving off, including observations and appropriate signals.

Who vulnerable road users are when moving off, such as:

- elderly pedestrians;
- children;
- deaf or partially sighted pedestrians;
- cyclists;
- motorcyclists;
- horse riders.

f The importance of selecting a safe, legal and convenient stopping location.

The importance of using a safe and systematic routine when intending to stop the vehicle, including the use of observations and appropriate signals.

The correct use of the parking brake when leaving a vehicle.

Why you must switch off your headlights, fog lights and engine when parking.

When you should use parking lights.

The potential consequences of opening a door when it is not safe to do so, in particular on the offside (driver's side) of the vehicle.

How the position of the steer wheels can help to make sure the vehicle is secure on a gradient.

The importance of securing the vehicle by:

- keeping luggage out of sight;

- locking doors;

- applying any additional security measures (such as anti-theft devices, alarm and/or immobilizer and visible security devices).

OUTCOME 3

Be able to drive and manoeuvre a vehicle safely on different road surfaces and in different weather conditions

What you need to be able to do

a Monitor and respond to information from instrumentation, driving aids and the environment.

Respond correctly to gauges and warning lights when driving.

Use switches and other controls in response to changes in road surfaces and weather conditions, as required.

b Use a safe and systematic routine such as 'mirrors, signal, manoeuvre' whenever manoeuvring.

Effectively indicate your intentions to other road users.

Make use of mirrors, and other aids, to effectively monitor other road users and hazards.

c Use the accelerator smoothly and effectively to maintain and change speed.

d Brake safely using appropriate techniques.

Stop accurately as and where necessary.

Make appropriate use of the parking brake.

Stop the vehicle safely and under control in an emergency.

e Steer your vehicle smoothly and effectively to maintain and change position on the road, on a straight course and in corners or bends.

Hold the steering wheel so that you are in full control.

Keep control of the steering wheel when changing gear or operating another control.

Use maximum steering lock where necessary when manoeuvring.

f Use the gears smoothly and effectively to maintain speed and minimize environmental impact.

Change gears smoothly and in good time.

Use a suitable gear for speed and driving conditions, and use selective gear changing.

Use an automatic gear box effectively if fitted.

g Coordinate the use of clutch, gears, accelerator, brakes (accelerator and brakes on an automatic) and steering to carry out the following manoeuvres safely, responsibly and accurately, with consideration for other road users and awareness of blind areas:

- reverse to left;
- reverse to right;
- perform controlled stops;
- perform parallel forward parking;
- perform parallel reverse parking;
- perform forward parking;
- turn in the road.

What you need to know and understand

a The meaning of dashboard warning lights and how to respond to them correctly.

What effect changing road or weather conditions might have on the handling of your vehicle.

How to operate ancillary controls in response to changes in road surfaces and weather conditions, for example:

- wipers;
- climate and ventilation controls;
- demisters;
- fog lights;
- traction control.

The rules on driving in adverse weather conditions, for example when to use dipped headlights.

The risks of not knowing the location of switches and controls while on the move.

b How to use a safe and systematic routine such as 'mirrors, signal, manoeuvre' so that:

- you know what is happening around you on the road;

- other road users know what you intend to do.

When and how to safely signal your intentions using indicators and, where appropriate, arm or hand signals.

When and how to use other 'signals', such as positioning on the road, to communicate or reinforce your intentions to other road users.

When and how to check mirrors to monitor the actions of other road users.

The use and limitations of internal and external mirrors.

How different types and shapes of mirror can make an object appear to be closer or further away than it is.

c How uneven use or overuse of the accelerator can reduce your ability to drive safely, especially in slow moving traffic.

How overuse of the accelerator can have a negative impact on the environment, for example by increasing harmful emissions or making too much noise.

What engine braking is and when to use it.

The use of cruise control systems, their potential benefits to the environment and their potential adverse impacts on driver fatigue and safety.

d How much pressure to apply to the brakes in varying road and traffic conditions.

The principles of varying braking systems, for example anti-lock, and how to use them to brake effectively.

How overall stopping distances:

- vary at different speeds;

- vary with different road and weather conditions;

- are broken into thinking distance and braking distance.

That while road and weather conditions may affect braking distance, thinking distance will be affected by your own physical and emotional condition.

The importance of looking well ahead so that you are able to stop within the area you can see to be clear.

The effect on your vehicle's stability if you brake on a bend.

How to stop your vehicle as quickly and as safely as possible in an emergency.

e The steering characteristics of your vehicle, such as its turning circle. How to steer smoothly and effectively, keeping complete control of the vehicle, when driving in varying road and traffic conditions.

What is meant by 'understeer' and 'oversteer' and how these affect the vehicle, for example, if you have to make a sudden change in direction.

That in certain conditions a vehicle can lose traction and skid, so that the wheels no longer grip and you cannot steer or brake effectively.

The use of systems that are designed to prevent you losing traction, such as 'ESP'.

How to avoid going into a skid, and what to do if you do.

f How to use the gears to progress safely and efficiently given the performance characteristics of your vehicle and the road conditions. How to coordinate the use of the clutch and the gears smoothly when moving away, changing gear or stopping.

How to use the clutch to control the speed of the vehicle when manoeuvring in a very tight space.

The problems and risks of not fully releasing the clutch, or 'riding the clutch', during normal driving.

The environmental impact of inappropriate use of gears.

The effect that carrying passengers or a load will have on the gears you use.

The importance of timely gear selection when ascending or descending gradients.

The use of gears when parked on a gradient.

The use of various automatic and semi-automatic transmission systems.

The use of 'kick down' to a lower gear on vehicles with automatic transmission.

The use of 'lock up' on automatic transmissions.

g The importance of coordinating the use of clutch, gears, accelerator, brakes and steering, and the effects of failing to do so. How to select a safe, convenient and legal location for manoeuvring.

The relevance of a safe and systematic routine such as 'mirrors, signal, manoeuvre' when preparing to carry out, or during, a manoeuvre.

How to take effective observation when manoeuvring, with particular attention to blind spots and to vulnerable road users.

How to stop your vehicle under full control.

How to reverse safely into a side road on the left.

How to reverse safely into a side road on the right.

How to carry out any parking exercise safely, on road and off road, including judging how much space is required if parking on the road.

How to carry out a turn in the road safely.

The rules about where you may and may not carry out turns in the road or U-turns.

Why you should not reverse your vehicle further than necessary.

How to make controlled use of the accelerator, in conjunction with the brakes, when manoeuvring a vehicle with automatic transmission.

What is meant by 'vehicle creep' and its pros and cons.

OUTCOME 4

Know the legal constraints that apply and the principles of towing a trailer or caravan safely and responsibly

What you need to be able to do

a Identify whether you are qualified to tow a particular trailer or caravan.
Identify whether your vehicle is suitable to tow a particular trailer or caravan.

Correctly and safely couple and uncouple a trailer or caravan.

Make sure any load is correctly distributed between the towing vehicle and the trailer or caravan.

Make sure any load is secure.

Allow more time and brake earlier when slowing down or stopping.

Make allowances for the extra length of your vehicle, particularly when turning, emerging at junctions or overtaking.

Make allowances for the extra height or width of your vehicle, particularly when planning routes or driving unfamiliar routes.

b Safely steer a trailer or caravan in reverse.

What you need to know and understand

a The rules and regulations on the size and weight of trailer or caravan that you can tow on your licence.
Whether your vehicle is suitable to tow a particular trailer or caravan.

What is meant by 'nose weight' and how it affects the use of a trailer or caravan.

The safety procedures you need to apply when coupling or uncoupling a caravan or trailer, such as fitting additional mirrors.

How to fit and use stabilizers and other safety devices.

How to load and secure the contents of the trailer or caravan safely.

That a trailer or caravan may affect the handling characteristics of your vehicle and how to compensate for those effects.

How to make allowances for the extra length of your vehicle and the changed geometry of the combined units when turning.

That your ability to make effective observations may be affected by towing a trailer or caravan and how to overcome this.

The importance of checking whether height and width restrictions apply to your intended route.

The need to be prepared for the possibility of a trailer or caravan failing, such as:

- carrying a spare wheel and any other necessary equipment for the trailer;
- checking your rescue service cover will include a trailer or caravan.

b The principles of steering when reversing a trailer or caravan.

3: Driving a vehicle in accordance with *The Highway Code*

Aim

The aim of this unit is to help you understand why it is important to understand and comply with *The Highway Code*.

It is important that you do not think of *The Highway Code* as just something that you have to learn to pass your theory test. You should think about what it has to tell you each time you go out on the road. Each time you come across a new situation on the road you should be thinking about what *The Highway Code* has to say about that situation.

Know Your Traffic Signs contains information on the traffic signs and signals that you will come across when driving. *The Highway Code* contains a wide range of advice and rules about how you should behave in particular situations whilst driving. If you understand what to do when you see a particular signal, or what the *Code* advises about how to handle a particular situation, it will make it much easier for you to understand what is happening around you when you are driving.

Failing to follow the advice and rules set out in *The Highway Code* can result in serious consequences for you, your passengers and other road users.

Learning outcomes

On completion of this unit you will:

- be able to negotiate the road safely and responsibly in changing road and traffic conditions.

- be able to comply with signals, signs, markings and traffic calming measures.

OUTCOME 1

Be able to negotiate the road safely and responsibly in changing road and traffic conditions

What you need to be able to do

a Deal with all types of junction or roundabout safely and in line with the guidance given in *The Highway Code*.
Use a safe and systematic routine such as 'mirrors, signal, manoeuvre' to deal with junctions and roundabouts.

   Turn left, turn right and go ahead correctly.
   Cross the path of oncoming traffic safely when turning right.
   Emerge into the traffic stream correctly from both left and right sides.
   Interact safely and appropriately with other road users.

b Maintain a suitable position on the road. Keep to the left in normal driving, unless otherwise instructed.
Use lanes as described in *The Highway Code*.

   Keep a safe position in the lane. Change lanes safely and responsibly when necessary.

What you need to know and understand

a The issues you will face when dealing with different types of junctions. The signs and signals that you may see and the rules that apply to each type of junction, including T junctions, Y junctions, staggered junctions, crossroads and roundabouts.

b What *The Highway Code* says about how you should go ahead and turn left and right at junctions and roundabouts to make sure that you:

- are safe;

- do not delay other road users;

- do not put other road users at risk.

Why it is important always to use a safe and systematic routine at junctions and roundabouts including:

- effective observation;

- appropriate and timely signalling of your intentions.

How to cross the path of approaching traffic safely.

The signs and signals that you may see and the rules that apply when joining and leaving streams of moving traffic via controlled and uncontrolled acceleration or deceleration lanes.

That active traffic management systems (or managed motorways) may display signals that change the use of lanes and the priorities at junctions and on slip roads.

The importance of being aware of and giving consideration to vulnerable road users.

Why some road users may position themselves differently at junctions or roundabouts to the way you would expect them to.

c What *The Highway Code* says about positioning your vehicle on the road. The importance of maintaining a safe road position at all times. The importance of lane discipline and suitable lane selection, including when driving on one-way streets.

How to make effective observations and signal your intentions clearly and in good time before changing lanes.

How to judge where to position your vehicle and how to adjust your speed when approaching a bend, taking into account factors such as:

- the road type;

- weather conditions;

- how far you are able to see beyond the bend;

- possible hazards (such as pedestrians, cyclists and horse riders).

That you must not enter a road, lane or other route reserved for specific vehicles.

OUTCOME 2

Be able to comply with signals, signs, markings and traffic calming measures

What you need to be able to do

a When driving, respond correctly to:

- warning signs;
- information and direction signs.

When driving, comply with:

- mandatory and prohibitive signs giving orders;
- all lights that control traffic.

When driving, deal legally and safely with all types of:

- pedestrian crossing;
- railway or tram crossing.

b Comply with all markings on the carriageway.

c Comply with signals given by any authorized person including:

- police officers;
- traffic wardens;
- school crossing wardens;
- Highways Agency Traffic Officers;
- VOSA officials.

Respond appropriately to signals given by other road users.

What you need to know and understand

a The meaning of all signals, including lights, and all signs that you might encounter on the roads, including warning, mandatory, information and direction signs.

How you should respond to all signals and signs that you might come across on the roads, as detailed in *The Highway Code*.

The importance of observing the speed limits for the road you are on and your vehicle.

That your use of some roads, such as motorways, may be restricted by the category of your licence.

How to act when approaching all pedestrian crossings, whether controlled or uncontrolled.

How to act when approaching all railway or tram crossings, whether controlled or uncontrolled.

b What all road markings mean, including:

- lines in the centre or along the side of roads;
- lines at junctions;

- segregation markings for buses, tram and cycles;
- ghost islands;
- traffic calming measures;
- written signs.

How you should respond to all road markings that you find on the roads, in line with *The Highway Code*.

c Who has authority to stop or direct you on the road.
  The meanings of the hand or arm signals they may use to direct you.

  The importance of stopping when a school crossing patrol shows a 'stop for children' sign and what the law says about failing to stop in this situation.

  The signals that may be given by other road users, and the potential for misunderstanding what other road users mean.

  The risk involved in relying on a signal from another road user and the importance of making your own judgement in any particular situation.

4: Drive safely and efficiently

Aim

This unit focuses on:

- minimizing risk when driving;
- defensive and eco-safe driving techniques;
- the interaction between road users.

The aim of this unit is to help you understand how your own behaviour and attitudes, and those of other drivers, affect your ability to drive safely and responsibly. It gives you some tools to help you to work with other drivers. The final learning outcome focuses on how to deal with incidents that may occur when driving.

In this unit you may feel that you are covering some things again. This is partly true, but this is part of learning to drive. You can now bring together the skills and knowledge that you have built up in the first three units. You should see it as the stepping stone to being able to drive independently and safely to a consistent standard.

Learning outcomes

On completion of this unit you will:

- be able to interact appropriately with other road users in varying road and traffic conditions.

- be able to minimize risk when driving in varying road and traffic conditions.

- know how to behave appropriately at incidents.

OUTCOME 1

Be able to interact appropriately with other road users in varying road and traffic conditions

What you need to be able to do

a Give timely, clear and correct signals according to *The Highway Code*. Position your vehicle to support your signalled intentions.

Use horn and lights correctly to communicate with other road users.

Avoid showing aggressive or negative behaviour toward other road users.

b Actively scan the road space all around, both close up and into the distance.

Make sure that you are aware of all other road users (including pedestrians, cyclists and motorcyclists) and have time to plan what you are going to do.

Show awareness of other road users, anticipate what they are likely to do and give them time and space to manoeuvre.

Allow for other road users who may not react:

- as quickly as you expect;

- in the way that you expect.

Allow for others' mistakes.

Monitor and manage your own reactions to other road users.

Identify and respond correctly to vulnerable road users.

Respond correctly to emergency vehicles.

c Make progress on the road by:

- driving at a suitable speed for the road and conditions;

- overtaking when:
  - necessary;
  - legal;
  - safe.

Allow others to make progress.

What you need to know and understand

a The correct use of all signals according to *The Highway Code* and when they need to be given.

The importance of cancelling signals so that they do not mislead other road users.

How to link the use of signals to the application of a safe and systematic routine such as 'mirrors, signal, manoeuvre'.

How positioning of the vehicle can support or contradict the signals you are giving.

The rules on using the horn and headlights as a warning.

The rules on the use of hazard warning lights.

How negative behaviour (such as road rage) toward other road users, by you or your passengers, can lead to further negative behaviour by other road users.

How to manage your own behaviour while driving to:

- avoid aggressive or negative behaviour toward other road users;
- minimize aggressive or negative behaviour toward you.

That showing courtesy and restraint can have a positive effect on others.

b How awareness and anticipation of other road users, and planning your actions, can contribute to a safe and efficient driving environment.

The importance of giving other road users the time and space they need in varying road and traffic conditions, for example when overtaking.

That being patient and considerate generally results in everybody getting where they want to more quickly and safely.

The particular needs of road users whose ability to manoeuvre is limited in some way, such as by disability, age or lack of experience.

The particular need to make allowances for those:

- accompanied by young children;
- riding or leading animals that might behave unpredictably.

How to respond when emergency vehicles are on call and how to assist their safe progress, whether they are approaching from behind, ahead or from side roads.

c How to select a suitable speed for the road and conditions.

How to make progress and how failing to do so can lead to negative behaviour in other road users.

What to consider when deciding whether to overtake.

Where you may and may not overtake.

That if you decide not to overtake a slower moving vehicle you should leave a gap so that others can overtake you if they wish to.

OUTCOME 2

Be able to minimize risk when driving in varying road and traffic conditions

What you need to be able to do

a Drive defensively, which means that you:

- judge speed and distance correctly and effectively;
- create and maintain a safe 'driving space' around your vehicle;
- do not encroach unnecessarily on other road users' space;
- can stop safely within the distance you can see to be clear;
- always use a safe and systematic routine when driving, including effective scanning;
- look for clues for potential hazards and anticipate situations that might turn into a hazard;
- prioritize hazards and potential hazards effectively;
- ensure that your vehicle is in an appropriate position on the road, in the right gear and travelling at the right speed so that you can respond appropriately to any hazard;
- maintain your attention to the driving task when faced with distractions.

Be aware of your own physical and mental fitness and assess whether it is affecting your fitness to drive.

Where you identify weakness in your ability to drive safely and responsibly, take steps to improve that ability.

b Follow the principles of eco-safe driving, by:

- removing excess weight (including roof racks or storage) from your vehicle when not needed;

- planning well ahead, as you make progress on the road, so that you can accelerate, decelerate and brake smoothly and progressively to minimize fuel consumption;

- using the highest gear appropriate for the road and traffic conditions;

- using cruise control, where and when appropriate;

- making appropriate decisions about the use of ancillary equipment;

- turning off the engine, when appropriate.

What you need to know and understand

a How to adjust your separation distance from other road users and create a safe driving space when on the move and when stationary.

That your safe driving space will vary in different road and traffic conditions, for example when driving:

- on wet roads;

- in traffic queues;

- in tunnels.

The importance of adjusting your vehicle's speed to what you can see ahead.

The importance of the consistent application of safe and systematic routines.

The importance of active scanning and how anticipation can help to make sure that you are in a position to respond safely to a hazard.

Techniques for scanning in a systematic way.

What affects, and how to maximize, your zone of vision.

How to look for and spot the clues that point to potential hazards.

How to position your vehicle and make sure that you are in the right gear and travelling at the right speed to be able to respond to any hazard that emerges.

How distractions (such as disruption from passengers) can affect your ability to drive safely.

How to spot situations that could lead to a loss of attention or awareness in different driving situations.

How to maintain attention and awareness in different driving situations.

The importance of constantly reviewing your driving performance as:

- you gain experience;
- your life circumstances change.

b That you should not put eco-driving techniques above safe driving principles, although generally the two approaches are mutually supportive.

How carrying unnecessary equipment or luggage, such as roof-top boxes, can increase fuel consumption.

How to plan (linked to the early identification of hazards to avoid harsh acceleration and braking).

The importance of the smooth application of all controls, for example smooth acceleration, minimizing unnecessary revving.

The environmental benefits of using the highest gear possible, recognizing when to change down to avoid engine labour.

How to use cruise control, if fitted, to minimize fuel consumption.

How appropriate engine braking can benefit fuel consumption and reduce wear and tear.

The effects of using features such as air conditioning or heated windscreens on fuel consumption.

When it is of benefit to turn the engine off, for example at a level crossing traffic queue.

The operation of automatic engine cut-off systems, where fitted.

OUTCOME 3

Know how to behave appropriately at incidents

What you need to be able to do

a If your vehicle breaks down:

- stop your vehicle in a safe place to minimize future risk and switch off the engine;
- where appropriate get out of your vehicle;
- make sure any passengers, loads and animals are managed safely;
- make sure, where practical and safe to do so, that you provide adequate warning to other road users to minimize risk;
- get appropriate help.

b If you are witness to, or involved in, an incident:

- where appropriate, stop your vehicle in a safe place to minimize future risk and switch off the engine;

- provide warning to other road users, where practical and safe to do so;
- get appropriate help;
- complete legal requirements accurately and in good time.

What you need to know and understand

a If your vehicle breaks down when in motion, how to:

- control your vehicle;
- bring it to a safe stop;
- make sure that the engine is switched off.

Where you have the option, the importance of selecting a safe place to stop and wait for help.

The risks associated with staying in your vehicle in some situations, such as on a dual carriageway or motorway.

The need to make sure that passengers, particularly young children, do not wander onto the road.

That you must leave animals in the vehicle unless there is a very good reason for taking them out, such as the risk of fire. If you do take animals out of the vehicle you must keep them under control.

When and how to warn other road users, by use of hazard warning lights or a warning triangle.

How to contact appropriate help.

b What the law requires you to do when involved in an incident, such as stopping and giving your details.
What the law requires you to do when you are a witness to an incident.

That it may not always be appropriate to stop immediately when you are witness to an incident, especially if by stopping you may put yourself or other road users at risk.

Where you have the option, the importance of selecting a safe place to stop.

When and how to warn other road users, by use of hazard warning lights or a warning triangle.

When it is appropriate to contact the police or emergency services and how to do so.

What documentation you are required to complete or information you are required to supply if witness to or involved in an incident.

This chapter contains information licensed under the Open Government Licence V2.

Disabilities and impairments   12

As a professional driver trainer you should have a reasonable working knowledge of how to teach someone who has a disability. This chapter includes the main points to consider, including topics such as making preliminary assessments, vehicle modifications and adaptations, methods of teaching, notes on some disabilities, how to apply for the driving test, how the test differs, and driver licensing. The chapter also deals with other factors that can affect the driver's performance, including learning difficulties, physical stature, ill health, drugs, stress, illness and ageing.

Assessing the needs

Many thousands of people with disabilities have passed the driving test and are regular, safe and competent drivers. Teaching driving to people who have disabilities is essentially the same as teaching anyone else. The subject matter is exactly the same – you merely have to adapt how you teach it, and take into consideration each individual pupil's needs and their medical conditions.

This type of driving instruction can be extremely rewarding. Very often pupils with some form of disability are highly motivated to do well and gain or regain their independence. You are also likely to be teaching experienced drivers to adapt to a different method of car control; this may involve a different style of teaching/coaching than with novice drivers.

You will need to assess your pupil's personal requirements with regard to any necessary vehicle adaptations. For many, all that may be required to control the car effectively could be:

- a car with automatic transmission;
- a steering ball on the wheel;
- power-assisted steering;
- wedge-style cushion.

Adapting your car will mean that you can attract a wider range of clients. Some of the more common modifications include:

- hand-operated accelerator and brake;
- accelerator pedal swappable to the left side of the brake pedal;
- bolt-on extensions to the pedals;
- panel attached to a steering aid for operating secondary controls.

For pupils with more complex conditions, a range of high-tech adaptations may need to be considered. Current technology allows vehicle controls, such as joystick steering and remote control devices, giving the freedom of driving to someone with little movement or strength.

Preliminary assessments

Car adaptations may be all that are required for people with physical disabilities such as arthritis or those caused through spinal injuries. However, if there is a possible difficulty with a person's learning capability or ability to cope with the cognitive demands of driving, then a more comprehensive assessment will be required. This type of assessment may be particularly appropriate for people diagnosed with:

- stroke;
- hydrocephalus;
- cerebral palsy;
- head injuries;
- marked general learning difficulties (even in the absence of physical disability).

Several specialist assessment centres around the country offer 'medical fitness to drive' assessments. This type of assessment forms an invaluable information resource for the pupil and the instructor, providing information on relevant aspects to be especially aware of during tuition.

An assessment centre can provide information on:

- eligibility to apply/reapply for a provisional or full driving licence;
- possible learning or other difficulties during the learning/retraining period;
- suitable cars and adaptations;
- conversion specialists and local driving instructors registered to teach those with disabilities.

Notes on disabilities

Cerebral palsy

This condition is present from birth or infancy and can be caused by birth injury or by the baby and mother having incompatible blood groups. It can lead to stiffness, clumsy movement and difficulty with walking and expressive or receptive language difficulties. Speech problems sometimes mask an alert and lively intelligence. Extra work may be needed in practising coordination of car controls.

Spina bifida

This is caused when the spinal cord does not develop correctly. At its most severe it can mean deformity of the spine, loss of feeling from the waist downwards and inability to control the bladder and bowels. Gaining independence as a driver may involve the need for assessment at a specialist mobility centre for advice on transferring into the vehicle and wheelchair stowage methods. Sitting height and sitting balance may need attention. Reduced sitting balance can affect coordination of the controls.

Hydrocephalus

This means 'water on the brain' and may be associated with spina bifida or cerebral palsy. It will have been treated medically by the time people are mature enough to drive. It sometimes leads to damage to parts of the brain dealing with concentration, memory and perception. This may make learning slower and more challenging.

Stroke

This is caused by a bleed or clot in the brain that interrupts the blood supply to part of the brain. It is common to assume that the resulting physical paralysis of one side of the body is the only problem. The brain damage causing the paralysis can also cause visual perceptual disturbance (affecting vehicle positioning skills) and information processing difficulties (affecting quick thinking and decision making). Loss of visual field can cause lack of visual awareness on one side. Expert assessment is needed to ensure that the legal standards for driving are met and that difficulties can be overcome. An assessment at a specialist mobility centre prior to rehabilitative tuition is recommended.

Paraplegia

This affects the lower half of the body. It is nearly always caused by damage to the spinal cord as a result of an accident. The level of the injury determines the amount of weakness and whether the result will be a spastic (stiff) or flaccid (floppy) weakness. Transfer methods, sitting balance, pressure care and wheelchair loading as well as the choice of hand control styles will need assessing.

Parkinson's disease

This is a neurological condition caused by a lack of the brain chemical dopamine. It can result in reduced coordination and the ability to use the car controls efficiently. Initiating a movement is often difficult, making reaction times too slow. Later in the course of the disease, thinking processes can become slow and some dementia-like changes can occur. The involuntary movements of Parkinsonism can be controlled with medication. However, in some cases medication can be the cause of involuntary movements. It is important that the driver takes their medication at the correct time and that they are aware of how they are affected by the medication. An assessment may be required to help choose suitable vehicle controls.

Cerebellar disease

This is caused by a problem in the cerebellum such as a tumour, or can result from conditions such as multiple sclerosis. The person may stagger and lurch when walking, have difficulty with speaking and be clumsy in movement.

Multiple sclerosis

This is a condition in which the insulating cover of the nerves of the central nervous system and brain is damaged. Once the cover (myelin sheath) is destroyed, conduction down the nerve is impaired. It can cause alteration of feeling, loss of balance, difficulty with vision and, in the later stages, deterioration of the mental processes. It is a disease that 'comes and goes', so thorough and frequent assessment is needed for driving. MS can cause loss of position sense in a limb. It is common for the driver to have good sensation and action in the feet, but to have trouble in finding the pedals accurately. Coordinating feet and hands on the controls can be an issue. Nystagmus (eye wobble) can cause intermittent blurring of vision. Optic neuritis (inflammation of the optic nerve) can cause other temporary visual problems. Some people experience cognitive problems affecting speed of thinking and decision making. Denial of symptoms is a common coping strategy, making tuition more difficult.

Arthritis

This means inflammation of the joints. There are two common forms: osteoarthritis implies premature ageing and degeneration of the joints, which may be precipitated by an injury in earlier life. The other common form is rheumatoid arthritis whereby the lining of the joints and other tissues deteriorate with specific injury. It is important to preserve the joints by not straining them at all. If the hands are affected, all controls should have chunky grips, steering wheel cover and easy operation. Parking brake and gearshift releases are advised. Lightened power steering can help.

Myopathies

This is a disease of the muscles, and covers conditions in which there is progressive weakness. Most of these conditions are inherited. Often there is weakness round the shoulders and hips, so aids such as power-assisted steering may be needed. Frequent assessments are needed to make sure a person has not become unfit to drive. There are not usually learning problems with this type of disability.

Time of day for driving lessons and the driving test may have an impact on your pupil's performance. For example, a person with osteoarthritis would probably perform better in the mornings because their joints are usually more painful later in the day. Fatigue and energy conservation can be important factors to take into consideration. Find out from your pupil what suits them best.

Vehicle adaptations

A wide range of modifications is available for drivers with disabilities. In all instances, selecting the correct adaptation to suit the particular qualities of the physical limitation is a specialist exercise. A referral to an assessment centre such as QEF Mobility Services at Carshalton is strongly recommended. Mobility centres are able to offer advice on where to purchase the correct products. The controls available have been categorized under headings to explain the use of these controls. Many adaptations, however, will need to be fitted to cars with automatic transmission.

Seating

A wedge-style cushion is a useful item in your training vehicle. It brings the eye level up without lifting the feet away from the pedals. Any cushions used should always be securely fastened to ensure they do not move when your pupil is driving. Care with seating and posture will ensure your pupil has a good view of the road; they are stable when turning corners and fatigue should be minimized. There are small adaptations that can make getting into and out of the car easier; the seatbelt easier to reach; the parking brake easier to operate; and a simple attached bar to enable the indicators to be operated with the other hand. If necessary, an assessment is available to ensure awareness of correct seating and posture and exact positioning of appropriate cushions and wedges.

Steering

Power-assisted steering can be tailor-made to match the strength of the driver of the particular car. Certain manufacturers have this built into the car; for other makes it can be a specialist job. Other vehicles have options such as a 'city button'. This allows the driver to lighten the steering with the press of a button. Most pupils who use one hand to steer need standard power-assisted steering to help them in various situations such as reversing.

If only one hand is used for steering, various modifications are available. Remember that the one hand must also operate secondary controls, so a steering aid alone is insufficient for the one-handed driver.

Steering ball for either right or left hand. This is usually placed at 10 o'clock for the left hand or 2 o'clock for the right hand, but it can vary, depending on the pupil's sitting position.

Steering aids come in various shapes and sizes to suit the pupil, such as:

- mushroom grip – this has a broader flat top and usually suits people with smaller hands;

- tulip grip – this is the most common style and suits most people;

- quad grip – this is used by pupils who do not have any finger grip, but have sufficient strength in their wrists to turn a steering wheel;

- glove and peg – this is used where gripping the steering wheel is not possible;

- T bar – this is often useful for drivers with cerebral palsy who have high muscle tone and flexed wrists; they can comfortably hold the grip with the back of the hand towards the steering wheel.

A joystick system may be fitted to a vehicle with automatic transmission if a pupil is unable to turn the steering wheel. This can be fitted either to the right or left side of the steering column, and will turn the steering wheel without actually touching it.

Foot steering may be used by pupils who have no useful function in their arms, but have full use of both legs. Shoulder or foot steering can steer the vehicle. The size and angle at which the steering wheel is placed can also be altered.

Brake and accelerator modifications

Foot pedals

Both the accelerator and the brake pedal can be levelled to make pedal operation easier, or the pedals can have raised edges to keep the feet in place if using one foot over the brake and one over the accelerator. Foot pedals can be extended for a driver of short stature. A floor raiser would also be required. For those who cannot use the right foot on the accelerator/brake pedals, the accelerator may be moved over to the left of the footbrake on a car with automatic transmission. The use of flip-up pedals or bayonet or wing-nut fitting allows the accelerator to be switched back to the right. For a driver who is used to driving a manual car, the left foot will have a clutch reflex, which causes the potential danger of pressing the left accelerator pedal when intending to press the brake pedal to slow down or stop. Several hours of tuition with a considerable amount of manoeuvring are needed to retrain the driver. For this reason, a person with experience of driving manual transmission cars is usually advised to use alternative controls. An assessment centre would be a good place to seek advice.

Knee controls

If the feet are not reliable, but the hip and knee joints are functional, adaptations can be fitted to allow a driver to operate the accelerator/brake controls with the in and out movement of the thigh.

Hand controls

If the lower limbs cannot be used to accelerate or brake, then either hand can be used. The most popular modification is the single combined lever for accelerator and brake. This is placed near the steering wheel and the hand normally pushes away to brake, using the driver's body weight. The accelerator is controlled by pulling towards the steering wheel. There are, however, various types of hand control such as a radial accelerator and a trigger or satellite accelerator. These usually require some form of steering aid. A ring accelerator allows the use of both hands for steering; with a split control the driver pulls the separate levers towards the steering wheel for accelerating and braking, and in a radial servo vacuum unit the driver pushes down towards the floor to brake and pulls up to accelerate. The last two systems mentioned have power-assisted braking.

Joystick

A joystick can also be placed either side of the steering wheel if the driver is unable to use other methods mentioned for accelerating/braking. There is also a four-way joystick system for use in an automatic vehicle, which enables a disabled pupil with only one usable limb to drive. These are extremely sensitive controls and specialist training and an off-road track for initial training is necessary before teaching someone to drive using this type of system. The joystick can be placed either side of the steering wheel, and the driver pushes the stick to the right or left for steering and pushes forward and backwards for the accelerator/brake.

Tiller

This system combines steering, accelerating and braking. The steering wheel is replaced by two handles either side of the steering column, and is steered like a motorcycle. Acceleration is achieved by twisting one of the handles, and braking is achieved by pushing the whole steering unit downwards.

Gear selector

This can be modified to suit a driver's restricted movement, either by extending the lever, removing the depressant button or lightening the tension required to move the lever. If this is not possible, an electric system can normally be fitted anywhere in the vehicle.

Parking brake

This can be moved to the right-hand side of the vehicle if the left hand cannot be used. If the left hand can reach the parking brake, but the button cannot be depressed, various aids can be fitted to assist with this. Electric parking brakes are available in some cars as standard equipment. A vehicle converter can place a parking brake switch anywhere within the car. An extension to the parking brake can be made for convenient use. A foot-operated parking brake can also be fitted to suit the driver.

Secondary controls

Indicators

The driver must, of course, be in complete control of the car and must be able to operate all secondary controls while maintaining efficient, coordinated control of the primary controls.

The minimum requirement, when using the single combined-lever hand control, is a trafficator thumb switch attached to the top of it. Some drivers also have the horn and headlamp beam control fitted.

For the one-handed driver, an infrared or Bluetooth switch panel attached to the steering aid is essential. Up to 18 secondary functions can be operated using press buttons or flick switches on the panel while still holding the steering aid.

Both of the above systems are very important from the instructor's point of view, as they enable the driver to indicate correctly and in good time. All secondary controls, however, can be placed anywhere in the car to suit the driver's ability, including in the head restraint, using the head to operate.

Mirrors

Additional mirrors can be placed in or on the vehicle to suit a pupil who has restricted neck movement. A panoramic mirror is most frequently used. This is fitted over the normal rear-view mirror and gives more visibility, especially when reversing. This mirror, used properly in conjunction with the two side mirrors, will satisfy safety standards. Other mirrors can be mounted internally or externally to enable safe observation at various types of junction and blind spot areas.

Impaired vision

Distance vision

The driver must be able to read an old-style number plate from a distance of 20.5 metres, or a new-style plate from 20 metres. If a person has a defective or lazy (amblyopic) eye, at no time should he or she attempt to drive with his or her good eye covered (occluded).

When assessing whether a driver can read a standard number plate, it is advisable to note the following:

- Whether the eyes are being screwed up noticeably. If so, this may indicate the need for glasses or a change of lenses. The driver should be referred to an optician. If glasses cannot bring the vision up to the required standard, sometimes contact lenses can.

- Whether the driver is adopting a noticeable head posture, which may be:
  - chin elevation or depression;
  - face turned to one side;
  - head tilted to one side.

  A head posture may be adopted for the following reasons:
  - to help overcome double vision (diplopia);
  - to bring a reduced field of vision to the central position;
  - to steady a fine wobble in the eye (nystagmus) if this reduces the vision;
  - to try to improve vision when incorrect glasses are worn.

If the head posture is significant, it is advisable to suggest that the driver seeks the advice of an ophthalmologist regarding the cause and possible treatment.

- Whether there is a tendency to close one eye. This may indicate diplopia (double vision). If so, and treatment cannot be given to eliminate it, the driver is permitted to cover one eye, provided the visual field in the uncovered eye is sufficient. For driving in the UK, we advise covering the left eye when the vision in the right eye is satisfactory, as the field of vision to the right is the more useful. Sometimes only partial occlusion of one lens is all that is needed, but the advice of an ophthalmologist should be sought. The presence of a squint does not necessarily mean that diplopia is likely to be a problem.

Squints

These present no problem for driving, provided that a person sees adequately and that there is no double vision (diplopia).

Double vision

There are varying degrees of diplopia depending on the level of vision in each eye and the separation of the images. Diplopia is usually at its worst when drivers are tired and therefore, if control of the diplopia is possible, they should be instructed when feeling least tired. Prisms are often used to correct this, and if recently given, the driver may need a little time to get used to them. In all cases with constant diplopia, one eye must be covered (occluded) for driving.

Colour vision

Defective colour vision is no bar to driving in most countries. However, it is always advisable to check that a person can assess traffic lights correctly by the position of the colours. Traffic signs are designed to be readable even with no colour vision; however, particular attention should be paid to *Highway Code* studies so that the pupil can recognize all types of signs.

Visual fields

People with constricted vision may drive, provided that there is at least 120° in the horizontal field and that it spans the central area. No one may drive with homonymous hemianopia (half the field missing with a vertical or horizontal cut-off through the centre of the field), or with a total quadrant loss (quarter missing).

Monocular vision

These drivers have no depth perception (stereopsis). Forty degrees of their visual fields will be missing on one side and night-time driving may prove more difficult. They may also find it difficult to judge the speed of approaching vehicles.

Impaired hearing

Deafness is not classed as a driver disability. No restrictions are placed on a full licence when someone who has a hearing impairment passes their driving test. It is beneficial for anyone who has a hearing problem, especially someone who is profoundly deaf, to disclose this on the driving test application form. This will ensure that the driving examiner is properly prepared. Some mobility centres, such as QEF Mobility Services, teach deaf pupils to drive. There is also training for teaching driving instructors how to teach deaf pupils.

Other impairments and barriers to learning

Illiteracy, dyslexia and non-English-speaking pupils

Some pupils have difficulty with reading – some may not be able to read at all. This is not a disability and does not necessarily mean that they will have difficulty with learning to drive. There are various ways in which you can help these pupils and these are discussed in the 'Methods of teaching' section of this chapter.

Autism

There is a range of disorders in this spectrum. Symptoms can include difficulty communicating and relating to other people. There is often a tendency to work by rules and an inability to work out the more abstract concepts of driving, making it difficult for such pupils to deal with unusual driving situations.

This can include situations where the *Highway Code* rules need to be supplemented when you are dealing with a situational analysis, for example, a reading of another driver's non-verbal responses in traffic situations such as when vehicles from all directions arrive simultaneously at a mini-roundabout.

The theory test can be a barrier for these pupils as they usually use the English language in a literal sense.

Physical stature and ill health

Physical discomfort such as toothache, cramp and natural functions can distract drivers. The performance of even the most skilful of drivers can deteriorate when they are feeling unwell. Alcohol and drugs affect every aspect of the driver's physical and perceptive processes, and some simple cold cures contain drugs that affect driving performance. Common drugs to be avoided while driving include sleeping pills, tranquillizers, antihistamines, amphetamines, anti-depressants, pain killers, opiates and belladonna.

Drivers with the following conditions may be taking the above drugs:

Anxiety	Depression	Insomnia
Asthma	Toothache	Indigestion
Headaches	Hay fever	Period pains and premenstrual tension
Colds/flu		

One of the difficulties with helping clients with some of the less obvious difficulties is that they can often go unnoticed for a long time, throughout which period the learners simply struggle on as best they can. Some people with a relatively minor disability may be embarrassed by it and so don't mention it. Others may not admit to having one through ill-founded fears that the instructor might be reluctant to take them on or simply through self-denial. Tact and understanding must be used when dealing with these problems.

In some cases, a properly secured cushion may be all that is required. Pedal extensions can be used for people with short legs or small feet. The floor of the car can be easily raised by placing a board (or similar object) under the heel of the foot (make sure it cannot interfere with the pedals). Mirrors can often compensate for trunk and neck restrictions of movement. None of us feels well all the time, and your pupils will be no exception. Women in particular may feel less well one week in every four due to the menstrual cycle. Mothers-to-be are not invalids and most of them will not appreciate being treated as such. However, they must be given some consideration, particularly with regard to ensuring the happy event does not occur during the driving test (or, for that matter, during a lesson!). Plan the lessons and test sensibly. Opinions in this respect vary considerably, and the final discretion must be exercised jointly by the instructor and pupil in relation to both lessons and test. Where there is any doubt, the client should seek her doctor's advice.

Prescription and non-prescription drugs

Drugs impair driving ability by reducing attention levels, the perception of risk and the ability to make sound decisions quickly and respond promptly to the road and traffic scene. Instructors should be particularly cautious when clients have some temporary illness for which they may be taking drugs. They should be advised to ask their doctors whether any prescribed drug will affect driving ability. They should carefully read instructions on the labels of non-prescribed drugs. It may also be appropriate to offer advice on the use of illegal drugs and their effect on driving.

Amphetamines speed up the nervous system and help users to keep going. While taking this type of drug, users may feel more alert and confident, but when the effect wears off they are likely to feel very tired and depressed.

Barbiturates are used to calm the nerves. They have an effect similar to that of alcohol, but when the effect wears off depression may follow. A combination of barbiturates and alcohol can cause severe depression. Tranquillizers are used by people with nervous and emotional conditions. They cause drowsiness, and the people who take them often combine their use with alcohol, with the likelihood of severe or even fatal consequences.

Marijuana is an hallucinogen which can act as either a stimulant or depressant. It slows mental responses and physical reactions, affects the judgement of time and space, and limits the ability to concentrate on more than one thing at a time.

Fatigue

Fatigue is a temporary condition that impairs the ability of all drivers. It reduces the ability to concentrate, impairs vision and the other senses, makes decisions more difficult, and makes drivers more irritable and so less tolerant with other road users. Fatigue can be caused by a medical condition or can be a side effect from medication, constant pain, hard work, lack of rest, emotional stress, boredom, or carbon monoxide poisoning. Contributory factors may include illness, overeating, an overheated car, driving for long distances without rest, bright sunlight or glare from oncoming headlights. Fatigue of physical action and of thinking skills can occur in many neurological conditions, and may be particularly common in a driver with, for example, multiple sclerosis.

Carbon monoxide is discharged by the car's exhaust system. If this is leaking, or if boot seals are not effective, or if the tailgate of an estate or hatchback car is not fully closed, carbon monoxide may find its way into the passenger compartment. It is colourless, odourless, tasteless and poisonous. Keep plenty of fresh air circulating through the car. The effects of fatigue on driving performance are not always obvious to the driver. They are:

- concentration becomes more difficult;
- the eyes become less active;
- decreased thinking time;
- a slowing of physical reactions;
- increasing difficulty with making decisions.

Symptoms for the instructor to be aware of are:

- consistent late braking;
- slow or erratic decision making;

- reduced hazard awareness and anticipation;
- a general impression of the driver driving on the brake lights of the vehicle in front.

Emotions and stress

Extremes of emotions, such as fear or anger, affect attention levels, perception and response to everyday traffic situations. They limit the driver's ability to reason quickly and logically.

Some medical conditions such as a brain injury have effects on personality, mood and emotional control. Aggression, impulsivity or a volatile nature can be symptomatic. Lack of appreciation of danger is common. Driving is in itself a stressful activity. High levels of frustration or stress can be felt because of the vehicle and traffic environment. Stress can cause excessive overreaction, and this adds even more fuel to the fire. On the other hand, these overreactions may (particularly in the case of new drivers in situations they are not yet competent to deal with) be associated with poorly developed hazard recognition skills, resulting in additional stresses due to late reactions and lack of confidence due to deficient car control skills.

Aggression is characterized by the hostile feelings or behaviour that some drivers display towards others. Mentally healthy people are able to tolerate a degree of aggression towards themselves without retaliation. Some experts claim aggression is linked to an individual's desire to dominate another and to compensate for feelings of inferiority or inadequacy. Others describe it as a surge of destructive feeling provoked by frustration. It is unlikely that aggression can be completely suppressed, and when it manifests itself in new drivers, instructors should direct their attention towards their own driver error rather than other road users.

After brain injury, aggression can be a contra-indication to driving. A specialist assessment is recommended. Young people are generally more at risk because they are less able to control hostile feelings. However, aggressive behaviour is not restricted to any particular age group or gender if drivers are pushed beyond their limits.

Anxiety

Most people get upset and anxious from time to time, particularly when faced with a threat of some kind. Anxiety describes the psychological disturbance characterized by feelings of apprehension. Some people are more susceptible to anxiety than others. This may be due to feeling helpless and alone, or experiencing a deep sense of inadequacy. These feelings are all normal in themselves but they can become over-obtrusive. Anxiety ranges in intensity from a vague restlessness to extreme uneasiness, and is usually accompanied by some kind of physical distress such as a tightness of the chest, dryness of the throat, sweating, trembling or tears.

Anxiety can be caused by financial or business difficulties, uncertainty about how to behave in some circumstances, fear of failure or fear of the consequences of an action. Intense anxiety can sometimes result from seemingly insignificant matters; for example, having dirt on one's shirt or blouse when meeting a stranger. Such exaggerated cases may indicate some subconscious cause relating to forgotten experiences. Anxiety makes it difficult for learners to think, reason or make judgements. It reduces their level of awareness and makes it difficult for them to concentrate on driving or any point under instruction. It results in a low level of retention of new information and skills, panic, reduced physical coordination, forced errors and a high degree of risk taking (to flee the situation). Instructors can assist over-anxious students by:

- creating a confident but relaxed and caring atmosphere;
- giving more reassurance and encouragement;
- using common sense over the task demands to help build up confidence – for example, letting them drive more slowly on routes with reduced task demands until confidence grows;
- seeing if shorter training periods and frequent breaks help;
- ensuring students understand what is expected and why;
- demonstrating and presenting information as graphically as possible.

Illness

From time to time, everyone has a temporary minor illness such as a cold, toothache, headache or stomach upset. Any of these can reduce attention, impair vision and upset judgement, timing and coordination.

Ageing

Ageing can reduce perception. Thinking processes become slower and manipulative coordination can be impaired. Older people are more set in their ways and will generally find learning to drive more difficult. They tend to be more anxious and their reactions are generally slower. Instructors should not place them under too much pressure or compare their progress with that of younger learners.

Regular eyesight tests are necessary, as deteriorating visual acuity can be so gradual that the driver does not notice. Difficulty dealing with headlight glare at night is common in the older driver, and many give up driving at night as a coping strategy. Choosing quieter times of the day to drive and avoiding right turns are other common strategies for continuing to drive safely up to an older age. Most mobility centres, such as QEF Mobility Services, offer assessments not only of people with disabilities, but also the elderly, who may have concerns about their driving safety as a result of ageing.

Methods of teaching

The rules, regulations and subject matter of driving remain the same. However, you will need to adapt your teaching methods and lesson programmes to suit the needs of each of your pupils.

Physical disabilities

For those with mobility difficulties, you may need to allow extra time for getting into and out of the car, and for finding the most comfortable driving position.

Some conditions cause people to tire during the day. It is important for you to discuss this with your pupil and arrange lessons at times of the day when they are more likely to achieve the best results. This should also be taken into consideration when you apply for the driving test so that his or her concentration and confidence will be at a peak. Consider shorter lessons for people with pain or fatigue or longer lessons for people with learning needs.

Hearing problems

The following is an extract from *Teaching the Deaf to Drive* and is reproduced with the kind permission of the Institute of Master Tutors of Driving:

> As the age of 17 must have been reached before a provisional licence can be issued, deaf youngsters, having received their education mainly in special schools or units, have some speech, although this may be difficult to follow. Usually sign language is used, and in addition they will be able to lip-read to a certain extent.

> Lip-reading, however, depends as much on the clarity of the speaker's lip movements as on the ability of the person who is deaf. Young people may have a reading age much lower than the natural age. Consequently, the ability to read

and write may be limited. They can, however, be just as bright and intelligent as their hearing peers, and with understanding and patience from the instructor will assimilate all that has to be learnt to drive a motor vehicle. The problem for the instructor is to learn the best way to impart the knowledge and the skill to the pupil. The essential is, what is the best way of communication?

You do not need to learn the sign language, but it is necessary to use simple, straightforward words, which only have one meaning. For example, 'Do not hug the middle of the road'. The word 'hug' to someone who is deaf has only the literal meaning of someone putting arms round another. Again, 'traffic jam' would not be understood; 'jam' is something one spreads on bread and butter.

It is essential to speak slowly and distinctly, and move the lips to form each word. Do not talk through your teeth. It will be appreciated that this approach means it has to be a face-to-face conversation and can therefore only be utilized in a stationary situation. Never shout – the pupil is deaf.

Due to the lack of hearing, it is vital that all 'conversations' be reinforced by demonstrations. Always be patient. Unsatisfactory response is likely to be the fault of the teacher rather than the pupil.

People who are deaf can normally speak, but it is not always easy for the hearing to understand what they are saying. It is difficult for them to make the sounds we are used to, as they are unable to hear their own voices. Always have a writing pad ready to hand, and ask the student to write down questions.

Learning the *Highway Code* can be helped if you simplify your language. Formulate questions in written form and have the answers following in the same easy wording. You may benefit from getting in touch with local associations for deaf people or Action on Hearing Loss (formerly The Royal National Institute for Deaf People), 19–23 Featherstone Street, London EC1Y 8SL (tel: 020 7296 8000). They are always very ready to help with any difficulties which may arise.

Several DVDs are available with sign language translations of the Multiple-choice Theory Test questions and explaining the Hazard Perception Test. Various courses can be found to help you teach people with hearing difficulties.

Reading and understanding problems

If you have any pupils with difficulties such as dyslexia, or pupils who are non-English speaking, there are various ways in which you can help. Making more use of visual aids during in-car training sessions will help pupils to understand when introducing new topics. Showing them pictures of road signs and markings and explaining their meaning should also help. They will understand *The Highway Code* rules better if they can apply them to on-road situations as soon after learning them as possible. It can be helpful to discuss with family or close friends the subjects currently under instruction, and encourage them to help the pupil by giving some in-between lesson revision and learning exercises.

Keep your terminology as simple as possible, and to avoid confusion, make sure you are consistent with the words and phrases you use. It may be advisable to obtain the services of someone known to the pupil to act as interpreter. This can be particularly useful during the training stages because, when the pupil attends the driving test, you will not be able to act in this capacity and the person who has already been present on lessons would be familiar with what is required. Try to give as much encouragement as possible to all of your pupils, perhaps by emphasizing their successes at the practical skills. In no way should you embarrass them or make them feel inadequate – this will do little to grow their confidence in you or themselves. You should introduce independent driving as early as practicable during the training so that this is not a surprise during the driving test. Speak with your local examiners to find out how they can help your candidate through this part of the test.

Applying for the driving test

The procedure outlined in Chapter 9 should be followed when applying for tests for people with disabilities, taking into consideration the following notes. When completing the application form DL26, try to give as much information as possible about the disabilities. If there is not enough room on the form to explain the disability and how the candidate is affected by it, write out the extra information and attach it to the application form. Supplying this information in advance will avoid any possible embarrassment to both pupil and examiner from questions that have to be asked on the day of the test.

When booking a practical test, please let the DVSA know if your candidate:

- has severe hearing difficulties;
- is in any way restricted in their movements;
- has any physical disability.

No matter how complex a disability might be, the pupil will still be taking the same driving test as every other test candidate. However, more time is allocated for the test. This is to allow the examiner to talk to the candidate about his or her disability and any adaptations fitted to the vehicle. If the candidate is dyslexic, supplying this information beforehand will allow a suitable means of communication to be devised. The senior examiner at the test centre should be informed at least two days before a test appointment where any of the following exist:

- impaired hearing;
- minor restrictions are experienced;
- abnormal stature;
- any disabilities not noted on the application form.

Providing such information may explain to an examiner why certain actions are taken by the candidate and allowances can therefore be made for them. For example, if an examiner knows in advance that a candidate has restricted neck movement, not classed as a disability, and uses the mirrors for making rear observations when manoeuvring, this will be expected and allowed for. If the information is not volunteered, then the examiner can only assume that correct observations are not made and there is no reason for it.

When preparing for the test

By this time you should have ensured that the adaptations used by each individual pupil overcome his or her disability as far as possible. If they do not, then you should advise on any further adaptations that you think are necessary, allowing plenty of time to get used to them. The time allotted for the examiner when testing people with disabilities spans two normal test periods. You should bear this in mind when entering the appointment in your diary.

Attending for the test

Make sure you allow plenty of time for getting to the test centre if the candidate has difficulty getting out of and into the car. Where it is not practical for the candidate to go to the examiner, you may go into the waiting room to inform the examiner that the pupil has arrived. The content and length of the driving test are the same as for standard driving tests but allow more time in your diary for the examiner to complete paperwork with the candidate. At the beginning of the test, the candidate will be asked if there are any additional disabilities that are not noted on the application form. Encourage your pupils to be frank about this as it will help the examiner to make an effective and objective assessment. The examiner will also ask about the vehicle's adaptations. Where there are hand adaptations, more emphasis will normally be placed on downhill junctions to check that control is adequate. If a candidate has neck or vertebrae problems, emphasis is normally placed on the ability to make frequent observations at those junctions where sight-lines are restricted.

At the end of the test

The examiner has two decisions to make. Does the candidate have the ability to drive? And do the adaptations overcome the disabilities? If the examiner is satisfied that the candidate is competent to drive all unadapted vehicles in the category on which he or she was tested, and in any additional categories covered, a normal pass certificate for that category is issued. If the examiner considers that the candidate can drive unadapted vehicles only of the category on which he or she was tested, but not the additional categories covered, then the pass certificate is issued for that category (eg category B) and a D255 should indicate that the candidate should be restricted to category B vehicles. If the examiner considers the candidate can drive only a vehicle with suitable adaptations, this is indicated on the pass certificate. All candidates, whether they pass or fail, are given a copy of the driving test report form. If a candidate fails and the examiner feels that some other adaptation might enable him or her to pass, an indication of this may be given.

Instructor courses

If you are interested in teaching people with disabilities, training courses are available at QEF Mobility Services, 1 Metcalf Avenue, Carshalton, Surrey SM5 4AW (tel: 020 8770 1151; fax: 020 8770 1211; website: **www.qef.org. uk/our-services/mobility-services**).

APPENDIX I
Associations and organizations

The Driver and Vehicle Standards Agency (DVSA) encourages you to join approved driving instructor (ADI) associations and organizations so your interests are properly represented in talks. However, you don't have to join one to be an ADI.

Each association and organization has its own terms and conditions.

There are also local associations and organizations as well as the national ones listed here.

These are national associations and organizations that represent and support ADIs:

Approved Driving Instructors National Joint Council

The Approved Driving Instructors National Joint Council (ADINJC) was established in 1973 to act as a central hub uniting individual driving instructor associations. It is a non-profit organization, with no commercial interests, premises or salaried staff. Its objectives are to further the professional and financial interests of ADIs and to keep members informed of developments within the industry. It is, as its slogan says, 'ADIs working together for the benefit of other ADIs'.

Membership is made up of local driving instructor associations, but individual ADIs can join as members of the 'Driving Instructors Group'.

Telephone: 0800 8202 444
secretary@adinjc.org.uk
www.adinjc.org.uk

Chairman:
16 Grosvenor Close
Lichfield
Staffordshire
WS14 9SR

The ADI Federation Ltd

A non-profit organization for individual ADIs.
Telephone: 01933 461821
www.theadifederation.org.uk

Kingsmith House
Marshalls Road
Raunds
Northamptonshire
NN9 6EY

The DIDU Association

DIDU membership is open to all Approved Driving Instructor and Potential Driving Instructors in the UK.

Telephone: 07812 644825
rob@didu.co.uk
www.didu.co.uk

DIDU Chairman:
10 Hendomen Drive
New Acre Wood
Montgomery
Powys
SY15 6RB

Driving Instructors Association

The DIA was founded in 1978 to represent the interests of the professional driving instructor and is the largest UK instructor association. It provides a range of valuable membership benefits, training and education opportunities, advice and information on road safety, driver education and advanced motoring topics, as well as lobbying and representation on behalf of members on key issues affecting the driver training industry.

The DIA offers a comprehensive range of membership services for driver and rider trainers. Each member receives regular copies of *Driving Instructor*, a leading instructor-focused membership magazine.

Telephone: 020 8686 8010
training@driving.org
www.driving.org

11 Gleneagles Court
Brighton Road
Crawley
Sussex
RH10 6AD

Driving Instructor's Branch of Unite the Union

Telephone: 020 8800 4281
robert.harper@unitetheunion.org
www.unitetheunion.org

National Chairman:
Unite the Union
33–37 Moreland Street
London
EC1V 8BB

Driving Instructors Scottish Council

The aim of DISC is to represent, inform and support driving instructor associations in Scotland and to have a role in the strategy, policy making and development of driver training at a national UK level.

DISC is a voluntary organization with no paid positions – its current structure was formed in 1995, and has grown in membership over the years, reaching a position where it now represents most Scottish driving instructor associations.

Any driving instructor association in Scotland can apply for affiliation to DISC, and associations from across the country are represented. DISC has full consultative status with the DVSA and works in partnership with all the other UK National Associations with consultative status.

Telephone: 0131 538 0984 or 07885 975 851
discchairman@virginmedia.com

DISC Chair:
95 Muirhouse Green
Edinburgh
EH4 4RF

Motor Schools Association

MSAGB was formed in March 1935, just before the driving test was introduced. The association's main aims, then as now, are to keep members informed of all matters of interest to them; to represent the views of members to government, its departments and various agencies; to provide services which will be of benefit to members; and to set standards of professional and ethical behaviour for driver trainers.

Full membership of MSAGB is only available to ADIs. However, anyone training to become an ADI may join as a probationary member and when qualified is converted to full membership at no extra cost.

MSAGB is a company limited by the guarantee of its members and is run on behalf of members by the Board of Management, members of which are all working driving instructors.

Telephone: 0800 026 5986 or 0161 429 9669
Fax: 0161 429 9779
mail@msagb.co.uk
www.msagb.com

The Motor Schools Association of Great Britain
101 Wellington Road North
Stockport
Cheshire
SK4 2LP

APPENDIX II
Useful contacts

Driver and Vehicle Standards Agency (DVSA)

The Axis Building
112 Upper Parliament Street
Nottingham NG1 6LP
Tel: 0115 936 6666
www.gov.uk

Theory test applications and booking support

DVSA
PO Box 381, M50 3UW
English bookings: 0800 200 1122
English enquiries: 0800 200 1188
Welsh bookings: 0800 200 1133
E-mail: **Customercare@pearson.com**

Practical test enquiries and booking support

DVSA
PO Box 280
Newcastle-upon-Tyne NE99 1FP
English: 0800 200 1122
Welsh: 0800 200 1133
E-mail: **Customer.services@dvsa.gsi.gov.uk**

DVSA Training and Development Centre
Harrowden Lane
Cardington
Bedfordshire MK44 3EQ

Driving and Vehicle Licensing Agency (DVLA)

DVLA
Swansea SA6 7JL
Tel: 0300 790 6801

Driving licence enquiries: 0300 790 6801
Driver check service: 09061 393 837

Drivers' medical enquiries

DVLA
Swansea SA99 1TU
Tel: 0300 790 6806

Vehicle registration and tax enquiries

DVLA
Swansea SA99 1AR
Tel: 0300 790 6802

Northern Ireland

Driver and Vehicle Agency

County Hall
Castlerock Road
Waterside
Coleraine BT51 3TB
Tel: 0300 200 7861
www.nidirect.gov.uk

Training aids and services

Desk Top Driving Ltd
Tel: 01903 882299
Fax: 01903 885599
www.desktopdriving.co.uk

Driving School Aids
Tel: 0113 281 8199
E-mail: info@drivingschoolaids.co.uk
www.drivingschoolaids.co.uk

Driving School Supplies
Tel: 0121 328 6226

E-mail: **sales@d-ss.co.uk**
www.d-ss.co.uk

Grade 6 supplies
Tel: 01353 749807
E-mail: **customerservices@gradesixsupplies.com**
www.gradesixsupplies.com

He-Man Dual Controls Ltd
Tel: 023 8022 6952
E-mail: **mail@he-mandualcontrols.co.uk**
www.he-mandualcontrols.co.uk

Porter Dual Controls
Tel: 0208 601 3566

RCM Marketing Ltd
Tel: 01202 949474
E-mail: **info@rcmmarketing.co.uk**
www.rcmmarketing.co.uk

Royal Society for the Prevention of Accidents (RoSPA)
Tel: 0121 248 2233
E-mail: **help@rospa.com**
www.rospa.com

The Stationery Office (TSO)
Tel: 0333 200 2401
www.tsoshop.co.uk

Disabled drivers' assessment centres

QEF

Leatherhead Court
Woodlands Road
Leatherhead
KT2 0BN
Tel: 01372 841100
E-mail: **mobility@qef.org.uk**
www.qef.org.uk

QEF offers practical advice, assessment and training for those wishing to drive or increase their mobility through assistive technology, personal mobility vehicles and adapted cars.

A specialist team of qualified and experienced instructors offer training for customers who have special needs, including pupils who are deaf.

Driving Mobility (was Forum of Mobility Centres)

2 Prince's Street
Truro
TR1 2ES
Tel: 0800 559 3636
info@drivingmobility.org.uk
www.drivingmobility.org.uk

A network of 17 independent local organizations offering information, advice and assessment to people who have a medical condition or are recovering from an accident which may affect their ability to drive.

APPENDIX III

Reference books and recommended reading

DVSA publications

The Official Highway Code
Know Your Traffic Signs
The Official DVSA Guide to Driving – The essential skills
The Official DVSA Guide to Learning to Drive
The Official DVSA Guide to Better Driving
The Official DVSA Theory Test for Car Drivers
The Official DVSA Theory Test for ADIs – DVD-ROM
The Official DVSA Guide to Hazard Perception – DVD

DVSA recommended books

Practical Teaching Skills for Driving Instructors, 10th edition by John Miller – published 2017

Published by Kogan Page and are listed as recommended reading material for the ADI exams.

All books are available from

DeskTop Driving Ltd
Gaugemaster Way, Ford, Arundel BN18 0RX
www.desktopdriving.co.uk
Tel: 01903 882299

and

TSO shop
PO Box 29, Norwich NR3 1GN
www.tsoshop.co.uk
Tel: orders – 0333 200 2425; customer services – 0333 202 5070

as well as from other suppliers and most bookshops.

APPENDIX IV
Answers – Theory mock test (Chapter 2, page 41)

1 At traffic lights, amber means:

c) Stop, unless it would be unsafe to do so.

2 A theory test pass certificate is valid for:

d) 24 months.

3 Signs giving directions are usually:

a) Rectangular.

4 A long white line with short gaps down the centre of the road is an indication of:

c) A hazard.

5 *The Highway Code* says that you should never reverse:

c) From a minor road onto a major road.

6 Reflective studs along the left edge of the road are:

d) Red.

7 Pupils should apply for the theory test:

b) When they have studied and the ADI advises them to do so.

8 Unless exempt, passengers travelling in cars must wear seat belts in:

b) Any seat of the car.

9 You must report to the licensing authority any medical condition that:

c) Is likely to last more than three months.

10 Car passengers under three years of age are the responsibility of:

d) The driver.

11 The speed limits for learner drivers are:

a) The same as for full licence holders.

12 You should control the speed of your car when driving downhill by:

b) Slowing down and then changing to a lower gear.

13 What is 'client-centred learning' about?

c) An ongoing conversation with the pupil to ensure that you understand their learning needs.

14 To ensure uniformity of tests, examiners are:

c) Closely supervised by a senior examiner.

15 A full driving licence is valid until the driver's:

c) 70th birthday.

16 If you are involved in an accident and do not have your insurance certificate with you, it must be produced at a police station within:

d) Seven days.

17 Children under 14 should wear seat belts.

a) If travelling in the front or rear of the car.

18 In built-up areas, a 30-mph speed limit applies unless there are:

a) Signs indicating otherwise.

19 A provisional licence holder is allowed to drive a vehicle of up to:

b) 3.5 tonnes.

20 Using the gears to slow down should:

c) Not be normal practice.

21 Groups of people marching on the road should:

b) Keep to the left.

22. Approaching a green traffic light, you should:

d) Be ready to stop if the lights change.

23 When walking with children, you should:

b) Walk between the child and the road.

24 Unless you are receiving higher-rate Disability Living Allowance, the minimum legal age for driving a car is:

a) 17.

25 As a general rule, driving test routes are designed to incorporate:

a) A wide variety of road and traffic situations.

26 The ADI regulations are part of:

   a) The Road Traffic Act.

27 When turning right, at a junction where an oncoming vehicle is also turning right, the DVSA book, *Driving – The essential skills*, advises:

   b) Turning offside to offside where possible.

28 According to *The Highway Code*, you should not park on:

   d) A road marked with double white lines.

29 *The Highway Code* says that, at night, you should use:

   b) Dipped headlights in built-up areas.

30 Serious faults committed by the pupil in the first few minutes of a driving test:

   d) May result in failure.

31 One of the basic teaching principles is:

   c) Explanation–demonstration–practice.

32 When attending for a theory test, candidates must produce:

   a) A current valid provisional driving licence.

33 The instruction for turning left should be:

   d) Take the next road on the left, please.

34 For an instructor to accompany a pupil on test, the:

   a) Candidate must ask the examiner.

35 *The Highway Code* says that the minimum tread on tyres should be:

   b) 1.6 mm.

36 A white stick with a red band is used by someone who is:

   c) Deaf and blind.

37 A pupil on test who commits only one serious fault will:

   b) Fail the test.

38 To cancel a driving test without losing the fee requires:

   a) Three complete working days' notice.

39 When first introducing a novice to the use of mirrors emphasis should be placed on:

   a) Correct adjustment.

40 For a first attempt at reversing most emphasis should be on:

   b) Maintaining control of the car.

41 According to the DVSA book, *Driving – The essential skills*, it is:

   b) Doubtful that the 'perfect driver' exists.

42 Anyone supervising a learner driver must:

   d) Be at least 21 and have held a full driving licence for that type of vehicle for at least three years.

43 If an examiner has to take action, this will be recorded on the driving test report as a:

   d) Dangerous fault.

44 Who, of the following, may accompany a learner on a driving test?

   a) Anyone the candidate wishes.

45 The purpose of the examiner's driving report, which is given to all successful test candidates, is to:

   a) Help overcome any minor weaknesses in the candidate's driving.

46 So that learners get the most benefit from each lesson, instructors should organize their teaching plan:

   b) In short, attainable stages.

47 Setting very difficult objectives for a learner driver may:

   b) Slow down the pupil's learning.

48 At the end of each lesson the instructor should:

   d) Recap on what has been learnt.

49 When passing stationary buses you should:

   b) Pass slowly, looking for people getting off.

50 When students reach a 'plateau' in their learning you should:

   c) Return to a previous topic for reinforcement purposes.

51 Extreme emotions such as fear or anger:

   d) Can reduce your concentration levels.

52 The exhaust system:

   a) Gets rid of burnt gases.

53 If your car breaks down on a level crossing and the bells start ringing, you should firstly:

  c) Stand well clear.

54 An ADI who is disqualified from driving for 12 months would be barred from giving driving instruction for a total of:

  c) Five years.

55 You can only be issued with a trainee licence if you:

  b) Have passed Parts 1 and 2 and are sponsored by an ADI.

56 If you are first to arrive at the scene of an accident and a casualty stops breathing, you should:

  b) First check that their airway is clear.

57 If you are involved in an accident which involves someone else, you should first of all:

  d) Stop immediately and exchange details.

58 If a police officer asks you to produce your documents, they must be taken to:

  b) A police station of your choice.

59 The three main factors involved in a skid are:

  d) Driver, vehicle, road.

60 You should 'make progress' by:

  d) Driving at speeds to suit the conditions.

61 In fog, when waiting to turn right into a side road, you should:

  a) Keep your right foot on the brake pedal.

62 Approaching a junction in an unfamiliar area, you should:

  b) Be guided by the signs and road markings.

63 When driving downhill, gravity makes:

  c) The brakes less effective.

64 Parking at the kerb on the left facing uphill, you should:

  d) Turn the steering wheel to the right.

65 When driving on multi-lane roads you should keep:

    c) In the centre of your lane.

66 Before crossing a one-way street, pedestrians should look:

    c) Both ways.

67 The PSL routine is used:

    b) As part of the MSM routine.

68 You may wait in a box junction when:

    a) The exit is clear and you intend to turn right.

69 *The Highway Code* states that you must not reverse for more than:

    d) The distance that is necessary.

70 At zebra crossings, you must not pass:

    a) The moving vehicle nearest the crossing.

71 Anti-lock braking systems:

    d) Are designed to prevent the wheels locking during heavy braking.

72 People with disabilities are:

    d) Permitted to drive any type of car, depending on their disability.

73 Flashing headlights should be used:

    a) As a warning of your presence.

74 When turning from a main road into a side road, give way to:

    d) Pedestrians who are crossing the road.

75 Approaching a roundabout, you should:

    b) Keep moving if the way is clear.

76 For pedestrians, the flashing green man at pelican crossings means:

    b) Do not start to cross.

77 When crossing a dual carriageway you should:

    c) Take into account the width of the central reservation before deciding on how to cross.

78 The main reason for a skid to occur is the:

    c) Driver not responding to the conditions.

79 When reversing in a van, it is usually better to:

a) Reverse into an opening on the right.

80 When waiting to turn right at a box junction where there is oncoming traffic you should wait:

a) In the yellow box.

81 A green filter arrow means:

b) Proceed if it's safe to do so, regardless of the other light.

82 Learner drivers should use mirrors to:

a) Decide if their actions will be safe.

83 High-intensity rear fog lights should be used:

a) If visibility falls below 100 metres.

84 If a candidate attends for the practical test in a car that appears to be un-roadworthy:

d) The test may be cancelled, with no refund.

85 When following other traffic on a dry road, you should leave a time gap of at least:

d) Two seconds.

86 Driving test candidates who make a lot of driving faults, but which are not considered serious or dangerous:

a) May fail the test.

87 *The Highway Code* recommends the use of an arm signal when:

b) Stopping at a pedestrian crossing.

88 Your following distance on wet roads should be:

a) Doubled.

89 According to the DVSA book, *Driving – The essential skills*, the only safe separation distance is:

b) Your overall stopping distance.

90 Pedestrians should show their intention to cross at a zebra crossing by:

d) Putting one foot on the crossing.

91 At 70 mph the braking distance is:

   c) 75 m (245ft).

92 Fuel economy can be maximized by:

   d) Using the highest gear possible.

93 When applying for a test for a pupil who has a slight disability, you should:

   b) Give as much information as possible.

94 When dealing with bends the speed of the car should be lowest when you are:

   a) Entering the bend.

95 Flashing headlights mean the:

   a) Same as sounding the horn.

96 If you break down on a level crossing you must first of all:

   c) Get your passengers out.

97 Before emerging at a junction, your pupil should:

   d) Look effectively in all directions.

98 The clutch separates the:

   c) Drive between engine and wheels.

99 *The Highway Code* advises signalling:

   b) To warn or inform others.

100 If the road ahead is flooded, you should:

   a) Stop and check the depth of the water.

APPENDIX V
Code of Practice for ADIs

The Driver and Vehicle Standards Agency (DVSA) and the driving instruction industry place great emphasis on professional standards and business ethics.

This code of practice has been agreed between the DVSA and the bodies representing ADIs listed at the end of this document. These bodies expect their members to adhere to this code of practice. It is a framework within which all instructors should operate.

The code has been updated in the light of developments in social media and the increased public awareness of matters such consumer expectation and the duty of care that we have to our clients. It provides guidance on how trainers can fulfil their duty to do all that is reasonable to protect the health, safety and welfare of pupils. It covers both their personal conduct and their business dealings.

Personal conduct

Driver trainers will be professional, comply with the law, keep clients safe and treat them with respect.

The instructor agrees to:

- at all times behave in a professional manner towards clients in line with the standards in the 'National standard for driver and rider training';
- at all times comply with legislative requirements including:
  - the protection of personal freedoms;
  - the prevention of discrimination based on age, disability, gender, race, religion or sexual orientation;
  - not using mobile devices like phones when driving or supervising clients' driving and only when parked in a safe and legal place;

- demonstrating a high standard of driving and instructional ability, upholding safety standards including showing consideration for all other road users, particularly pedestrians, cyclists, motorcyclists and horse riders;

- consumer, workplace and data protection regulations, the handling, storing, use and dissemination of video or audio recordings made in or around their tuition vehicle.

- avoid inappropriate physical contact with clients;

- avoid the use of inappropriate language to clients;

- not initiate inappropriate discussions about their own personal relationships and take care to avoid becoming involved in a client's personal affairs or discussions about a client's personal relationships, unless safeguarding concerns are raised;

- avoid circumstances and situations which are, or could be, perceived to be of an inappropriate nature;

- respect client confidentiality whilst understanding the actions to take if a pupil reveals concerns about their private life;

- treat clients with respect and consideration and support them to achieve the learning outcomes in the 'National standard for driver and rider training' as efficiently and effectively as possible;

- ensure that their knowledge and skills on all matters relating to the provision of driver training comply with current practice and legislative requirements;

- use social network sites responsibly and professionally:

  - ensuring that clients' personal information is not compromised;

  - ensuring when using social media for marketing purposes that what is written is compliant with privacy and data protection legislation pertaining to digital communications, the laws regarding spam, copyright and other online issues;

  - treating other users of social media including clients, colleagues and their views with respect;

  - being careful not to defame the reputation of colleagues, the DVSA, driving examiners or the ADI Register;

  - not distributing, circulating or publishing footage taken of driving tests from in-car cameras without permission from the DVSA and the client.

Business dealings

Driver trainers will account for monies paid to them, record clients' progress, advise clients when to apply for their driving tests and guide them fairly through the learning process.

The instructor agrees to:

- safeguard and account for any monies paid in advance by the client in respect of driving lessons, test fees or for any other purpose and make the details available to the client on request;

- on or before the first lesson make clients aware of both this code of practice and their terms of business which should include:

  - the legal identity of the school/instructor with full postal address and telephone number at which the instructor or their representative can be contacted;

  - the current price and duration of lessons;

  - the current price and conditions for use of a driving school car for the practical driving test;

  - the terms which apply to cancellation of lessons by either party;

  - the terms under which the refund of lesson fees may be made;

  - the procedure for making a complaint.

- check a client's entitlement to drive the vehicle and their ability to read a number plate at the statutory distance on the first lesson and regularly during their training;

- make a record of the client's progress, which will include the number of lessons provided, and ensure that the client is aware of their progress and future training requirement to achieve their driving goals;

- discuss with and advise a client when to apply for their driving tests, taking account of the DVSA's cancellation rules, local waiting times and the instructor's forecast of a client's potential for achieving the driving test pass standard;

- not cancel or rearrange a driving test without the client's knowledge and agreement. In the event of the instructor's decision to withhold the use of the school car for the driving test, sufficient notice should be given to the client to avoid loss of the DVSA test fee;

- ensure that, when presenting a client for the practical driving test:

- the client has all the necessary documentation to enable them to take the test;
- the vehicle complies with all aspects of motoring law, displays the instructor's certificate or licence correctly and is fitted with an extra interior rear-view mirror and correctly positioned 'L' or optionally 'D' plates in Wales.

- accompany the client on their practical test and listen to the debrief, when requested to do so.

Advertising

Driver trainers will take care to advertise and promote their businesses in a clear and fair manner.

The instructor agrees that:

- the advertising of driving tuition shall be clear, fair and not misleading;
- any claims made in advertising shall be capable of verification and comply with CAP Advertising Codes;
- advertising that refers to pass rates should not be open to misinterpretation and the basis on which the calculation is prepared should be made clear.

Conciliation

Driver trainers will deal promptly with any complaints received and aim for speedy resolution of any grievances

The instructor agrees that:

- complaints by clients should be made in the first instance to the driving instructor, driving school or contractor following the training provider's complaints procedure;
- if, having completed the procedure, the client has been unable to reach an agreement or settle a dispute, further guidance may be sought;
- if a client believes that their instructor is not providing a satisfactory business service they can contact their local Citizens Advice Bureau for guidance;
- if clients are unhappy with their instructor's professional service, the client can contact the ADI Registrar by e-mailing **adireg@dvsa.gov.uk**.

Endorsement by ADI consultative groups

This code is endorsed by the following ADI consultative groups who represent driving instructors and schools:

- Approved Driving Instructors National Joint Council (ADI NJC).
- Driving Instructors Association (DIA).
- The Motor Schools Association of Great Britain (MSAGB).

INDEX

Note: Page numbers in *italic* indicate figures or tables.

CPSIA information can be obtained
at www.ICGtesting.com
Printed in the USA
BVHW02s1232070918
526814BV00024B/565/P

9 780749 483937